UX

FOR

DUMMIES®

A Wiley Brand

by Donald Chesnut
and
Kevin Nichols

FOR

DUMMIES®

A Wiley Brand

UX For Dummies®

Published by **John Wiley & Sons, Ltd,** The Atrium, Southern Gate,
West Sussex, PO19 8SQ, England

E-mail (for orders and customer service enquires): cs-books@wiley.co.uk

Visit our home page on www.wiley.com

Copyright © 2014 John Wiley & Sons, Ltd, Chichester, West Sussex, England

Published by John Wiley & Sons Ltd, Chichester, West Sussex

For general information on our other products and services, please contact our Customer Care Department within the U.S. at 877-762-2974, outside the U.S. at 317-572-3993, or fax 317-572-4002.

For technical support, please visit www.wiley.com/techsupport.

Wiley also publishes its books in a variety of electronic formats and by print-on-demand. Some content that appears in standard print versions of this book may not be available in other formats. For more information about Wiley products, visit us at www.wiley.com.

British Library Cataloguing in Publication Data: A catalogue record for this book is available from the British Library.

ISBN 978-1-118-85278-1 (pbk); ISBN 978-1-118-85271-2 (ePub); 978-1-118-85279-8 (ePDF)

Printed and bound in the United States by Bind-Rite.

10 9 8 7 6 5 4 3 2 1

Contents at a Glance

Introduction 1

Part I: Getting Started with UX 5
Chapter 1: Defining UX and the Process 7
Chapter 2: Examining Why You Should Use UX 25
Chapter 3: Determining Your Users 37
Chapter 4: Modeling the Experience 57
Chapter 5: Understanding UX as (R)evolution 77

Part II: Components of Design 89
Chapter 6: Taming the Beast: Understanding What You Do and Don't Have 91
Chapter 7: Developing Content Strategy 111
Chapter 8: Designing the Content Strategy 131
Chapter 9: Building the Information Architecture 155
Chapter 10: Designing for Specific Channels 175
Chapter 11: Diving into Visual Design 201

Part III: Your UX in Action 217
Chapter 12: Testing: How It Can Save Your UX 219
Chapter 13: Measuring Your UX to Keep It Relevant 235
Chapter 14: Making It Past the Finish Line 257

Part IV: The Part of Tens 271
Chapter 15: Ten Reasons Why the User Is Your Most Important Consideration 273
Chapter 16: Ten Ways to Ensure That Your UX Is Best in Class 279
Chapter 17: Ten UX Principles That Never Change 285

Glossary 289

Index 299

Table of Contents

Introduction 1

    About This Book 1
    Foolish Assumptions...2
    Icons Used in This Book 2
    Beyond the Book 3
    Where to Go from Here..3

Part I: Getting Started with UX 5

    Chapter 1: Defining UX and the Process 7

        What Is UX, Really?..8
        The Promise of Good UX Design....................................9
        UX Components 9
            Information architecture..10
            Content strategy 10
            Interaction design 10
            Usability 11
            Visual design 11
        UX Is a Big Deal 12
        How UX and Usability Work Together 13
            The basics of usability 13
            Comparing UX to usability....................................14
        Necessary UX Inputs 14
            Business objectives 15
            Competitive landscape..15
            Technology architecture 16
            Design inputs...16
            Content inputs...18
        Considerations before Beginning UX 19
            Understanding your target users............................19
            Deciding on a new project or redesign 19
            Identifying the technology......................................20
            Maintaining the experience 20
            Ensuring consistency 20
            Determining your level of comfort 20
            Understanding what makes a good UX designer 21

How a Typical Project Works...21
Define phase 22
Design phase 23
Build phase 23
Test and launch phase 24
Maintain phase 24

Chapter 2: Examining Why You Should Use UX....................25
Realizing UX for All Channel Benefits 26
Understanding How UX Benefits Your Business 28
Understanding How UX Impacts Your Users 33
Seamless information discovery...33
Ability to accomplish desired tasks 34
Fashions the experience around the user 34

Chapter 3: Determining Your Users 37
User Experience versus Customer Experience.................................38
Gathering Data 39
Online surveys...41
User interviews 41
Focus groups 42
Ethnography and contextual inquiry 42
Analyzing the Data to Create User Profiles 42
UX: Why is behavioral segmentation so critical? 44
Putting the data into action 44
Prioritizing Who's Most Important..48
Bringing Users to Life through Personas..49
Using personas...50
What should a persona contain? 50
Keeping it simple 52
Introducing Phyllis..52
A Final Example...54
Building Upon Your Understanding 56

Chapter 4: Modeling the Experience 57
Creating User Scenarios...58
Defining the user in the user scenario 59
Defining the user's goals 59
Defining user expectations 60
Identifying why the user engages here 61
Understanding and Designing User Journeys 62
Identifying the goals for your journeys...64
Identifying the tasks within the journey 65
Understanding how personalization can impact your journeys ...66
Identifying the tasks for a purchase decision 69
Developing user journeys for omnichannel experiences 72

Chapter 5: Understanding UX as (R)evolution 77

Figuring Out Your Strategy..78
Defining a Sustainable Model..82
Advancing the Future with a UX Process 85
Responsive design 86
Adaptive design...86
Considering channels..87

Part II: Components of Design *89*

**Chapter 6: Taming the Beast: Understanding What You Do
and Don't Have... 91**

Assessing Your Current and Future States 92
Understanding UX as an iterative approach 92
Performing an assessment...93
Getting an expert opinion: heuristic assessments 94
Assessing your current-state analytics 96
Understanding what's happening — not why it's happening 97
Conducting a visual systems audit...................................98
Using scenario-driven assessment 99
Completing a contextual interview with a user 100
Surveying Your Competitors to Build a Better Experience.................102
Defining and Prioritizing Features and Requirements....................105
Ascertaining fundamental requirements 106
Prioritizing features 107

Chapter 7: Developing Content Strategy........................ 111

Defining Content and Content Strategy 111
Making Your Content Work...113
Understanding the Content Inventory and Audit....................115
Completing a content inventory 116
Completing a content audit 122
Interviewing Stakeholders for Content Requirements.............125
Creating the Content Strategy Audit Report and Future-State
Point of View (POV)...128

Chapter 8: Designing the Content Strategy..................... 131

Getting Started with Content Strategy.....................................131
Identifying the Necessary Content Types 132
Creating Experience-Level, Section-Level, and Page-Level
Content Strategy 137
Creating a Content Model...138
Creating a Taxonomy 140
Identifying Content Life Cycles for Each Type of Content 143
Creating a Governance Model...148
Creating an Editorial Calendar and Production Tools.............152

Chapter 9: Building the Information Architecture...............**155**

Benefits of Good Information Architecture..156
Creating a Sitemap as the Framework of Your Experience....................156
Assessing your content..157
Creating a high-level sitemap...158
Creating a sample browse path 160
Templates versus pages..161
Templates as part of the design system 164
Template inventory 165
Constructing a Blueprint with Wireframes 166
Examining components of a wireframe..167
Annotating your wireframes..169
Maintaining sitemaps and wireframes 171
Wireframing navigation..171
Limitations of wireframing...173

Chapter 10: Designing for Specific Channels **175**

Changing Trends in UX 176
Preparing Your Design for Multichannel...177
Considering content for multichannel 179
Ensuring a multichannel approach...180
Designing for Home Desktop, Laptop, and Large-Screen Computers...183
Designing for Mobile Phones 185
Mobile website design best practices..186
Special functionality for mobile sites..191
Accounting for feature phones 192
Designing for Tablet Experiences 193
Designing UX for Other Channels...196
Other digital experiences...196
In-store kiosks 197
Considering E-mail and SMS 197
Print materials...198
Considering the Role of Social Networks 199

Chapter 11: Diving into Visual Design.........................**201**

Wearing a UX Hat for Visual Design 202
Layout: Information architecture versus visual design 202
Defining the benchmark based on screen sizes
and platforms...203
Starting with brand guidelines 204
Understanding the Basics of Visual Design..204
Master template and grid...205
Grids in action 206
Using color appropriately...207
Leveraging the power of type..207
Other key components of the visual system................................208

Conceptualizing Visual Design..209
    Mood boarding...209
    Creating a page comp...210
Validating the Visual Design..211
    Replacing placeholder text with actual content and copy..........211
    Validating visual designs with stakeholders....................212
Creating and Using Style Guides...213
    Common components of a style guide............................213
    Guidelines for voice and tone within content and copy..........215
    The bigger picture...216

Part III: Your UX in Action............................. 217

Chapter 12: Testing: How It Can Save Your UX 219

Eight Common Testing Myths in UX...220
The Power of Prototypes...221
Deciding on Your Testing Strategy..222
    Identifying what to test......................................224
    Choosing a testing method.....................................224
    Identifying research participants.............................225
    Selecting a location for testing..............................227
    Incorporating stakeholders into the process...................227
Using Participatory Design Testing Methods.................................227
Conducting a Card Sorting Exercise...228
Usability Testing Primer...231

Chapter 13: Measuring Your UX to Keep It Relevant 235

Measuring UX Performance as UX Strategy.....................................236
Understanding Goals, Objectives, and Metrics...............................238
Putting the Performance Approach to Work...................................241
    Considering goals and objectives for your experience..........242
    Defining specific metrics to measure..........................245
Understanding Channel-Specific Requirements................................251
    Desktop experiences...252
    Smartphone experiences..252
    Tablet experiences..253
    E-mail/SMS experiences..253
    Social media metrics..253
Capturing and Reporting on Metrics...254

Chapter 14: Making It Past the Finish Line 257

Determining When You Should Consider Bringing in
    Additional Assistance...258
Supporting Large-Scale UX Projects with
    Additional Information Architects.............................259

Bringing in Visual Design Experts 260
    Sources of visual design talent... 261
    Developing specific visual assets: Photography,
      illustration, and video.. 262
Assisting with Content and Copy 263
    Content strategy assistance 263
    Written copy and copywriting assistance 264
Supporting User Testing Activities 264
Enabling the Technology Architecture through Expert Help 265
    Complex technology architectures 265
    Platform-specific technology assistance 266
    Rich media asset development 267
Where to Find UX Help 267
    Browsing great web resources... 268
    UX Magazine 268
    Smashing Magazine 268
    UX Booth 268
    LinkedIn 268
    UX Books 269
    Attending UX conferences 269

Part IV: The Part of Tens *271*

Chapter 15: Ten Reasons Why the User Is Your Most Important Consideration 273

UX Is Based on User-Centered Design 273
UX Focuses on How Services Are Used 274
Users Vary in How and What Content They Consume 274
Users Share Their Experiences — Positive or Negative........................ 275
Users Change Over Time 275
User Experience Trumps Brand Messaging 276
Your Competitor Is Only a Click Away 276
Your Users Are Not You 276
Experience Is Personal.. 277
Experience-Focused Companies Out-Perform the Market 277

Chapter 16: Ten Ways to Ensure That Your UX Is Best in Class 279

Ask Your Users 279
Conduct a Heuristic Assessment... 280
Monitor Your Analytics 280
Focus on the Enjoyment Factor 281
Keep the Experience Fresh... 281
Structure the UX to Reflect User Needs.. 282
Reuse Components... 282

Support Multiple Platforms...282
Don't Lose Your User..283
Create the Experience That Competitors Copy......................................283

Chapter 17: Ten UX Principles That Never Change. 285
The User Is Rarely Wrong..285
Usability Is an Absolute Requirement..286
Content Is King..286
Don't Underestimate Visual Design 286
Prototypes Are Powerful Tools 287
UX Is an Art and a Science...287
Good UX = A User's Approach 287
Less Is More 287
Consistency Is Key 288
The Experience Is the Brand...288

Glossary *289*

Index.. *299*

Introduction

· ·

*T*he methodology of user experience design shapes many products and services that surround us on a daily basis. It informs the websites we use, the applications on our mobile phones, the software packages that pervade our worlds, and even the physical products and environments in which we live.

How are these experiences designed to ensure they work seamlessly and easily for users? What are the best practices to follow to ensure an product is useful and usable? User experience design can provide the answers.

User experience — or UX for short — is a field growing in popularity and visibility in business today because great user experiences help ensure that products and services are adopted, used, and even enjoyed by their target users. Although a variety of inputs go into UX design, the practice of UX design is not necessarily complicated. This book shows you how easy it is to get started with designing great UX.

About This Book

You can use this book in a variety of ways. Naturally, you can read the book from start to finish, which will give you a broad understanding of the critical components of UX in a linear fashion. Alternatively, you can use this book as a chapter-by-chapter reference guide — a tool that gives you a better understanding of specific topics, themes, and challenges as you encounter them. You may also choose to read just the first few chapters together to get a basic understanding of UX, and then use the remaining chapters as an ongoing support guide.

In general, think of *UX For Dummies* as a basic guidebook to the major components of UX. UX is a commonly misunderstood domain — many people think of UX as just usability, but it is so much more. There are subdomains, such as information architecture, content strategy, visual design, user research, testing (including, naturally usability testing), and many others. The topics, terms, and subjects can be confusing to the newcomer, and the primary objective of this book is to shed some light and help to alleviate some of the confusion.

Foolish Assumptions

The practice of UX is relatively new — only 15 to 20 years old, and it was borne out of the field of Human Computer Interaction (HCI), which focused on how people interacted with early forms of computers and related technology. UX is also continually evolving, expanding, and iterating to address new types of experiences and technologies, such as tablets and smartphones, or new interaction methods, like touch and voice. This book aims to give a broad-brush understanding of the world of UX, but always keep in mind that what is relevant now will change as new technology emerges. New topics and approaches are constantly being developed to address our ever-changing world.

UX design is used for many different experiences, including websites, mobile apps, tablet apps, desktop software, kiosks, game design, and many others. In addition, though, UX methods are sometimes used to design physical products and real-world environments like retail stores or bank branches. However, in most cases, UX refers to the process of designing digital experiences, and that's our focus of this book: to highlight how UX is applied to many types of digital challenges.

This book highlights a variety of types of digital platforms, but the book intentionally does not dig too deeply within any one of these subjects specifically. Naturally, entire books can be written (and have been written!) on the sole topic of web design, software interaction design, or mobile app design. The basic building blocks of UX are applicable to all of these types of challenges, and this book is a guide to UX in its most fundamental form.

Although UX is design practice that was borne out of technology experiences (web, mobile phones, and software),UX is not really a technological field. It deals with technology but is focused on understanding how the user interacts with technology rather than focusing on the technology itself. It is a common misconception that UX is a technology development process. In reality, UX is more aligned with other forms of creative design and production processes, such as advertising or product development.

Icons Used in This Book

Icons are those little pictures that you find in the margins of this book. We use them to grab your attention and steer you toward key bits of information. Here's a list of the icons we use in the book and what each one means:

Some of the points made in this book are things you should consider committing to memory. These are important details that will serve you well in years to come if you remember them.

These are the insider's tips that we have gathered over the years. These can help you ensure success, as well as avoid many of the common pitfalls along the way.

 Years of experience in the world of UX has taught us a lot about what works in the world of UX, and what does not. These points help identify the most common mistakes and misconceptions made during a UX project.

 The Technical Stuff icon marks information of a highly technical nature that you can normally skip over.

Beyond the Book

To read more on topics related to UX, check out the following things:

In addition to this book, we supply content online that feature the following information:

- ✔ **Cheat Sheet:** The UX cheat sheet is a quick reference guide for some of the primary themes discussed in this book. You can find it at the following www.dummies.com/cheatsheet/ux.

- ✔ **Dummies.com online articles:** We've written some articles about content strategy, information architecture, user research, and testing resources. You can also read "Ten Things to Prepare Your UX for the Future" at www.dummies.com/extras/ux.

Where to Go from Here

Welcome to the world of UX. If you are reading this book (and obviously, you are, for which your humble authors thank you deeply) then your curiosity has been awakened into designing experiences with a new and different focus — the user. Our recommendation is you should read Chapter 1 and then take it from there. If after the first chapter you want to focus on a specific topic, then jump right to it. Good luck!

Part I
Getting Started with UX

In this part . . .

- ✔ Understand the basics of user experience design and how it's focused on the wants and needs of the user.
- ✔ Recognize the importance of UX and the business value it can bring.
- ✔ Define basic models for understanding users and find out how those models can be used during the UX design project.

Chapter 1

Defining UX and the Process

In This Chapter

▶ Orienting you to what UX is about and why it's important

▶ Understanding how to use UX

▶ Defining the various components that comprise the world of UX design

Any darn fool can make something complex; it takes a genius to make something simple.

— Albert Einstein

Maybe you think UX is a high-tech term that applies only to folks who work with computers. And prior to picking up this book, you had no reason to understand anything about UX. Or maybe you develop code for a website and want to learn how to more effectively work with folks in UX. Regardless, it is safe to bet that UX has impacted your life in numerous ways, quite possibly every day or even every hour. If you've ever browsed a website, purchased a product online, checked the weather via an app on a smartphone, used an electronic kiosk at an airport to print a ticket, or interacted with an interface on your television to watch a movie, you have touched on the world of UX. There is a UX that surrounds many types of products, from home appliances such as the interface on microwave ovens to the dashboard of your car. Empowering so many of today's everyday products and digital experiences is the art and science of UX: making our interactions and transactions seamless, effective, and oftentimes invisible for people who use them.

UX is known by several other names, such as UXD (user experience design), user-centered design, human-computer interaction (HCI), and experience design. Although there are subtle differences in these expressions, regardless of what you call it, UX plays a critical role in making our physical and digital lives frictionless and enjoyable. When good UX practices are not deployed, the result is interactions that are frustrating, confusing, ineffective, or just plain useless or ugly. If you have ever used a website and walked away from the experience so frustrated that you wanted to throw your monitor out a window, you know what it means to encounter bad UX design.

Perhaps you are thinking of launching your own website, designing a blog, or maybe you just want to better understand the basic design considerations of the world of digital media. Maybe you have a website but it is not accomplishing your intended goals. Or you have to ramp up quickly on UX so that you can work with a UX professional. Regardless of your starting point, taking a look at UX will help you think differently about the digital phenomenon that is changing our world. This chapter helps you get started on the UX journey.

What Is UX, Really?

UX, simply put, stands for user experience. You may be asking, "Why not UE?" But in the world of user interaction, *X* takes precedence over the letter *E*. *User experience* is the design practice that focuses on creating experiences — typically digital experiences like websites, for example — that are easy to use and satisfying for users. It focuses on a design practice that puts the user at the center of all considerations, so that the eventual experience provides interactions that are intuitive, helpful, and even enjoyable.

Although user experience can apply to many different types of products and designs, the scope of this work is to focus primarily on digital interfaces. In this context, user experience design is changing all parts of our world, including:

- **Websites:** Content sites, social media, and e-commerce
- **Mobile apps:** Smartphone applications
- **Tablet experiences:** Apps for tablets
- **Kiosks:** Seen in airports, shopping malls, and so forth
- **Software:** Standard software applications such as spreadsheets and word processing
- **Product Interfaces:** GPS systems, interfaces in automobiles to control audio and climate, digital interfaces to common household appliances such as TVs, and microwaves

From a business standpoint, UX best practices help to define how your brand or business will be experienced by customers through digital media.

Good UX can ensure that customers use and actually enjoy the experiences you design. If you've ever used a website, software application, or product interface that confused you, you've probably experienced a design process that did not leverage UX best practices. In addition, UX can be a key component in establishing customer loyalty and goodwill.

The Promise of Good UX Design

Good UX design has three fundamental measurements, and they are widely known throughout the UX digital design industry. Any UX design should embody all the following components:

- ✔ **Useful:** The solution provides content, features, or functions that meet common user needs; in short, the experience must be useful in all aspects. As an example, an e-commerce website could include the capability to see if a specific product is in stock or not — a simply useful feature.

- ✔ **Usable:** The solution provides functionality that is easy to use and intuitive, for which basic functions do not require much active concentration to accomplish. Given the e-commerce example just used, this could mean that the process to purchase a product is simple and quick.

- ✔ **Desirable:** Good UX designs enable experiences that are desirable, or even delightful. So not only does the solution provide useful features that are easy to use, but it also does so in a way that engages the user — often through great visual design, content, and copy. To continue with the e-commerce example, the capability to purchase a product online should be so compelling and enjoyable that users are likely to come back again sometime soon or even share the experience with others within their friends and family.

If the user experience is not all these things — useful, usable, and desirable — it is very possible the shopper will find other ways to purchase your product or will purchase a similar product from another source. For example, if a user gets frustrated because your website makes her do all sorts of things she does not or cannot understand, she will quite likely jump to a competitor's website to purchase a similar product. And if you are really unfortunate, she might post her experience in social media, such as on Yelp.com, Twitter, or Facebook, adding further insult to injury and informing others to not use your experience!

UX Components

UX design is a particularly multidisciplinary practice that integrates a number of components. The following sections highlight these components to help you better understand what makes up UX. In later chapters, you find out more about each of these areas.

Information architecture

Information architecture is one of the most fundamental components to good UX design and refers to breaking down a solution, website, or screen into the most basic contents, including these:

- ✔ **Navigation:** How a user navigates on a site
- ✔ **Content organization:** How information is organized, into which modules or "containers" it is placed, and where the modules go
- ✔ **Visual priority of page elements:** Where things fall or reside on the screen
- ✔ **Interaction design:** What the interaction model is (defined later)

Information architecture is most often brought to life during the design process through a *wireframe:* a black-and-white sketch of a web page or an application screen, much like an architectural blueprint that provides a basic illustration of a house under construction. Wireframes and information architecture also typically include technology and functional requirements, which help to define how the experience will change (or not) when a user interacts with it.

Content strategy

Content strategy determines how, why, where, and when content will go into an experience. Content refers to any type of information that is recorded (video, images, copy, text, information). The content for the experience is another of the basic components to defining the user's overall experience. Content strategy is similar to the overall editorial strategy for the experience, outlining the objectives and defining characteristics of all the content, whether that is written content or functionality. All content within an experience should have a purpose and must be meaningful in helping a user achieve a task. Digital content must be written for "scanability," understanding that most users digest written content on a screen quickly, and oftentimes without reading the full page.

Interaction design

Interaction design defines the rules for how a user interacts with an experience: what happens when users navigate, choose buttons, and follow links, for instance. Interaction design helps to define the journey a user goes through to accomplish a task. Say a user wants to interact with online support on a website. What does the user do before, during, and after that experience? What types of interaction should the website include so that all the user's needs are met? The area of interaction design is growing as the types of interactions with digital products increases. For example, most smartphones allow for touchscreen interactions, providing new models of interaction design that include touch, swipe, and pinch.

Usability

Usability refers to how well the experience performs against users' interactions with it. For example, if Sheila wants to check on her prescription using a digital kiosk in her local pharmacy, can she quickly find the status of whether the pharmacist has filled it? Is the kiosk useful to her, or is it just an oversized gizmo unnecessarily taking up store real estate? Is the experience clear and intuitive to users, or does it require active concentration to complete basic functions or needs? Poor usability is an experience killer in today's world of digital media. And an experience killer can mean a death in the relationship between you and your user.

You should know your users — those who interact with your product, service, brand, company, or all of the above via a digital interface — as well as you know your best friends (or even better). This means you need to get into their minds and understand how they think, act, look, and behave. This book explores how you begin to understand your uses, generally through user interviews, usability testing, and other techniques that are explored later in the book. You also have to stay on top of your users' needs. Just as with friendships, user needs and behaviors change. The better you know your users, the more likely the experience you build will resonate with them, which translates into success for your business.

Visual design

The visual aspects to any user's experience are the most visible components of the solution. *Visual design* not only helps to ensure a solution is aesthetically pleasing, but it also helps ensure that the solution follows brand consistency. In addition, though, visual design helps a user digest all the content on any screen, so it's a key contributor to the usability of an experience.

Of course anyone who pays a professional to build an interface wants it to look good. But sometimes, this becomes the main priority — color and imagery take the front seat to all other design decisions. Although visual design is the final icing on top of an effective UX, it's imperative that the other aspects of UX are also represented in any final solution. A beautiful website that contains difficult or unintuitive navigation will impress no one and may ultimately compromise a business's goals.

UX Is a Big Deal

Simply put, good user experience is good business. Many companies — as big as GE and as small as your local web design shop — are now focusing on the discipline of UX. It's just as important for Tom's Tavern in Eliva, Wisconsin, to embody good usability so customers can easily order food for takeout as it is for a Fortune 100 company to have a robust user experience to sell products online. Apple, for example, is known for simplicity in the UX of its products and software. Just how important is UX to the business bottom line? As shown in Figure 1-1, companies that provide an outstanding customer experience outperform in the S&P.

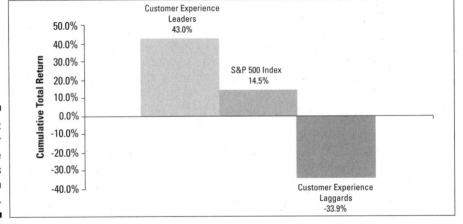

Figure 1-1:
Customer experience leaders outperform the market.

Here are some areas in which good UX can have a significant business impact:

- ✔ **Customer satisfaction and loyalty:** The better the experience with a product or service, the more likely customers are to continue to use it, and to recommend it. The quality of the experience is becoming an increasing factor in overall customer loyalty. If you use online banking and recently switched banks, it's easy to compare which bank has better online banking services, more useful tools and features, and is easier to use. Most consumers feel more loyal to the bank that offers a better user experience.

- ✔ **Revenue:** Clarity and consistency in UX will help ensure shoppers can get through the online purchase process quickly and efficiently. For big box retailers like Walmart, Target, and Amazon, clarity in the UX of the shopping and checkout process can mean the difference in millions of dollars in sales on any given shopping day.

✔ **Traffic:** The better the UX on a website, the more likely users will spend more time on the site and are more likely to return at a later date. Increased traffic and dwell time have a direct correlation to rankings in search engines like Google, and the higher the rankings, the more additional traffic that will visit the site. In short, better experiences help deliver more customers.

✔ **Brand expression:** and finally, the better the UX, the better the impression of the brand overall. A famous designer, Clement Mok, once was quoted as saying, "the Experience is the Brand." In his words, the user experience is an active expression of the brand: a bad experience leads to poor brand perception. A good user experience leads to positive brand impressions and higher longer-term brand value.

How UX and Usability Work Together

UX and usability are often confused. Certainly, there is a close relationship between the two, but these two concepts are fundamentally different. In short, UX is a broader design practice that ensures the usability of a solution, but UX is focused on broader objectives, such as usefulness and overall engagement. Usability is an output of the UX, and within UX seeks to test the performance of the solution. The following sections help to clarify how UX differs from usability.

The basics of usability

Usability is an area of research and testing that primarily ensures that any digital solution works, and is easy to use and intuitive. It also tests to make sure that a user can accomplish the goals embodied by the digital solution. For example, a local car dealership may want a website so that a user can locate the shop, identify which cars are currently in stock, schedule service for an existing car purchase, or call the shop to discuss a new car. The usability of a solution can be tested and explored in many ways, and several of those methods are explained in Chapter 12. Consider usability testing to be a primary method of answering the question, "How easy is a solution to use?" Following are some examples of common problems that usability testing can identify in a solution:

✔ **Navigation:** How does a solution work, where does a user click to accomplish key tasks, and is the website or application structured to make sense to a user?

✔ **Content:** Is the content clear, and is it the right level of content at the right time?

✔ **Dead ends:** Are there navigational pathways that don't lead to the completion of a user's task; dead links; nonworking buttons; or links that take users to features they did not expect?

✔ **Cognitive overload:** Are you asking the user to digest too much information or complete too many functions or fields, or have you designed a user flow that is too complicated?

The most important measurements for usability are clarity, consistency, and ease of use. Thus, if you build an experience that is clear, concise, and easy to use, then chances are your solution will be effective and you will please your users.

Comparing UX to usability

UX, on the other hand, has a broader set of focus areas beyond just usability. If usability aims to answer the question, "How easy is a solution to use?" the world of UX design also aims to answer the questions, "How useful was the solution?" and "How enjoyable was the solution to use?"

Making a solution easy to use is one of the key objectives behind user experience design, but UX also focuses on making sure a solution contains content, features, and functions that are most useful to a user (not simply features that work well). UX also focuses on how satisfying and engaging a solution is, which is determined by factors other than how simple it is to use. Factors like visual appeal, the tone of written content, and how the website or system responds are all key components to determining how engaging and desirable the final solution will be.

Necessary UX Inputs

One of the goals of UX is to make complex interactions and transactions easy and enjoyable to accomplish. That said, it may not surprise you that many considerations go into designing the experience to ensure that it feels seamless. The building blocks of the UX design process focus on a number of things: business goals, target users, enabling technologies, and content, among others. All these topics become strategic inputs to the UX design process.

Strategic inputs include the following: business objectives, competitive landscape and technical architecture, design, and content input. You should consider all these areas when building a user experience, as each impacts the overall experience. The relationship between each input and user experience is examined in the following sections.

Business objectives

The most fundamental input in the UX design process is a solid understanding of the underlying business objectives. What are you trying to accomplish? Do you want to sell products? Provide customer information to reduce phone calls? Engage and entertain users? A clear definition of the business goals and objectives is the first and most critical step.

For example, Deborah, a bakery owner in Portland, Maine, wants to build a website for desktop, mobile, and tablet devices to promote her business. Her business goals in doing so include promotion of her business by generating buzz about her shop; selling more products by providing customers the capability to order online; and, competitively differentiating herself from other bakeries in her area by building a best-in-class website. To create a successful experience, Deborah must first consider what constitutes success and then identify ways to demonstrate its value.

After you define these objectives, you also have to determine how you will measure success. It's critical to define the key success metrics, or key performance indicators (KPIs), at the start of the project because they will impact all other decisions you make throughout the process. These metrics also ensure that the final experience aligns with your original goals.

In addition, though, you must consider other operational business objectives, which may be equally important. How will the experience be maintained? Who will update the content? How will the experience be modified and enhanced over time?

Competitive landscape

Before you begin the design process, it's important to consider the competitive landscape: Who else possesses a similar product or service that is on the market? Has he built a user experience to promote, sell, or support his product or service? What can you learn from assessing the UX of that service? What do you like? What features or content may be missing?

Assessing your competition means that you assess what others in the same industry are doing, especially around any types of user interaction they create. For example, when Deborah, mentioned earlier, decides to build a web presence, she reviews all the competitors in Portland to see what they offer. Who has a website and who does not? With those who do, what features do they offer their users on their websites? Deborah also looks at websites for similar businesses in other cities to determine if there are any other ideas she can glean about building a best-in-class user experience.

Given the iterative nature of digital design, where websites and applications are continually updated and enhanced, it's particularly useful to take a deep look at any similar experiences (products or services) that exist on the market. You can learn a lot from quickly assessing these services, and avoid many of the UX pitfalls that are common in design today.

Technology architecture

This input includes which technology is necessary to support the solution you are building. Which technology is necessary to create, produce, publish, and maintain your user experience? Also, where will the user experience exist (for instance, a website on mobile, tablet, and desktop)? What technology will support you solution?

Taking time to assess the underlying technology architecture will ensure that the design choices you make throughout the process will be supported by the underlying technology. Some of the more simple technology questions that need to be addressed are: Which web browsers will be supported? Will the solution be used via mobile devices, and if so, which operating systems will be supported (Apple, Android, and so forth)?

If you are designing an e-commerce or more complex solution, you need to explore additional areas, including:

- Is there a system to publish and manage content, such as a content management system?
- If you are selling products, how will the product catalog be updated and maintained? How will you process payments?
- Will the website or app require a user to register or authenticate herself?

These topics can get very technical, very quickly, so it is critical for all team members on a UX project to have a common understanding of the technologies that will enable the experience. They play a critical role in the eventual experience.

Design inputs

Design inputs include the components necessary for thorough and robust design experiences. Two considerations form these inputs: profiles or personas, and customer journeys or scenarios.

Profiles and personas help frame which user behaviors are necessary to consider in your ultimate experience, while scenarios and journeys provide the different paths a user may take to accomplish a task within the experience.

Profiles or personas

Another fundamental building block of UX is an understanding of your target audience: Who are they, how will they use your solution, and what do you know about them? If you want to design successful user-centered solutions, profiles and personas provide a helpful understanding of how your user is critical.

Frequently, though, one of the bigger challenges with respect to understanding your target user is not the lack of information about users, but the challenge of *prioritizing all the information* you know about users. For example, for most solutions, not all users are equally important. It's important that you document which type of user may be your top priority. For a baby goods company, the priority persona might be expectant mothers, rather than soon-to-be uncles and aunts (gifters), who may be important, but not as critical as expectant mothers.

User information is typically distilled into simple and digestible formats, called user profiles or personas. Personas help to bring to life the target user for your solution, highlight mission-critical information about that user, and strip away the unnecessary details. You use these personas throughout the entire project lifecycle.

Scenarios and journeys

To help bring a prospective solution to life, a persona is typically paired with a scenario or a user journey. Scenarios tell a simple story of the process a target user goes through, and how your new solution is used along the way. For an e-commerce example, your scenario might explain the process that an expectant mother goes through to purchase products for the nursery.

The user journey, similarly, tells a story, but it's typically a higher-level story, with broader reach and impact. For example, a scenario may illustrate how the mother-to-be researches a crib for the nursery, while the user journey shows the broader process of getting the nursery ready overall.

Brand guidelines

You will want to understand any brand requirements your organization may have, because these may impact the eventual user experience. In some cases, such as a small business building an entirely new website, no brand guidelines may exist. For larger companies, these guidelines typically come in the form of brand guidelines, which outline color palettes, logo usage, and fonts, among other details. For smaller projects and smaller businesses, it's helpful to identify and assess any existing collateral that will help inform the visual look and feel you will be creating. This information can be in the form of printed brochures, corporate identity, or even product specifications.

Experience models

And finally, one last artifact that is critical for larger, more complex UX engagements is the experience model. The experience model aims to document the entire life cycle of an experience, stepping back from any one moment during the process, or any one website, application, or tool. The experience model is a critical tool for the overall understanding of users, and how all the products, services, marketing, and communications can fit into how users experience your world.

For example, experience models could help define the overarching process mothers go through in having children: whether from adoption, surrogacy, or becoming pregnant, to preparing for new babies within their lives, and possibly repeating the process. It is the highest-level model of all our artifacts, going more broadly than scenarios and journeys. The same experience model can be used by business for years, without the need to update or modify them, while scenarios and journeys typically need updating as technology, tools, and behaviors evolve.

Content inputs

Content input is critical to successful user experiences because it informs what types of information are made available to your users. The next two sections highlight content models, matrixes, and taxonomies, and the role each plays in the user experience design process.

Content models and content matrix

The content model and matrix help you to organize the content that is in your experience and prioritize it effectively. A solid model also establishes any rules around the content (such as ensuring that the rotating carousel on the home page serves up five images with headlines, and is updated weekly). It can also enable personalization (for example, for people in Nebraska, serve up X content; for people in Tokyo, serve up Y content). Chapter 8 details exactly how to build the content model and matrix. A successful content model means that your users will get the right content in the right place at the right time.

Taxonomy

Taxonomy is not the art of stuffing animals. That's taxidermy. *Taxonomy* is the science of figuring out how to organize and label information so that your users can find what they need, where they need to find it, and when they need it. The manner by which information is organized in a library (by author, title, subject, and so forth) is an example of a taxonomy. Also, a grocery store is organized around a taxonomy (Meat > Beef > Steaks > Sirloin). If you have purchased any product online, you probably have interacted with a taxonomy without even realizing it. Taxonomy is critical to organizing information so that users can find it; as you see later, it is critical for enabling search capabilities, whenever search functionality is present within an application or website. Without a proper and robust taxonomy, your users may not be able to find what they need.

Considerations before Beginning UX

Some of the best user experiences make the complex look very simple, but that simplicity often masks the large number of considerations that the UX designer takes into account during the development process. Just how complex will your project be? Take some time to consider all the variables that will help to determine a successful outcome for your solution. The following sections can guide you in this thought process.

Understanding your target users

What do you know about your users? How much information do you have about them? Can you easily picture your target users and describe them? Is there more than one type of target user, and, if so, how different are those users from one another? Given that UX is a user-centered process, it is critical you have a good understanding of whom you are designing for: who they are, how they behave, and their wants and needs.

If you don't know a lot about them, do you need to conduct user research? User research can be enormously effective for not only generating strategic insights into a solution, but also for inspiring the design process for how the solution will fit into a user's lifestyle.

If you think there are gaps in your understanding of your target user, a myriad of user research methods, tools, and approaches can help fill in some of the blanks. And many of them are easy, inexpensive, and quick to execute. Some of them are outlined in the following section.

Deciding on a new project or redesign

Many UX projects are redesigns of existing experiences, such as updates to existing websites, applications, or mobile apps. If this is the case, what data might be available from the existing experience that you can take into the start of your redesign analysis? Before you begin the redesign process, identify all sources of existing data that may be relevant, including current website analytics that outline which content is used most frequently, for example.

Identifying the technology

How complex will the solution be? If it is a content-heavy solution, consider how content will be created, maintained, and even retired. What system will enable this? By identifying your target user, you can identify the technologies that will need to be supported. For example, if you are targeting 20-year-old students for your new experience, it's likely you'll need to consider Android and Apple's iOS platform support to enable smartphone use as well as laptops for accessing websites. Without getting too deep into the technology, assess how technical you think your solution will be, and make sure the correct resources are aligned for supporting the project life cycle.

Maintaining the experience

Although your UX project has not even begun, it's never too early to stop and think about the longer-term maintenance of the final solution. How will the system be maintained once it has been built and launched to the public? How will new features be added? Spend some time to think about the longer-term needs before the design process begins. The plan for maintaining the solution can greatly impact the choices you will make during the UX design process.

Ensuring consistency

What guidelines currently exist that may impact the look and feel of visual design? Are brand guidelines available? If so, get them on hand before the project begins. Furthermore, it's also helpful to get any other guidelines that may assist in developing written content. Many brand guidelines also include specifications for written content: guidelines that define the tone of voice and standards for written copy.

Determining your level of comfort

And finally, just how comfortable are you with this process? The world of UX is multidisciplinary, spanning business strategy, creative design, market insight, and technology (among other areas), but no one UX designer is equally strong in all these areas. Many UX designers come from one specific area, such as visual design or information architecture, and have only fundamental knowledge and skills in the other areas. It is also common to see UX designers who come from a technology or site development background. You won't need to do it all, but do identify where you might need more assistance and align the appropriate additional resources.

Understanding what makes a good UX designer

UX designers possess a mixed set of skills. Some skew more heavily toward user research; others skew more toward creative design. Some of the best UX designers have a good blend of experience in the creative design and a deep understanding of the business objectives and strategic goals, and are also great team project managers (able to pull all the pieces together). Figure 1-2 illustrates the ideal combination.

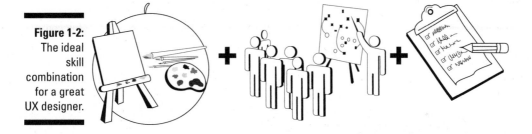

Figure 1-2: The ideal skill combination for a great UX designer.

How a Typical Project Works

A wide variety of UX methods and approaches have been developed over the years, all reflecting the varied nature of today's digital experiences (websites, mobile apps, software design). And while some projects are enormously complex and will span years in design and development, others can be completed in just a few weeks.

Underneath all this diversity, though, is a set of common practices that are standard across the vast majority of UX projects. This approach can be scaled up or down to support projects of any complexity and duration. Each of the phases below can span hours or days for simpler projects, to months or years for more complex projects. Figure 1-3 illustrates this process.

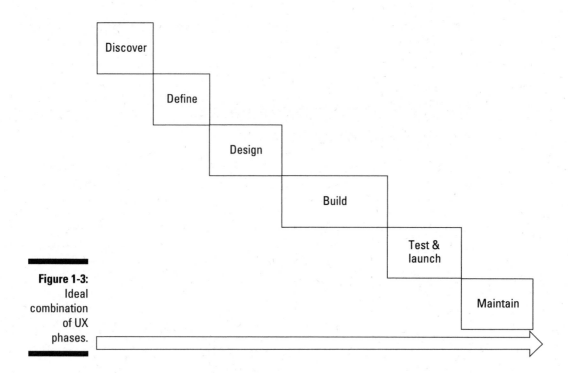

Figure 1-3:
Ideal
combination
of UX
phases.

Define phase

The define phase frames the first phase in a typical UX project, also referred to as discovery. The work involved in this phase helps define the core building blocks of the solution, and helps ensure that the creative design process that follows is well grounded with insights and clear goals. The following are tasks that are commonly included in the define phase:

✔ **Define the business goals:** A clear definition of what business objectives the UX solution should accomplish, with clear metrics defined so that success can be evaluated.

✔ **Benchmark current experiences:** An assessment of any current experiences (if the project is a redesign), identifying what works well and what does not work well. In addition, a look at any competitive services: What insight can be taken from all existing experiences?

✔ **Develop user personas:** A clear and useful understanding of your target user, in the form of user profiles or personas. Personas can be created from existing data on target users, or can be created by conducting some user research to inform the UX process, if necessary.

- ✔ **Audit content:** A look at all content you'll have to work with during the design process. This can be existing website content (in the case of a redesign), or content that is used for other uses (such as printed materials).

- ✔ **Brand audit:** An assessment of any existing visual guidelines you have for the look and feel of the experience, as well as for the tone of written content.

- ✔ **Technology assessment:** A review of all technologies that will be involved in the final solution. This includes underlying technologies, as well as a "browser benchmark," which defines all versions of web browsers that should be supported, as well as key platforms (web, mobile, tablet, and so forth).

Often discovery and define are broken into two phases, with the discovery phase encompassing business goal definition, benchmarks and competitive analysis, audits, and user persona definition. Define includes sitemap creation (or the initial sitemap), content strategy framework, user flows, and technology assessment.

Design phase

This phase is where the creative process kicks into high gear. Wireframes and sitemaps are created to provide a high-level blueprint of the experience. Mood boards and visual design comps are created to illustrate the visual nature of the solution.

A key output of the design phase is a high-level design that shows key pages or screens: the home page and primary secondary pages or screens. All major creative design decisions are made during the design phase. Additional deliverables, all of which are explored later in the book, include wireframes, content matrix and guidelines, and detailed functional specifications.

Build phase

The build phase involves building out all lower-level pages and screens, according to the design decisions that were made during the design phase. This work involves the development of additional templates and visual designs for all lower-level pages, as well as the creation of additional page modules.

Typically, a large amount of work during the build phase is to create all the content that will fill all the pages and screens for the final solution. Some of this work can begin in the design phase, but in general the bulk occurs during the build phase. This content includes written content and visual assets (such as photographs and illustrations), as well as technical functions. While the majority of the larger creative decisions are made during the design phase, it's the heavy lifting of the build phase that determines how great the detailed experience will be.

Test and launch phase

Before an experience design is completed, it needs to be thoroughly tested for bugs, technical glitches, and any remaining usability problems. Depending on the complexity of the solution, the testing process can be extensive.

Maintain phase

Finally, given the iterative nature of digital design, once a website or application has launched to the public, ongoing effort must be made to maintain the quality of the experience. Is the content still relevant, or does it need to be updated or retired? Has the technology evolved, and if so, will it require enhancements to the user experience you created? The best user experiences are those that contain content and features that are still relevant and fresh, and it's the maintain phase that ensures how often the experience will be updated.

Chapter 2

Examining Why You Should Use UX

In This Chapter

▶ Understanding why UX is a big deal

▶ Assessing the impact UX has on your business or organization

▶ Revealing how UX helps your users to accomplish their goals

In business you get what you want by giving other people what they want.

— Alice MacDougall

*U*X can play an important role in helping a business realize its goals and contributing to its bottom line of generating revenue. Good UX also provides customers and users of a product, application, or service with an enjoyable, productive, and engaging experience, thereby facilitating a positive relationship between the user and the business. The ability to understand your customers' and users' unique needs, thinking, and behaviors may also provide you with a competitive edge. A compelling UX may help you outperform your competition and even win over some of their customers. Regardless of your type of business, understanding your users and their goals, motivations, and desires is tantamount to speaking to them and connecting to them in a way that is beneficial to you and them.

In the world of digital and interactive experiences, the relationship between the user and the business *ideally* functions symbiotically — in other words, the ideal relationship mutually benefits both the user and the business. Given the multichannel universe in which your business lives — whether you want it to or not — creating an experience where users and businesses not only peacefully coexist, but also thrive together separates an exceptional business from one that just survives. This chapter first quickly explains why a solid UX approach is more important than ever. Then it surveys how UX helps achieve business goals and describes how UX can benefit your users.

Realizing UX for All Channel Benefits

Considering that many people live in an increasingly "always-on" and "always-connected" world with all these technological gadgets and gizmos, you can infer why user experience matters more and more in your everyday life. But how does this importance translate to helping you realize your business or organizational goals via your users? To understand the impact of user experience in the technologies around you, first consider two key concepts at play in your life today: *multichannel* and *omnichannel* experiences.

You may have heard the term *multichannel* before without truly grasping its meaning. In essence, the term refers to more than one channel to which content or an experience resides: TV, desktop, mobile, in-store, and so forth.

You also may have heard folks use an even more impressive sounding term: *omnichannel*. But what does one mean by putting the all-encompassing term *omni* in front of the word *channel*? Was Omni not a doomed 1980s car model and currently, a popular higher-end hotel and resort chain? Yes to both accounts, but Martha Stewart also uses the term for her company's name, Omnimedia, and her use of "omni" provides insight into its importance for you. Stewart named her company Omnimedia and made it an overarching business goal of the company to proliferate all media and channels in ways that capitalize on each medium's unique capabilities. For example, a magazine highlights a feature story about artisanal foods, such as cheese from an organic farm; a television program showcases "how-to" content, such as how to create the perfect place-setting; and a cookbook contains recipes. In many ways, all three of these unique channels offer complementary content, and in this case each channel can easily point to the other — that is, the magazine can reference a recipe in the cookbook that uses the featured cheese and the television segment on dinner place-settings can feature the recipe upon the table.

But how is omnichannel important to UX and why is understanding its role paramount to uncovering the potential of UX for you and your business in today's world? Omnichannel provides information at every place a user interacts with your brand or organization, and it considers the time, manner, and place that the interactions occur. It includes analog, digital, in-store, and person-to-person interaction and captures the entire end-to-end customer or user experience. Omnichannel recognizes that in today's world, a user interacts with a product, service, or business in many different channels or mediums and that most user engagement with a brand exists in several channels. Table 2-1 illustrates some common uses of different channels.

Table 2-1	User Engagement with Channels
Channel	**Experience**
Television	Viewing an ad on TV
	Selecting "learn more" on the TV in response to an ad (available on smart TVs)
Radio/newspaper	Hearing/seeing an ad that points to a website
Desktop	Interacting with a website, a banner ad, or social media such as Facebook, Twitter, Instagram, or Tumblr
	Receiving e-mails on a purchased product
	Conducting research on a product, service, or company
Mobile (smartphone or tablet)	Scanning a QR code in a store
	Clicking to call or clicking for a map
	Sharing a product photo on social networks
	Receiving SMS updates, such as coupons, when standing in front of a retailer storefront
Kiosk (in store)	Seeing a product in action
	Ordering accessories for a product
	Interacting with an interface to "virtually" try out a product
Product package	Obtaining registration information
	Viewing an opt-in for social media
	Reading product support instructions or being directed to the support section of a website

Omnichannel is important for UX because a good and well-informed UX experience across channels translates into a seamless user experience with your product, service, or brand. A good omnichannel experience places the user at the center of the engagement and looks at how she interacts with channels across her life cycle with a product or service. Figure 2-1 demonstrates this concept.

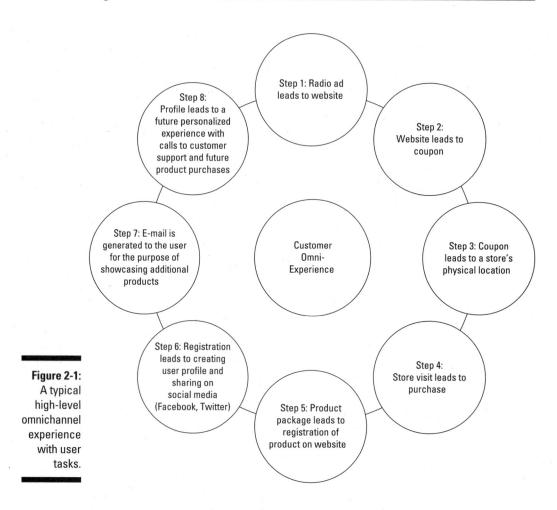

Figure 2-1:
A typical high-level omnichannel experience with user tasks.

To develop a solid UX strategy, you need to look at the overall customer life-cycle and its channel engagement; from that, you derive the best experiences necessary per channel. When you understand this approach, you harness the power that a solid UX strategy brings to your business and its goals.

Understanding How UX Benefits Your Business

A robust and effective UX benefits a business in many different aspects, depending on the nature of the business. First, well-informed UX can help you sell more products efficiently and effectively as well as support those products after customers have bought them. UX can also change the perception of your brand or organization by showing users how you serve your community and employees through engaging company information, such as videos on sponsorship of local charities. Cost savings may arise out of fewer errors in applications and interaction experiences: Taking the time upfront to build user-friendly experiences means not reworking these in the future. This section of the chapter and the next explore these benefits by demonstrating how you should define your business goals with UX in mind and how UX provides specific benefits for your business.

If you are like most of us, you own a business, work in one, will be working in one, or are starting one up. To determine how UX benefits you, you first start with an understanding of your business goals and objectives. This book does not help you define your larger business goals; you should know these already. However, your business likely has some specific goals that UX can directly impact. This section explores those areas. For a more thorough list of these business goals and how to measure them, see Chapter 13.

Make UX integral to your business by calling it out specifically as a business goal. This approach demonstrates a commitment to your users and inspires an ongoing financial and organizational investment to quality UX. Businesses that make UX a priority receive several benefits, including higher brand recognition, greater financial returns, and improved customer satisfaction.

UX is not something many users notice unless it is poor or broken. In those cases, users do notice the experience, and it reflects poorly on your product or service and your company as a whole. In today's world, when a customer endures a bad experience with a brand, he is likely to talk about and share that experience. Online peer-to-peer ratings and reviews, such as Yelp and Angie's List, make sharing one's experience quick and easy. A poor UX — whether on your website or within a product itself — can prove costly and detrimental to your business.

Your business should have goals and objectives, as outlined by a business plan, a mission statement, product positioning, or in any of a variety of strategic business objectives or annual reports. Identifying specific business goals impacted by UX proves helpful in determining the benefit of UX to your business. Following are some goals that are typical for businesses that build a website:

- ✔ **Retaining current customers** by providing them a useful experience and supporting their relationship with the brand (through customer support, news on their previous purchases, and value-added content that suits their current and future needs).

- ✔ **Generating new customers** through a variety of efforts, such as providing functionality and information in the user experience that competitors fail to provide, making it easy to accomplish user tasks and goals, and effectively marketing the experience in areas such as search engines.

✔ **Selling a product or service,** by either selling a new product or cross-selling an accessory or item to go along with the product — for example, when a man buys a suit online, he receives a recommendation to purchase shoes and a belt to go with the suit.

✔ **Providing information about the company,** such as investor relations information; information about the organization's social responsibility; and news about company activities, such as a new product release or changes in management. This information can be presented in a variety of ways, such as articles, videos, and infographics (charts and graphics).

✔ **Procuring new employees** through listing current jobs, providing compelling information on why to work for the company, and showcasing current employees.

Some likely benefits of a robust UX include the following:

✔ **Increase in customer satisfaction:** Because UX is user-centric, adhering to UX best practices means developing functionality, features, and content relevant to users and their needs. Being attentive to the users and what is relevant to them helps keep them happy when they engage with your brand. When a user is happy with a brand, he will engage with it again and again. He will also refer it to his friends. For many users, this means posting a positive experience on a social media site. The following example illustrates this point.

A popular amusement park in Owl's Head, Maine, recently attempted to reduce the impact of waiting in long lines by making it less cumbersome and agitating. Sheila experiences this effort firsthand while she and her child stand in line at an amusement park behind approximately 100 other people. She sees a sign with a QR code that reads: "Journey Away from a Long Line: adults (scan here), teens (scan here), or children (scan here)." Upon scanning, she is prompted to download an app that allows her child to interact with a rollercoaster cartoon while solving a puzzle. The child is appeased despite a 20-minute wait. The app "senses" Sheila's placement in line, so it tailors the experience specific to her location: When she reaches the front of the line, the game is over. At the end of the line, an additional scan enables her to share her experience on Twitter and receive a coupon for free cotton candy. Sheila recommends the theme park to all her friends with children. The entire scenario is facilitated through user research, user testing, and a solid UX strategy.

✔ **Impact on the sale of product or service:** When a UX is easy for a customer or potential customer, the overall sales process improves because the user has an overall purchase experience that is simple, enjoyable, and intuitive. But there are additional benefits to a solid UX. When a user feels that a website is credible and understands her needs, she more likely trusts the site (and brand). When a brand builds a user's trust, the user is more likely to follow through with purchasing a product or signing up with a profile because he feels more secure in providing his personal information.

Consider the following example: Yu wants to buy a new pair of heels for a gala event. She notices her favorite retail website fails in providing the style she hopes to procure. She completes a search on Google, which directs her to a website with thousands of shoes. On the site, she notices that the shoe section contains a size chart, tips for various types of feet (narrow versus broad soles), and a color coordinator tool. The site even recommends a belt and necklace during the checkout process! Yu opts in to receive e-mails on future offers because of her overall positive experience. The website's functionality increases sales of products and decreases the number of returned purchases due to improper fit.

✔ **Reduction in customer support costs:** A good UX considers the user even after he commits to your brand by purchasing a product or service. By supplying the user with the necessary information to support the product and service within your website, you reduce the amount of overhead to support the actual product. You also decrease the amount of product or service returns due to users feeling that they cannot effectively use the product or service. The following scenario demonstrates this point.

Ted is one day away from flying with an airline he has never flown on before. Twenty-four hours prior to departure, he receives an SMS and e-mail prompting him to check-in for the flight. To do so, Ted uses the smartphone app he downloaded after purchasing the ticket, and the app guides Ted through a series of informative options about the cost of checked baggage, seat selection, and instructions for where and when to arrive at the airport. There are also tools for first-time air travelers or first-time travelers with the airline. At the end of the experience, Ted is prompted to complete a 60-second survey, which he agrees to answer. Ted is very happy with the information and realizes that unlike his last flight experience, he will not have to call the airline to ask for a flight confirmation or rules for baggage. The airline decreases the number of calls to its customer support line and saves money. By surveying the user, the airline also solicits feedback for future improvements to the app. Finally, because Ted can check-in with the app and can have the e-ticket downloaded to his smartphone, he can bypass the long lines at the airport and go directly to security if he chooses to not check baggage.

✔ **Reduction in costs to build or maintain the interface:** By putting the user at the center of the design process, UX ensures that the user needs are met. Up front, as opposed to at the end of the development process, you can determine the most critical functionality to build in your interface through user research and testing, and not worry about developing superfluous features — features a user would never engage. You will not have to launch an interface that is flawed in a way that fails to account for most users' needs. Thus, less rework will be required. You can altogether avoid the *gotcha* moment of realizing a critical piece of functionality or feature after the interface is built (or worse yet, by receiving negative user feedback or user attrition because the interface is not usable). You can also think of this benefit in terms of uncovering user issues with the experience early on within the design and development process.

You may think that the most important role and goal of UX includes procuring new customers and selling a product or service. But you should equally consider your existing users in your goals and objectives. Do you provide them with enough information to support your product or service? Do you connect with them regularly and keep them up to date on future releases and new product features, and do you recognize them on a birthday or product purchase anniversary? Keeping existing users happy means repeat business and increases overall satisfaction with your brand.

 If you understand where a user converts from a user to a customer in your sales process, you can create experiences that make this transition efficient and pleasant for them. Sales and marketing teams often use a tool called a purchase or sales funnel to demonstrate a user's decision-making process in the sales life cycle. (Read more about this tool in Chapter 4.) See Figure 2-2 for a typical model of the funnel.

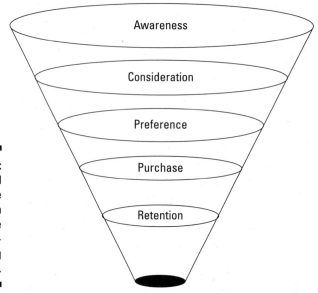

Figure 2-2:
A typical purchase funnel with steps in the decision-making process.

Understanding your users' paths to purchase or engage with a product or service provides you with the opportunity to figure out which features and content are necessary to push them through that process. When reflective of your users' decision-making processes, purchase funnels can yield significant insight on user behavior and show which features directly affect the decisions of a user.

Understanding How UX Impacts Your Users

UX has a direct impact on the user. An ineffective or inconsiderate UX almost always translates to a user leaving the experience dissatisfied, whereas a strong and compelling UX builds confidence, trust, and respect for a brand. A good UX means that a user can accomplish a task or goal. Good UX can also showcase additional products or services to her and at the same time, provide her with a manner to consume information in which she prefers. For example, some users may want quick information that summarizes a product's description, benefits, and key features and that take 30 seconds or less of their time. Other users may prefer a much more detailed assessment with a tool to compare your products with similar products. And some other users may prefer to watch a short video that showcases the product's key features and benefits. As you can see from these different scenarios, a good UX provides a variety of options to meet the different needs and desires of users. A rigorous UX approach provides the user with the right information at the right time in a manner in which he wants to consume it.

UX always considers the user as the primary influencer in design decisions (for example, what should go into the experience, how is it architected, who will use it, and so forth). Thus, the user's needs, goals, behavior, and desires (what she wants to see and when she wants to see it) are considered. By definition, a "good UX" is always beneficial to the user because it considers the user's needs and reflects those needs within the experience.

The following sections describe several benefits of UX for the user.

Seamless information discovery

Chapter 7 explains how to figure out which content to serve which users. Effective UX offers users the information they need to accomplish a task. Thus, they get the information they seek, when they need it. Put another way, thoughtful UX ensures users have the content they need to achieve the tasks relevant to them. Facilitating information discovery means that the user finds what she seeks effectively and easily. So, when she goes to a mobile site seeking to find a company's physical address, she easily finds the information replete with a click-to-map function (this functionality provides a map at the click of a link or icon).

When users find what they need, they gain confidence in a business and its capability to deliver on its brand promises. Users trust the product or service with which they are engaged, and frustration and dissatisfaction diminish. On the other hand, when a user cannot find information he desires, he becomes impatient and disenchanted with the experience. He may leave angry or resolve to not return.

The following example conveys how good information discovery facilitates user satisfaction and helps a user achieve his goals. Vishal recently moved into a new apartment and now he requires a cable and Internet services provider. On his mobile smartphone, Vishal conducts a search for cable and Internet service, which leads him to a well-known cable company. The link directs him right to a page that highlights the Internet and cable services. A prompt asks him for geo-location recognition — meaning he is asked permission to allow the site to determine his exact location — which he agrees to, and then another page launches that provides specific services for his location. While Vishal is perusing the information, a friend calls him. After Vishal hangs up the call, he notices that a chat pop-up box has appeared to prompt him for any questions he may have. (This appears once the site senses he spent a certain amount of time on the site and may be unable to find what he needs.) He quickly chats with the service agent and asks specific pricing questions. He then decides to purchase a contract for the service.

Ability to accomplish desired tasks

If robust UX benefits the user in any way, perhaps the most important benefit embodies the fact that a user can achieve what she desires to achieve. If a user wants to find a product, she can find it; if she wants to view a company profile, she can view it; if she wants to pull up directions via GPS, she can easily do so and then reroute the itinerary if she discovers that construction impedes her original route. Good UX fundamentally understands the needs and the behaviors of the user, and this understanding anticipates the user's tasks, journeys, and the most likely (and unlikely) interactions.

Fashions the experience around the user

UX seeks to learn who the user is, what motivates her, and how she thinks and behaves when she interacts with an experience. In this context, good and effective UX fashions an experience around a user. In the digital and interactive industries, UX practitioners often refer to this approach as *user-centric design*. User-centric design is exactly what it states, a UX design approach in which the user is the fundamental consideration within the design process. When an experience is fashioned around the user, the user is satisfied and finds an enjoyable experience. In some cases, the user might even feel gratitude and loyalty. In general, good UX is beneficial to the user, which is good for the organization that created the experience and for the relationship between the user and the organization.

Chapter 3

Determining Your Users

● ●

In This Chapter

▶ Understanding the role the user plays in UX design

▶ Defining an approach to prioritizing user types

▶ Creating a compelling portrait of a sample user

● ●

Quality in a service or product is not what you put into it. It is what the client or customer gets out of it.

— Peter Drucker

*T*he UX process is, by definition, a user-centric approach to solving business problems and achieving business goals. It requires that the entire project team, who is responsible for the UX, has empathy for target users, understanding who they are, what they want, and what they need. In addition to these things, the team needs an understanding of how experiences may be designed to better support the target users and further the organization's goals. User understanding will help ensure the way you sell your goods reflects the ways that people want to buy them rather than being the easiest or cheapest way to put those goods online.

In the world of UX, you are designing business interactions from the viewpoint of the user, not solely from that of the business. Understanding the user is arguably the most important step in the UX methodology: Without good user understanding, it is unlikely that the solutions you create will have the stickiness that most consumers today have come to expect.

Stickiness refers to how effective an experience is in keeping users within it or getting them to return to it. A solid stickiness means a user spends time within an experience because he finds it useful, compelling, interesting, and relevant. In many cases, he might return to the experience so he can consume more content or achieve additional tasks. Many different factors contribute to stickiness, but some key ones include interesting and meaningful content; engaging experiences with useful tools; new and timely information, such as new videos each day; and experiences that are easy to use and navigate.

This chapter describes the following core steps that are necessary for you to understand your target users:

1. **Gathering data:** Collecting what is known on current users and target users

2. **Analysis:** Looking for the similarities and differences in user types

3. **User profiling:** Developing a baseline profile of each user type

4. **Prioritizing users:** Identifying the most important user types for your design

5. **Persona creation:** Designing a compelling portrait of your target user for use by a variety of project team members

Understanding your target user can be a deceptively challenging process. Many businesses feel they know a lot about their target customers, but the UX process requires that you understand users at a level of detail that is often overlooked by marketers, customer service agents, and business owners. You need to understand who your users are (for example, "Soccer Moms"); you also need to understand their key behaviors and attitudes that will help you design your services (such as, "Soccer Moms who organize yearly holidays for their family and friends"). Having a more deeply nuanced understanding of your target user is a critical step in the UX design process because the user should be your ultimate litmus test for what you should and should not design.

User Experience versus Customer Experience

You might be asking why UX design is focused on *users* and not *customers,* and why you need to distinguish between the two. You are not the first person to have wondered that; we hear those questions all the time.

For one, not all of your target users are actually customers — in many cases, you will be designing experiences that will support existing customers as well as potential customers, so thinking of UX design merely as customer experience design leaves off a critically important target segment: *prospective customers.*

In other cases, you might have users who have no desire to purchase a product, particularly if you are a non-profit organization or an information provider. Also, you may want to develop a specific digital experience for your internal users, such as a tool that your employees can use to track and monitor their daily tasks.

In addition, the fact that UX design focuses on the "user" helps amplify a core tenant of UX design overall: the focus on how people *use* a website, mobile app, product, or software package. Understanding how users behave — how they use a service — is a critically important part of the user understanding process for you. Whereas many marketing and branding approaches have traditionally focused on who target consumers are (through the study of demographics), the UX approach also seeks to illustrate how those consumers *behave,* so the services you create are in line with people's basic behaviors.

Finally, the term "customer experience" is often referred to mean all types of customer interactions with a brand: digital, via phone, and in person. In comparison, UX is typically meant to refer specifically to digital experiences.

Gathering Data

As your first step, you develop a useful understanding of your target users by consolidating and reviewing everything that you already know about the target users. UX practitioners sometimes call this process *secondary research* because it encompasses a review of existing research materials. Common sources of existing data on users can include

- **Market research:** The data collected from market research that was conducted in the past. This research includes analysis of users, their preferences and purchasing patterns, trends within the industry and any types of information that indicates consumer or user patterns with regard to the industry.

- **Customer segmentation:** An existing framework for understanding customer types. Customer segmentation is typically used by sales or marketing teams to understand how and where to engage consumers most effectively. Customer segmentation breaks customers or users down into categories based upon shared characteristics, such as age, geographical location, gender, and economic income bracket.

- **User feedback:** Feedback from existing websites, mobile apps, or other services. This information is gathered when the user actually provides some type of feedback on the experience, either through a form, survey, call center, or to a customer service agent.

- **Sales and customer service teams:** Teams that currently sell or support services to existing customers can be sources.

Just as there are very helpful sources of insight into your users, there are also sources that tend to be less helpful to understanding who your users are. One example is analytics — data gathered from existing experiences such as a website or app that shows which content and pages are used more often than others. (For more information, see Chapter 13.) Although this type of data can be very helpful in evaluating the effectiveness of the current website, it doesn't tell you much about your actual users. Website analytics illustrates which content is viewed frequently, but it does not answer the question of *why the user is viewing that content* (for example, what are users' needs?). Website analytics show a user's typical pathway through a website, but that data does not answer the question of why the user took the pathway in the first place (which could be because of the design of the site).

Whereas analytics generally do not provide much information on user needs and who users are, sites that track that information because users have provided it can offer valuable insights into users. For example, Facebook provides detailed demographics, such as age group (for example, 18 to 24) and region of a country and world. If you know a substantial number of users come from Facebook, you can figure generational and location information about your users, such as whether they are Millennials (people born after 1982 and before the mid-1990s) or baby boomers (people born between 1946 and 1964). This provides valuable information because a lot has been written about these groups.

In short, be careful about making broad interpretations about your users based upon a limited data set.

After taking stock of all your existing data on customers, assess whether you feel you have all the information that you need. You may have a lot of data on users, but are you confident you have the right kind of data? Or do you lack data on critical aspects of your target users? Here is a list of simple questions to ask yourself as you look at what you know about your target users:

- ✔ **How old is the data?** Are you confident the data is still relevant? Or do you have reason to believe your target users may have changed in some important aspect?

- ✔ **Has your business evolved?** Has your business changed significantly since the data was created? As businesses change the products and services they offer, this evolution can influence how customers perceive and interact with the company. If your business has changed significantly, it may indicate you need to rethink what you know about your target users.

- ✔ **Has technology evolved your experiences?** As digital services, such as mobile apps and tablets, increase in popularity, you need to understand whether your target users have changed how they interact with your UX. Newer technologies, such as "wearables" (for example, the smart watch or eyewear that capture videos and images) may even further evolve user behaviors and expectations.

- ✔ **Does the data cover the type of customer you are targeting?** Frequently, businesses possess a lot of information about their current customer base, but they may not have as deep and clear of an understanding of other types of people who are not yet customers. If extending your customer base to additional types of customers beyond your current base is part of your core business goals, then consider how different these new customers may be from your existing customers. For example, a printing business that targets small business owners may also be interested in broadening its customer base to include large- to medium-sized businesses. The processes these larger businesses use to purchase printing services may differ significantly from a small business, so it may be worth finding additional sources of data on this newer target user.

✔ **How easy is it to extract insights?** Does the data exist in a format that users can easily digest? Can you easily manipulate the data during the analysis process?

✔ **Does it inspire you?** This last question is important: Does the data help paint a persuasive and compelling picture of target customers — one that inspires you? In analyzing the data, do you get a sense of the real people who make up these customers — their real-world wants, needs, and pain points? One of the critical functions user insight plays in the UX process is to inspire project teams in the design, content development, and feature development process. As part of this process, the picture you have of your users should inspire and compel you to think about new products, services, and experiences.

If reviewing any of these questions leads you to think that you might need to add to your current understanding of your target user, you probably need to think about conducting some firsthand research on your target user, called *primary research.* Do not worry, though; customer research does not have to be a costly or time-consuming process. Furthermore, it can be one of the most helpful steps in the UX design process, signaling the difference between a successful project and a failed one.

User research not only can inform the design process by grounding it in an up-to-date understanding of target users, but it can also provide great inspiration into the design process. User research methods and approaches are constantly evolving, but the following sections describe the most commonly used methods.

Online surveys

If you are redesigning an existing website or application, polling current users for their feedback on what works well and what does not provides great insight. A variety of off-the-shelf online survey tools are easy and inexpensive to deploy. Zoomerang (`http://zoomerang.com`) and Survey Monkey (`www.surveymonkey.com`) are two popular choices. Online surveys can typically generate larger samples of quantitative data in short amounts of time, rather than the other methods we describe, which take longer. However, although sample sizes will be larger, the depth of topics that can be explored is very limited, given the nature of an online survey.

User interviews

The most fundamental of user research methods for the UX design process is the one-on-one user interview, where target users are interviewed, sometimes using the current website or app (in the case of a redesign) to guide the conversation. This approach yields highly qualitative results, but it is traditionally very effective in UX design engagements: It provides a clear picture of the types of people who make up your target users.

Focus groups

In a focus group, a facilitator brings together a collection of target users in a room for a guided conversation. This method was born out of the history and legacy of the advertising market research industry. Focus groups are used less commonly in the field of UX design, given the difficulty in getting a group of users to simultaneously navigate a UX solution as they would if they were using it individually. Focus groups tend to be more effective at exploring whether a bigger idea contained in an advertising or brand communications campaign is successful and relevant.

Ethnography and contextual inquiry

Ethnography is a research technique UX practitioners use that is based upon observing users in their natural environments. Research and design teams can find ethnography inspiring, but it can be time consuming to conduct. As an example, UX solutions that focus on vacation planning may involve ethnographic research studies that invite researchers into vacationers' homes to see how and where they plan their holidays, the sources of information they consult, and the overall process they use. Observing users in their own environments often generates additional insights beyond what is revealed in a standard user interview.

Analyzing the Data to Create User Profiles

After you collect data on your target users, you may step back and analyze it for patterns. The objective of the analysis is to identify groupings of users that have core similarities, including:

- ✔ **Behaviors:** What does the user *need?* Owners of a small gift shop understand that most customers come in during holiday shopping seasons looking for appropriate gifts. They will also understand that shoppers on Christmas Eve will have a specific set of behaviors associated with last-minute shopping.

- ✔ **Desires:** What does the user *want?* In addition to solving his basic needs, the user also typically has key desires he would like to fulfill. The gift shop owners might understand that a man shopping for a tenth-anniversary gift for his wife will probably want to show his wife just how much he cares, and is therefore looking for "that perfect gift." When the gift shop owners understand this desire, they can help the customer select the perfect gift and personalize the wrapping.

✔ **Pain points:** Finally, what are the common problems associated with accomplishing a key task for a target user? For example, finding the perfect gift for a significant other may prove a challenging process. However, attempting that task under the pressure of last-minute shopping also adds a specific pain point, which could be alleviated by shopping services that address the needs of a last-minute shopper with specific features and relevant content. If that user has very specific logistical and budgetary requirements, it can add further challenges to the process that are worth identifying during the user research process.

Identifying the similarities and differences across the fundamental areas of behaviors, desires, and pain points provides you with a great place to start in creating a useful breakdown of different user types. You can begin by grouping users according to the similarities across these dimensions. The next two sections explore the relationship between segmentation and user profiles.

As you look at data on your various users, consider the following questions. They can help you organize the users into to meaningful groupings:

✔ **Profit:** Who makes the business the most money? Of all your user types, which ones generate the most revenue and profit for the business? Of that group of users, are there meaningfully different types of users? For an airline, this may be the very frequent business travelers, who collectively make up a small percentage of the passengers on board any given flight, but who generate a large part of an airline's overall revenues.

✔ **Cost to serve:** Who costs the business the most money to support? Many companies have defined types of customers that are expensive to support and may be effectively supported through self-service types of services and experiences. For the airline, this may be holiday travelers who may need more assistance and have special needs, but often buy tickets far in advance to save money. Although holiday travelers may be less profitable and more costly to serve for an airline, they are the largest majority of passengers typically on board any specific flight and are still a critical user segment for most airlines.

✔ **Complexity of needs:** Who has the most complex needs? Is there a type of user that may have the most complex needs, compared to those users who have very basic needs? Identify those "power users" who have the most complex needs out of all user types. In the airline example, these could be frequent travelers, as well as those people flying international, multi-destination itineraries.

When you analyze your data to identify patterns among the users that distinguish them into groups, you can begin to build user profiles for your target customers. Thomas Mann, a German author in the late 19th and early

20th centuries once noted, "People's behavior makes sense if you think about it in terms of their goals, needs, and motives." Within the field of UX, this sentiment certainly rings true.

UX: Why is behavioral segmentation so critical?

Advertisers and marketers have a variety of ways to understand their target audiences. One method is called audience or market segmentation. Historically audience segmentation was based on key demographic characteristics, such as age, gender, income level, and location. In recent years, though, advertisers and marketers have started examining attitudinal and behavioral information to form a more useful description of target audiences. In this respect, a marketing segment for an insurance carrier may have changed from "Recent Retirees" (a primarily demographically defined segment) to "Agent Loyalists" (which defines the segment according to their reliance on insurance agents for serving, but is less specifically aged-based). Knowing that Agent Loyalist users are likely to go through their local agent for all needs helps you identify (or remove) those features that do not address the desire for agent-oriented services. The Agent Loyalist example shows how key behavior traits have been used to define types of customers based upon how they interact with a business, and less specifically based up on their defining demographic characteristics.

The process of UX is oriented toward a deep understanding of behavioral segmentation. Because UX is primarily used to design interactive services and tools like websites, mobile apps, and software, it is critical not just to understand who users are (demographics), but how they behave and how they use a service. This ensures that you'll create an eventual experience that will prove useful and usable according to the way people are accustomed to accomplishing common tasks in their lives.

Putting the data into action

After you have started analyzing the data on your target users, your primary objective is to find meaningful similarities across users, as well as the meaningful differences. Considering both the similarities and differences within your users helps you identify where you need to define user profiles and to identify "like-users."

Consider the following example:

An e-commerce website that sells tickets to Broadway shows and similar events recently completed a redesign of its ticketing website.

A second look at users creates a better UX

A regional bank recently redesigned its website and focused its attention on its growing home lending business. The bank was originally working from a user segmentation that was primarily defined by its core product lines (home mortgage seekers, home equity seekers, and reverse mortgage seekers). However, as the bank analyzed the data it collected on users' needs, wants, and pain points, it identified a way to segment its core customers in ways that better reflected how customers behaved, rather than how the bank organizes its products. The bank's revised list of user profiles included the following user segments:

✔ **Home buyer:** Customers seeking a mortgage for a first or second home.

✔ **Rate reducer:** Customers seeking to reduce payments via refinancing to a lower-rate mortgage product.

✔ **Equity seeker:** Customers seeking to take equity from their house through a home equity loan or refinancing to a new mortgage.

✔ **Retiree:** Similar in goals to equity seekers, but for a specific life need (that is, financing retirement). Retirees are an independently named user segment due to the specific needs of customers nearing retirement and the specific requirements of the reverse mortgage products.

These revised user segments helped the bank better understand target users based upon shared behavioral patterns, desires, and pain points, rather than merely being product focused. The bank could work with Equity Seekers to better understand which product would be best for them (home equity loan or refinance), rather than being solely product focused. This example provides an excellent snapshot of user-centric thinking changing the way a business interacts with its customers.

As part of the initial discovery process, where the project team looked at the current site and its issues and future-state opportunities, the project team began collecting information on the people who used the site. In many respects, customers' goals seemed clear: Users would come to the site, select a show, browse for available dates, choose seats, and then purchase tickets. All users needed a clear and simple browse path and purchase process, so usability was a key driver for everyone. As the data on user types progressed, the project team soon realized that there were more meaningful ways to segment all the various users based upon more specific needs and behaviors.

A deeper look at fundamental business and demographic data on existing users showed the team that there were two primary types of customers using the site: out-of-towners who were visiting New York City (NYC) on a vacation, and locals who were planning a night at the theater.

All Broadway show attendees can be divided into these two groups, so the initial segmentation included those two groups with the following descriptions:

- ✔ **Tourists:** Tourists typically want a lot of information on the show, such as plot summaries, photos, videos, appropriateness for children, theater locations, and other details.

- ✔ **Locals:** Local users tend to get the basic show information from other media (TV news and newspaper reviews) and just want to focus primarily on ticketing of seats.

The project team recognized both user types as critically important for the business: Tourists generate the majority of the volume of traffic to the site (and to the theaters, in general), but locals also provide a significant amount of revenue, but with a different set of needs.

A deeper analysis of key behaviors, wants, and needs across these two user types helped break down these user segments into even more meaningful segments. The project team further understood the local audience to contain a variety of different types of customers, including some locals who attended the theater three times a month or more ("expert users" of the system), as well as those attendees who just went to the theater occasionally (once a year or so). As the team analyzed the demographic, behavioral, and attitudinal data, four meaningful segments emerged, as shown in Table 3-1:

Table 3-1	Theatergoer Customer Categories
Customer Type	*Description*
Urban Frequent Theatergoer	An NYC local who goes to the theater frequently (once or twice a month)
	Older, typically female
	Can be the Wednesday-matinee audience
Tourist	The "out-of-towner"
	Can be U.S. resident, or international traveler (non-English speaking)
	Wide variety of ages, backgrounds
Occasional Theatergoer	Attends the theater occasionally (once a year or less)
	Can be an NYC local, from the metro area, or out-of-towner
Theater Lover	Goes to the theater regularly (at least once a month)

These four distinctions of users became incredibly useful. For each user profile, the project team could begin to better understand key behaviors and pain points, which could then be mapped against possible content and features for the new site. (To understand how content is mapped to users, jump to Chapter 8.) And although all these user types would appreciate an easy-to-use site with great visuals, each of these user profiles has specific wants and needs that could be addressed in the new design.

The project team began fleshing out these user profiles with a bit more detail and also began identifying which functionality might support each user type the most effectively. Table 3-2 shows an initial breakdown of the four user profiles, mapped against potential features.

Table 3-2	User Profiles and Potential Features	
Customer Type	*Key Behaviors/Needs*	*Sample Functionality*
Urban Frequent Theatergoer	An NYC local who goes to the theater frequently (once or twice a month)	Clarity, legibility, and usability are key
	Older, typically female	Offers, discounts, and premium seats
	Can be the Wednesday-matinee audience — possibly retired	May have special seating needs — wheelchair accessibility, and so forth
	Typically knows what show he/she is looking for	Tends to be a "no-nonsense" kind of shopper
Tourist	The "out-of-towner"	Guidance for choosing a show or event (for example, is it appropriate for kids?)
	Can be U.S. resident or international traveler	
	Wide variety of ages, backgrounds	Event/availability comparison features
	Typically may need guidance for what show to see	Recommendations (what shows are good)
	Needs to know the basics about a show	Restaurants and special offers
		May be willing to purchase premium ticketing, but also may be very price sensitive

(continued)

Table 3-2 *(continued)*

Customer Type	Key Behaviors/Needs	Sample Functionality
Occasional Theatergoer	Attends the theater occasionally (once a year or less)	Show basics — plot summaries, audio, video, and so forth
	Can be an NYC local, from the metro area, or out-of-towner	Recommendations
	Has basic familiarity with Broadway	Special offers, discounts, e-mailed offers, parking information
Theater Lover	Goes to the theater regularly (at least once a month)	Advanced ticket and seat-finding features
	Knows exactly what show he/she is looking for and is often the "Expert User"	Special offers and pre-sale for hot tickets
		Very open to premium ticketing and exclusives
	Passionate about the theater, his/her experience, including the use of the ticketing site	Wish lists, group invites
		"What's New" features, alerts
		Does not need information on shows (knows it already)

Each of these user profiles describes a core type of customer, according to her basic needs, behaviors, and desires. This milestone proved significant in the UX design process: The team moved from trying to design for everyone based on a broad understanding of everyone who attended Broadway shows to having a more meaningful understanding of four basic user profiles.

But designing with four priority user types in mind can still be challenging, so the next step in the analysis process is to identify a smaller set of priority users.

Prioritizing Who's Most Important

One of your primary goals in the UX design process is to simplify design choices, such as which features to include and which to exclude, as well as to guide how those features are designed and brought to life. As part of that process, you should prioritize your user segments — identifying those user types who are most useful to the design process. This objective does not mean that you always design around the most profitable customer type, but it does mean you aim to identify one or two types of users whose wants and needs may be shared by most other users. Simply put, if you try to design for everyone, you will have no user-centric way to decide on which features are most important.

The most effective design processes typically identify one or two top priority user types that guide the design. Narrowing your focus to top priority users is an important step in simplifying the variety of design choices available later in the process.

Let's look at the Broadway ticketing example again. The team started to analyze which users had the most significant needs and which user's needs were shared by the other users. Certainly all user types needed good usability and design. Beyond that, though, the Tourist segment wanted a number of features to help decide which show might be best for their needs. They also needed clarity on basic show information, theater locations, and plot summaries. Therefore, guidance on the types of shows was a critical area of content and functionality for this target user segment. Upon analysis of the other user segments, though, the team realized that these needs were also shared by the Occasional Theatergoer and the Urban Frequent Theatergoer. So if the new design met the needs of Tourists regarding guidance for choosing the best show, the site would also simultaneously accommodate the wants and needs of the other two user segments.

However, as the team analyzed the needs of the Theater Lover, they also realized that this was another critical user segment (representing a significant amount of traffic to the site), but one that had distinct wants and needs. These site users wanted advanced features such as detailed seat location information (interactive seat maps), multiple options for seating, performance dates, presales for hot shows, and quick-purchase paths (since they used the site so frequently). Theater Lovers clearly had a core set of more advanced needs and were also a priority to the business.

As a result, the design team identified two priority user segments as the top priorities: Tourists and Theater Lovers. If the team could design an experience that met the needs of both types of customers, then it would be meeting the needs of almost everyone else. The design team then was able to focus the design process around those two user profiles, and the specific wants, needs, and pain points of each of them.

Bringing Users to Life through Personas

The final step in forming a meaningful understanding of users is to bring these user segments to life in the form of *personas*. Personas are an illustration of a user profile: a user profile that has a name, a face, and a backstory. Where user profiles can sometimes feel sterile, personas are intended to feel like real people. Like user profiles, they are archetypes of sample users (they are fictitious), but they should be created from a real-world understanding of the users they represent.

The goal of the persona is simple: to make what can be a dry and sterile description of a user profile into something that is inspiring, compelling, and believable. Personas should feel like real people, with wants, needs, and challenges.

The difference between the persona and the user profile is significant, despite the fact that each artifact contains similar data points. The user profile contains only factual information presented in a dry and academic manner; it's a collection of bulleted data points. The data provides useful points, but not necessarily inspiring ones.

Persona development began in the world of UX design over the last 15 years; businesses have expanded persona use in many different broader business contexts. Some businesses even focus their product organizational structure around persona types, in order to be fully customer-centric.

The next three sections provide details on developing and using personas.

Using personas

Many larger companies use personas to help keep their organizations focused on their customers. It is common to see poster-size personas mounted on the walls of the offices of marketing, customer service, or experience design teams. Keeping personas visible can help ensure all project teams are considering the effectiveness of their day-to-day contributions to the lives of the customers who mean the most to the business. GE is known to have whole project rooms dedicated to bringing its key personas to life in innovative ways. Business teams can visit the persona rooms to get a deeper and richer understanding of the consumers they are supporting.

Throughout the later stages of the UX design process, you will revisit the personas you have developed to understand and prioritize users. You will use key personas during the design process to make sure all project teams are focused on evaluating the design choices through the eyes of the personas.

What should a persona contain?

User personas have many different formats; there is no one specific set of contents requirements. However, most personas have contents that you can use as a guideline when thinking about how to create your own personas.

✔ **Name:** Give the persona a name. First name will do. Naming personas goes a long way in helping all project team members remember that they are designing for real people, not for "user types." Team members can then refer to the needs of the user by the user's name as they evaluate the design decisions they are making.

✔ **Photo:** A photograph or similar illustration helps bring the persona to life. Photos taken during user research are often used. However, if you haven't conducted user research as part of your user understanding process, try searching publicly available photo libraries (such as Google, Flickr, or Getty Images) for royalty-free photos or illustrations. It's quick, it's easy, and it's enormously effective. Putting a face to the name of the persona is critical in making these user archetypes come across as the real people they represent.

✔ **Quote:** A one-sentence quote, written in the voice of the persona. Next to the photo and name, the quote will give the persona a true voice.

✔ **Basic demographics:** The relevant details of the persona. What's relevant, though, is highly contextual: In some cases, you want to highlight age, income level, and location; in other cases, you may be concerned with age, number of flights taken per year, location, and job title. Capture whatever demographics you think will convey the basic facts about that persona.

✔ **Customer segmentation:** How does this persona map to other models of customers used within the business? If this persona maps to the "Road Warrior" marketing segment, then include that here. For banking clients, this could be used to identify "High Net Worth" customer segments and so forth.

✔ **Key needs/goals:** What are the key needs and behaviors this persona demonstrates? How does this persona go about accomplishing her relevant tasks? Given the importance of understanding behavior in the world of UX, try to highlight as much of the behaviors as possible.

✔ **Key pain points:** What causes problems for your persona in getting him to accomplish his goals? Identifying those things that cause your personas pain and discomfort can help you identify solutions during the UX design process.

✔ **Brand affinities:** What relevant brands does this persona purchase today? Using brand names in a persona helps give him a personality, and also helps to define him in context of competitors' brands. Understanding that a persona has brand affinities toward Lexus and Infiniti helps to identify that car buyer as a luxury car buyer, and a competitor to Cadillac.

✔ **Technology profile:** What technology does the persona use today: laptop, mobile phone, or tablet? All three? How computer-savvy is the persona? Identifying the persona's technology profile will help ensure you design solutions that meet that profile and leverage all appropriate channels.

✔ **General description:** How would you describe this person? A few sentences in a narrative description help give all the bulleted details broader meaning.

Although this may seem like a lot to consider, it typically does not end up being a lot of content. You need only a few helpful bullet points for each of these areas to create an effective model of a real-world person. The goal of the persona is to inspire teams to bring users to life, so remember to have some fun with them.

Keeping it simple

One of the key success criteria for creating a persona is to keep it as simple as possible. Personas do not need to contain a lot of content, just relevant and illustrative content. As a guideline, if you are considering adding content that may feel interesting but is not useful in differentiating that persona from one of the others, then it probably is not critical content and should be left out. All details contained in the persona should be useful in *defining and differentiating the persona from the other personas.*

As you contemplate adding detailed content to your personas, ask yourself, "Will these details help me to distinguish this persona from the others?" If your answer is yes, it's great content to include in the persona. If you aren't sure, then it's possible you're including detailed content that may only confuse team members by obscuring the other more meaningful content.

Introducing Phyllis

The best way to describe a persona is to bring one to life through an illustration. Using the Broadway ticketing website earlier in the chapter, the following user profile was identified:

> **Urban Frequent Theatergoer:** An NYC local who goes to the theater frequently (once or twice a month); is older and typically female; can be the Wednesday-matinee audience

This description may create a basic understanding of this type of user, but it doesn't sound much like a real person. Now meet Phyllis, the persona that the team created to bring to life the Urban Frequent Theatergoer, whose picture is shown in Figure 3-1:

✔ 73 years old.

✔ Lives on the Upper East Side.

✔ Widowed.

✔ Urban Frequent Theatergoer.

✔ Quote: "Now that I'm retired, I go to the theater regularly — with my sister and my friends."

✔ Theater experience

- Attends theater once/month.

- Subscriber to Lincoln Center and Metropolitan Opera.

✔ Key needs and behaviors

- Sometimes very price sensitive, sometimes not.

- Uses e-mail offers.

- Usually knows what show she is looking for before she enters the site.

✔ Pain points

- Special needs — her sister walks with a cane.

- Has trouble navigating through complicated websites.

- Has concerns about the security of credit card info on websites.

Figure 3-1:
Phyllis, the persona for the Urban Frequent Theatergoer category.

Phyllis goes to the theater at least a couple of times a month — it's the main catalyst for getting together with three friends and her sister. Each of them takes turns buying the tickets for the others.

As a former librarian, Phyllis is a member of Theater Development Fund. She loves a bargain on theater and also loves to read the e-mailed offers she receives from the various ticketing websites.

Phyllis uses the computer her daughter gave her last year, but ignores most of the bells and whistles the computer offers. Likewise, she isn't a big fan of the multimedia features of many websites she visits; she'd rather just be able to complete her tasks and get off the computer. She does most of her theater research through *The New York Times* and uses the computer only for purchasing. For that, she appreciates ease of use.

Phyllis uses the following websites:

- ✔ NPR.org
- ✔ TDF.org
- ✔ BroadwayOffers.com

The persona of Phyllis, on the other hand, provides the design team with an illustration of a real person (even though she is merely an archetype of a real person) who makes the data easier to understand. With the persona, you have a name, a face, a bit of a narrative story, and some characteristics that help you identify which content, features, and functionality would most support the user's needs.

For the Broadway ticketing website redesign, Phyllis became an easy-to-understand icon of a type of user. In addition, the other three user profiles were turned into full-blown personas of Shana (Tourist), Jonathon (Theater Lover), and Nate (Occasional Theatergoer). The subsequent stages of the design process were oriented around key decisions based upon what Shana and Jonathon might value the most, given that those two personas were identified as top priorities.

A Final Example

This section describes another real-world example of a customer of websites and mobile applications to help car owners troubleshoot problems with their current vehicles or to guide them in the decision-making process to buy a new vehicle.

Take a look at Figure 3-2 and the content used to describe Carl, the car-buying persona.

From a quick glance at this persona, any team member will understand the basics about Carl: He's divorced with two kids, he's 52, has a $72,000 salary, and lives in San Francisco. Team members can also understand that Carl has been labeled a "vehicle upgrader" — a segment used by sales and marketing teams to identify those customers who might be appropriate for a vehicle upgrade. He's also identified as "The Patriarch," which was the name of the user profile he brings to life. The Patriarch is a name given to possible purchasers of vehicles who aren't the actual drivers. In this case, Carl may be considering buying a new car for his daughter to drive to college. This user profile helped to bring to life the multiple people associated with purchasing and maintaining a car, as well as highlighting those people who have a key part in the decision to upgrade the vehicle.

Customer Persona & Scenario

Carl
The Patriarch

VEHICLE UPGRADER
LIGHT DRIVER

CAR BUYING
**CUSTOMER
JOURNEY**
Cross-brand Multichannel

"It would be great if vehicle technology helped me keep track of service and vehicle-related emergencies for my two children."

Divorced, 2 Kids

B.A. English

52
Years Old

72k
Household Income

Civil
Servant
Employed Full Time

Location: San Francisco
Role: Vehicle Owner
Brand Affinities: Jeep, Ford

Key Things to Know:
• Does most of the routine maintenance on family vehicles
• Concerned about maintenance and safety for his children while in the vehicle
• Technology is not very intuitive and he needs to ask his children for help
• Currently owns a 2002 Chrysler Sebring
• Vehicle is driven mostly short distances, to and from school and work

REAL LIFE SCENARIO

Daughter is away at college and her car breaks down.

Summary and Primary Goals
Carl's daughter attends a college that is a 7-hour drive away. The week before Thanksgiving weekend her car starts making funny noises. She was planning to make the drive home but is now worried that her car might be having problems. She calls her dad at work because he has always been able to deal with maintenance issues in the past. Carl's daughter is tech savvy but knows nothing about cars and wants her dad to look at the vehicle diagnostic info remotely and tell her if it's okay to make the drive home or if she needs to get service locally to be safe.

Additional Drivers
Carl knows his daughter is trying to be financially independent, so going to a service center will be an expense she bears herself. He is travelling for work right now so his time and internet access is limited. Further, he's unfamiliar with how to access vehicle diagnostic info but knows it's possible. He has his password and account info for his daughter's vehicle written down at home but can't remember what it is right now. If his daughter has to go to a service center he will want to be involved in the interaction with the maintenance workers.

Key Channels

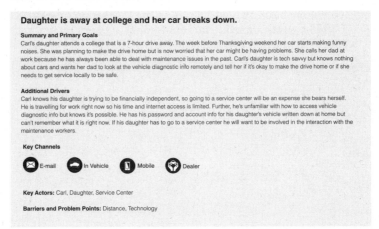 E-mail   In Vehicle   Mobile   Dealer

Key Actors: Carl, Daughter, Service Center

Barriers and Problem Points: Distance, Technology

Figure 3-2:
Carl repre-
sents the
Patriarch
user profile.

Finally, the quote that is associated with Carl aims to highlight the opportunity for web and mobile app services that may help Carl in his ownership experience. The quote clearly lays out how digital services that enable great communication and problem-solving between him and his kids could give Carl a better experience overall.

This persona is not too specific, or directional, nor should it be. It does not lay out specific recommendations or requirements. It merely brings to life an important type of customer, his personal pain points, behavioral drivers, and background details.

The Carl persona comes up in Chapter 4 that examines the journey he goes through in buying and owning a car. For now, we want to give you an example of how personas are used in real-world projects.

Building Upon Your Understanding

It's important to keep in mind that as technology and business evolve, so do your target users. Personas are very helpful models of real-world users, but keep in mind that like all market research, the data contained in them needs to be maintained and kept relevant. As the experiences you design evolve, make sure you also have a plan to update your understanding of your target users. This may require updating your personas, discarding a few, or creating new ones.

User profiles and personas take many shapes and forms, and they aren't the only tool UX designers use to capture relevant insight about target users. As you move into the next phases of the UX design process, you'll learn how to build upon the baseline understanding of users by adding scenarios, customer journeys, and experience models.

Chapter 4

Modeling the Experience

In This Chapter

▶ Learning what user scenarios are and how to create them

▶ Uncovering the user journey and learning how to harness its power

▶ Understanding the purchasing life cycle of a customer

▶ Evaluating why omnichannel is the future of many user experiences

Everything starts with the customer.

— Louis XIV

*U*X bases its approach on the user, and in doing so, relies heavily upon how users engage with particular tasks to achieve certain goals. When a user interacts with an experience, she always has a task with an end-goal in mind. The following examples provide different types of goals a user might try to accomplish within a digital experience:

✔ Reach a new level in the game she is playing

✔ Browse new back-to-school styles, and then purchase a product online

✔ Research salaries to see if hers is competitive, using Google

✔ Procure instructions using her tablet to connect to a newly purchased smartphone

✔ Submit a form to apply for a job

✔ Create a user profile when registering a newly purchased product

✔ Use a smartphone to shut off the lights in her house

✔ Complete an online bank transaction

In order to complete any of the preceding tasks, the user generally goes through a series of actions. Understanding how to map out these tasks and divide them into steps, as well as identifying which types of experiences are necessary at each point in a step, helps you to create an experience relevant for your users. This chapter covers the necessary tools to complete this effort and explains how to create user scenarios, journeys, and prototypes. The chapter also shows when and why to use each tool as well as how to construct each one.

Creating User Scenarios

User scenarios convey a narrative that captures what a user does to complete a task and his primary motivation behind doing so. This tool, written in the form of a story, captures the goal a user needs to achieve and then provides additional details on what drives him to use the interface. You should develop a user scenario to provide guidance around which content, features, and functions will appeal to a user. The scenario should address not only the goal a user wants to achieve, but also address how he would go about achieving that goal and why he desires to complete it. The primary components of a user scenario answer the following questions:

- Who is the user?
- What are his goals?
- What does the user need from the experience, and how will he accomplish his goal?
- Why would the user engage with the experience? What would lure him here?

The best user scenarios answer the preceding questions in a thorough but succinct manner in no more than four paragraphs. Because the scenario is a narrative, use a word-processing program like Microsoft Word to capture a one-page scenario for each user type. Ensure you address the primary goal the user wants to achieve. The next four sections answer each of the preceding questions, and show you how to generate a complete scenario.

User scenarios are similar to use cases, which are commonly used by testing and technology teams to ensure that a system supports key interactions with users. There is a slight different between use cases and user scenarios, however. The main focus with use cases is on the technical systems that are used within a user's interactions, and less on the actual user himself. Use cases are more frequently used in software development and technology, and less frequently used by UX teams.

Defining the user in the user scenario

Answer the question "Who is the user?" by referencing the personas created for the experience. This step assumes that you have already created personas to capture your typical users, their behaviors, and qualitative information about them. Chapter 3 provides specific instructions on how to develop personas.

Review the persona for each user type, then list specific details from the personas about who they are and how they think. Answer the following questions:

- ✔ What is the user's gender and how old is she?
- ✔ Where does she live and work?
- ✔ What is her education background?
- ✔ What is her income bracket?
- ✔ What makes her unique?
- ✔ What's important to her?

When answering these questions, be as specific as possible but also compile the information clearly and succinctly. The persona will not contain all the necessary information, and this exercise requires you to develop further the missing details from the persona. You should write no more than one brief paragraph for this exercise.

User scenarios are entirely based on a user and how she thinks and acts. Although personas provide some information about whom the user is, personas do not provide information about why the user wants to engage with the experience or what she hopes to accomplish. Personas are also more high level than user scenarios. For scenarios, it is useful to really "get inside the head" of an actual archetypical user. Although this is a creative exercise, the fewer assumptions made in user scenarios, the better. After you complete your primary user scenarios, validate the scenarios against actual users via testing to ensure your assumptions about the user are accurate. For more information on testing, see Chapter 12.

Defining the user's goals

When the user engages with a user experience, he does so with a specific task in mind, such as, "I want to buy a new watch." Capture the goal at this level and note any requirements necessary to accomplish the goal. The goal should not include all the tasks that may be required for its completion (for instance, "Go to Google, enter search term, and then click link."). Leave these details to the user journeys, explored in the next section of this chapter. Because you want the user to accomplish the goal without bottlenecks or choices, keep this part of the scenario simple. Limit it to no more than a paragraph and answer the following questions:

✔ What does the user need to achieve?

✔ What outcome does he expect?

✔ What is his budget (if applicable)?

✔ What are any constraints he has on accomplishing the goal (time frame, travel restrictions, budget, and so forth)?

Write no more than a five-sentence paragraph when answering these questions.

Defining user expectations

To define the expectations and needs of the user, start by reviewing the persona. From that, draw out specific motivations. Use the following questions as sources of inspiration when forming the scenario:

✔ What does the user require to fulfill her needs?

✔ What are her underlying motivations behind those needs?

✔ How does she expect to be treated during the experience?

Keeping the preceding questions in mind, ensure that you answer the following questions to complete this section of the scenario:

✔ What is the understanding of the task the user wishes to complete? Is she a first-time user or an expert?

✔ Does she value personalized or custom-tailored experiences to meet her needs?

✔ Does she want a lot of detailed information to make an informed decision, or is she content with a summary?

✔ What does she value?

- Convenience?

- Utility?

- Art- or design-focused experiences?

- Rich media (such as videos, tools, or apps)?

- Decision-making tools (product comparison tools, calculators)?
- Simplicity or complexity?

✔ How does she think? Some considerations include the following:

- Is she introverted or extroverted?
- Socially active?
- Socially minded?
- Methodical?
- Organized?
- Risk-adverse?
- A traveler or home-bound?
- Culturally literate (theater, books, and so forth)?
- Sports enthusiast?
- Motivated by money?
- Altruistic?
- A foodie?

By answering these questions, you will complete the third paragraph in the scenario. Just as with the previous sections, write no more than one paragraph. This paragraph will likely be the longest, but try to keep it under seven sentences.

Identifying why the user engages here

The last section of the scenario addresses why the user would choose your experience over that of another. The information you provide here helps you zero in on specific types of unique functionality or content that may differentiate your experience from that of others. To complete this section, answer the following questions:

✔ What brings the user to the experience?

✔ Why would he choose it over others? (Obviously, if the experience is not built, this involves factoring what would make it more appealing for the user.)

✔ How important is this destination for him to complete his goal?

Keep this information to one paragraph. Note any entry tasks to the destination, such as a referral from a friend or an Internet search. After completing this paragraph, the user scenario is complete.

Meet Joanna — a sample user scenario

Joanna Heidegger (30 years old; works in a flower shop in Munich, Germany; annual salary 50,000 Euros).

Joanna is very conscious of her spending, so receiving the best deals in everything she does is important to her. She is methodical, reads *Sueddeutsche Zeitung* (a newspaper) daily, and understands the political and social issues around her. She likes documentary film and goes to the opera monthly. She has a degree in business and understands the economics of business as well as personal finances. Joanna hates uncertainty and because she follows through on everything she does, she expects the same from businesses and other people with whom she engages.

Joanna has never traveled before and yearns to see her best friend from childhood, who lives in New York City. Her budget for the entire trip is 3,500 Euros, which includes round-trip airfare. She wants a vacation lasting a week and a half, and her trip doesn't include accommodations because she will be staying with her friend. Always someone who plans ahead, Joanna is looking to book the trip eight months in advance. Ideally, she will go to one place online, use her bank card, book the ticket, and receive confirmation immediately.

Joanna is web savvy but knows nothing about booking online travel, and while surfing sites, she prefers functionality over bells and whistles. Risk-adverse, she prefers security and safety over adventure and drama in her life. She is well organized (after all, she catalogues and inventories hundreds of flowers weekly for her job). She is quite adept at doing research, but wants all the information before making a purchasing decision. She expects the airline to anticipate and understand her needs — because this is the airline's business — and she doesn't want to feel like all the details are buried or that she has to read pages of disclaimers to understand the "real deal." She wants tools to help her make her decision, and values more information over less; thus, she cares about promotional content only if it advertises the latest, greatest deals.

Joanna doesn't want to go to an actual travel agent, but she values expediency and convenience. She wants to feel as if the information she receives is as specific to her needs as a travel agent would provide. She is motivated by "getting the best deal," but doesn't mind paying a little extra for quality. She chose one particular airline because it is based in Europe, a friend who had a good experience with it referred her to it, and she has read favorable reviews online of its services for first-time buyers. Joanna understands that the airline is customer focused and not just interested in turning a profit.

Understanding and Designing User Journeys

User journeys include the end-to-end processes a user follows to complete a particular task. Generally, the journey may include several steps in the process to complete it, and often includes more than one path to reach the desired result. Perhaps you read the *Choose Your Own Adventure* book series, in which you, the reader, become the protagonist and choose different options along the way, resulting in different outcomes —ideally resulting in a favorable ending. UX journeys look at a preconceived path and apply it to a group of users, with the intent of achieving a desired outcome.

The following example demonstrates how completing a simple task is more complex than meets the eye. From this example, you can see that user journeys contain several different decisions and steps before an end is reached.

Greg heard from a friend that No. 9 Park is Boston's best restaurant. He decides to book a reservation, so he does the following:

1. Launches a browser on his smartphone.
2. Goes to a search engine, such as Google.com or Bing.com, and inputs the search query: 9 Park Restaurant Boston, MA.
3. Taps the Search button.
4. Reviews the list of links.
5. Taps the first link, no9park.com.
6. Once on no9park.com, he taps the reservations link.
7. A reservations link prompts him to make a reservation via OpenTable.
8. After tapping the OpenTable link, he enters a date, uses a pull-down menu to select a time, does the same for number of people in his party, and then taps the Find a Table function.
9. The next screen prompts him to confirm the time he previously selected, which he does and which launches another screen asking for his name, mobile number, e-mail, and any special requests.
10. He enters the information and taps Complete Free Reservation, which launches a confirmation screen.

In the preceding example, Greg completed his task in ten steps. (What is Step 11, you ask? Enjoy the delicious meal when the date and time arrive, of course!)

If the previously described user scenarios provide insight on the user and his motivations, user journeys provide the most logical steps a user takes to complete a task. When defining journeys, you do not capture information about the user aside from the persona (who generically represents the person). User journeys provide many benefits and should be used whenever you want to personalize an experience or figure out which types of content would suit which types of users within an interactive experience.

User journeys also enable you to set a benchmark on the types of processes and tasks a user will undertake to achieve a goal. After your experience launches, you can test the journeys (see Chapter 13 for additional information) to ensure that the experience and content within perform optimally. User journeys offer the opportunity for you to continually optimize and ensure your solutions are relevant in the future, despite technological changes.

One of the worst, but most avoidable, mistakes that UX practitioners make when working on user journeys is to exclude other members of the project team (or the client, if they are developing an ultimate experience for a client). If you are building a user experience, then many other teams are involved with the effort. Ensure that you vet the user journeys through a member of the technology team as well as business stakeholders to ensure buy-in and to mitigate the risk of coming up with a set of expectations the technology team is unprepared to implement. Although such interaction may require more time, major pitfalls or rework later in the project can be avoided if transparency is employed throughout the process.

The following sections demonstrate how to construct user journeys by first identifying user goals and accomplishing the goals through a series of steps — that is, the specific tasks necessary to complete the goals. We also explain how to develop customer journeys specifically for users purchasing a product, and the final section explains how the omnichannel experience factors into user journeys as a whole.

Identifying the goals for your journeys

Before completing a user journey, you must first identify the user goals and the tasks associated with completing those goals. For example, to apply for a job, what are the tasks a user must undergo to achieve the goal? For defining the user goals, start with reviewing the personas, the user scenarios, and any business goals and objectives for the overall experience. You may also use experience briefs or creative briefs or any information about the project and its scope.

Come up with a list of goals you want the user to be able to accomplish. Each persona could have several goals. Then list the business driver behind the goal and tie that goal to a persona. Table 3-1 provides an example for this exercise and assumes that the user experience in question is a new website for a major airline.

Table 3-1   User Goals Tied to Persona and Business Objective

Persona	User Goal	Business Objective
Joanna: Neophyte traveler (new to airline)	Book a trip abroad	Generate revenue, acquire new customer
Molly: Casual tourist (infrequent flyer but airline loyalist)	Book family's annual vacation using some loyalty miles and some cash	Provide optimum value to loyal families
Donald: Road warrior (airline elite frequent flyer)	Retain Platinum status on airline	Retain frequent flyers through loyalty program
Donald: Road warrior (airline elite frequent flier)	Understand changes to benefits	Retain frequent flyers through loyalty program

Some guides for creating user journeys ignore the step of tying the journey back to a business goal. You could leave out this information and still capture a user journey. However, because journeys tie the user to an application and directly link her to the goals of a business, providing this relationship offers transparency for how the user journey affects the business itself. Obviously, the user only cares about her goals and most likely does not consider the goals of the business. Thus, the exercise is only important to appease internal stakeholders within an organization and demonstrate to them where user tasks impact business objectives. By going through this effort, you can later justify design decisions that may be more costly or unpopular because you tie these decisions directly to how each affects the business.

Identifying the tasks within the journey

After completing a list of user goals for the experience, you may now begin to create a set of tasks for the user. A workshop is an excellent mechanism to tease out user goals, journeys, and tasks to complete each. To accomplish this effort, ensure that the appropriate stakeholders are present. Ideally, you solicit input from a multidisciplinary team — including a member of the technology team and any pertinent business stakeholders — and ask these people to attend the workshop. If you are developing a user experience for a client, you should ask a member of the client team to attend. This might also include someone who represents a product line within your or the client's organization, and folks to represent sales and marketing. Although you can come up with the journeys on your own, development of the journey lends itself to a workshop involving various stakeholders. Their input will only enhance the overall solution.

For best practices, limit the workshop to no more than eight people. Create an agenda, and prepare a list of assumed user goals based on research and insights. For the best results, schedule the event far in advance and establish the following workshop ground rules:

- ✔ Capture lengthy discussions in a parking lot. A parking lot is a tool used in workshop facilitation where topics outside the scope of the workshop or topics that will consume the workshop are captured — generally on a whiteboard or in notes — with the intent to come back to at a later date.

- ✔ Forbid the use of cell phones or laptops.

- ✔ Ask that no side conversations occur.

- ✔ Obtain agreement that silence does not equal acceptance.

- ✔ Explain the concept of not beating a dead horse (decisions must be made, so discussion of a topic should be limited).

The following is a sample workshop agenda.

> Workshop objective: Validate user goals for the project and define user tasks to accomplish those goals.
>
> 1. Review and validate user goals; identify any new user goals.
> 2. For each user goal, define the end-to-end user tasks.
> 3. Identify issues and pain-points for the user.

To come up with tasks for each goal, look at the persona, the user scenario, and then the goal. Create a set of tasks necessary to accomplish the goal in sequential order.

One fun way to complete this exercise consists of capturing the goals on a whiteboard, breaking the workshop attendees into small groups, assigning a goal to each, and then having the participants capture the journey on sticky notes. Each group can reveal its findings and ask for feedback on the tasks identified. For this activity, ensure the users capture the tasks sequentially. This technique is an excellent way to bring users to life within a business context because workshop attendees are brainstorming around actual user journeys.

Understanding how personalization can impact your journeys

When you develop journeys, also think about areas in the journey where you can personalize information specific to who the user is or what his needs are. *Personalization* delivers specific content to an end user based on a specific context. It considers one or more of the following:

- ✔ Who that user is
- ✔ Her online behavior
- ✔ Where she consumes content
- ✔ When she accesses content
- ✔ What she uses to access content or the channel
- ✔ Why she is accessing content or what task(s) she is trying to accomplish

By personalizing experiences and content specific to a user, you present options and content specifically relevant to that user's needs. For instance, Ahmad, a young student who lives in Minneapolis, Minnesota, searches for accessories for mobile devices. The retail site he ends up on senses his device and makes recommendations specific to it. After he creates a user profile on the site and completes a purchasing transaction, when he comes to the site in the future, he continues to receive information pertinent to his previous purchases — for example, a recommendation on an item that complements his previous purchase or perhaps an alert that informs him of a recall.

With advances in technology, personalization has become a standard in user experience offerings. Thus, the journeys provided in this chapter include personalization as a primary consideration. Even if you don't require personalization in the immediate future, remember that a user journey can always be scaled back to meet implementation requirements, should an ultimate solution not support features such as personalization. If you think you will deliver personalization in the future, then account for it upfront, even if your initial launch doesn't use it.

For personalization in user journeys, also consider the different states of users within a personalization framework. Using a website example to convey these different instances, these various states include:

- ✔ **Anonymous:** Nothing is known about the user. But you can still personalize the experience by looking at where the user comes from, or how he gets to your experience (if you have that data). For example, the user searches for "kitty toy" in a search engine and lands on your website, but has never been to the website before, and has no known user profile or stored cookies that trace the user back to previous visits of the website. You know the user is interested in kitty toys and can serve up content to the user relevant to cats and toys as he browses the site.

- ✔ **Recognized:** The user is recognized but not known. Perhaps the user has visited the website in the past and a stored cookie indicates this fact. A cookie is a piece of code that many websites leverage; when a user goes to a site with a cookie, it is stored on her machine and then her behavior on that site is recorded. When she comes back to the site in the future, the data that is known from her previous behavior helps the website tailor a more custom experience to her.

- ✔ **Known:** The user is known on the website. Generally, this status is recognized if the user signs up for a user profile — registers with a site by providing personal information or completing a form for a user profile — and is logged into the website.

- ✔ **Influencer:** The user is known and she shares the experience with others (for example, sharing videos or posting to the organization's social media spaces such as Facebook or Twitter).

- ✔ **Repeater:** The user is an existing customer who continues to give repeat patronage.

Each of these instances of personalization provides different ways to tailor an experience to a user. Thus, each affects the journey a user may take to accomplish a task. Considering the preceding information, you can use a tool such as Microsoft Excel to capture user journeys and the associated tasks. Table 3-2 provides an example using the user goal of purchasing an interview suit. Note, in this example, Linda the surgical shopper is a persona developed for a person who carefully and methodically shops for products (a surgical shopper is not an impulse buyer).

Table 3-2	Personalized User Tasks		
Persona	*User Goal*	*User State*	*User Task*
Linda the surgical shopper	Purchase a new pantsuit to wear to an interview	Anonymous	Step 1: Searches for product in Google using the phrase: *professional pantsuit*
Linda the surgical shopper	Purchase a new pantsuit to wear to an interview	Anonymous	Step 2: Sees a perfect suit in a rotating carousel of product images on the page where she lands
Linda the surgical shopper	Purchase a new pantsuit to wear to an interview	Anonymous	Step 3: Clicks on the image of the suit and is taken to a product detail page that provides information on the suit and its specifications

After capturing the details in a spreadsheet, you can also visualize them in Microsoft PowerPoint or a visual design application, such as Adobe Photoshop.

Much of what is gleaned about a user for personalization is done so from analytics and metrics. Chapter 13 details the types of metrics necessary to capture this information. But personalization is dependent on a robust data strategy to inform which types of content are most widely used, where users are coming from, and what types of information they need to see. Because personalization often involves new content creation to support it, understanding which areas to make an investment in are decisions that come out of analysis of metrics.

Identifying the tasks for a purchase decision

As noted in Chapter 2, documenting a purchase funnel for a typical sales process captures the various stages a user undergoes, from the point of discovering a product to post-purchase behavior. Using such a funnel provides a powerful tool for creating user journeys for transaction experiences, or experiences where a user engages within a business transaction such as buying a product.

Figure 4-1 represents a typical funnel.

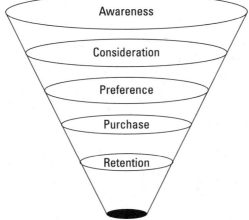

Figure 4-1:
The purchase funnel.

Note that the diagram also captures the state of a user after he has purchased the product. You should always understand that the engagement with your customer does not end with the purchase of a product. In fact, in many cases, your relationship with the customer really begins after the customer has purchased your product or service.

You can get very creative with the user journeys in a way that captures copious amounts of information in a very simplistic format. Consider Figure 4-2, which shows the various stages within a customer relationship for a user purchasing a car. Note the various channels that are used and how the post-purchase activities are also considered. When completing a journey, you can easily document this information in a spreadsheet and then transfer to a more visual format such as the diagram conveys. But don't worry if you don't have a fancy visual design application: You can sketch a process flow on paper for an equally compelling representation.

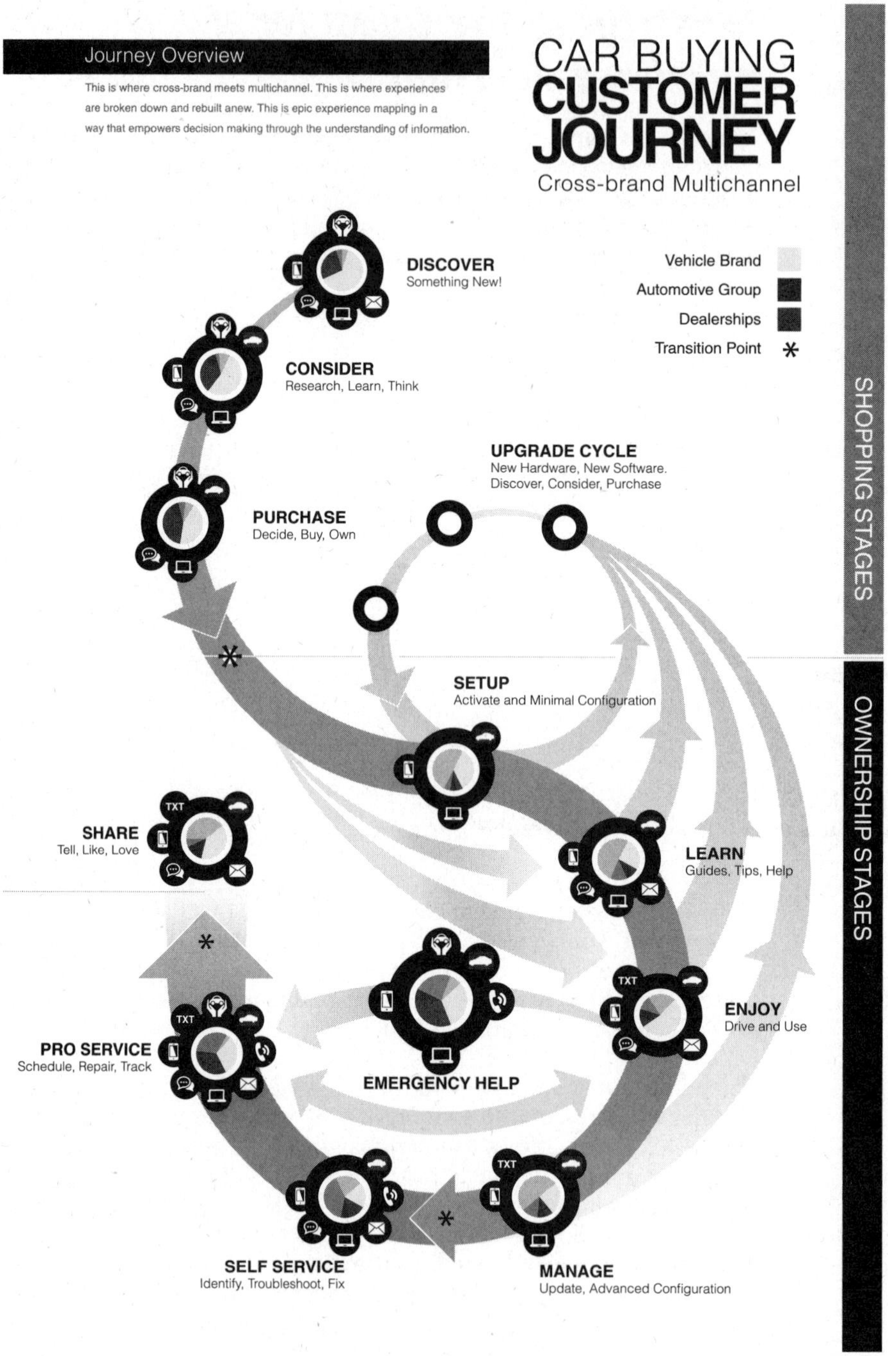

Journey Overview

This is where cross-brand meets multichannel. This is where experiences are broken down and rebuilt anew. This is epic experience mapping in a way that empowers decision making through the understanding of information.

CAR BUYING CUSTOMER JOURNEY
Cross-brand Multichannel

Vehicle Brand
Automotive Group
Dealerships
Transition Point ✱

SHOPPING STAGES

OWNERSHIP STAGES

DISCOVER
Something New!

CONSIDER
Research, Learn, Think

PURCHASE
Decide, Buy, Own

UPGRADE CYCLE
New Hardware, New Software.
Discover, Consider, Purchase

SETUP
Activate and Minimal Configuration

SHARE
Tell, Like, Love

LEARN
Guides, Tips, Help

PRO SERVICE
Schedule, Repair, Track

ENJOY
Drive and Use

EMERGENCY HELP

SELF SERVICE
Identify, Troubleshoot, Fix

MANAGE
Update, Advanced Configuration

Figure 4-2:
Car-buying
customer
journey.

The diagram in Figure 4-3 breaks down what happens during one of the stages in the user journey: the manage stage. Note in this case, the high-level life cycle, evident in Figure 4-2, breaks down into subjourneys within the larger paradigm. This next scenario maps out what happens when the user experiences engine problems with the car. Notice how the key customer activities incorporate information that you would glean from completing a customer scenario and persona.

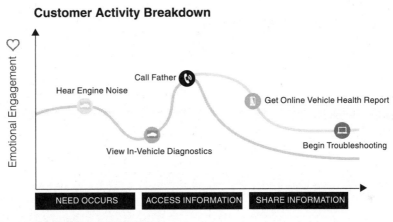

Customer Activity Breakdown

Emotional Engagement

Hear Engine Noise

Call Father

Get Online Vehicle Health Report

View In-Vehicle Diagnostics

Begin Troubleshooting

NEED OCCURS   ACCESS INFORMATION   SHARE INFORMATION

MANAGE STAGE / College Breakdown Scenario

KEY CUSTOMER ACTIVITIES

Hear Engine Noise
Inner Dialog: "Oh no! Is something wrong? I need this to be okay right now. This is the worst possible time!"
Motivators: I need to drive home this weekend.

In-Vehicle Diagnostics
Inner Dialog: "What does this red icon mean? Is this issue serious?"
Motivators: Wants to quickly understand a nontechnical summary.

Call Father
Inner Dialog: "Dad always knows what to do. He'll tell me how to fix it."
Motivators: I need help dealing with this.

Get Online Report
Inner Dialog: "I want my daughter home for Thanksgiving. I need this information now to help her."
Motivators: Wants to be the hero for his daughter.

Begin Troubleshooting
Inner Dialog: "Okay, there are several issues, some are just fluid levels. The other might be a problem but I need to look it up..."
Motivators: Wants to avoid a visit to the dealership for his daughter while he is away on business.

Figure 4-3: Stage-by-stage breakdown of user journey.

Developing user journeys for omnichannel experiences

Omnichannel factors into the entire user experience across all channels. As noted in Chapter 2, your users experience your product, service, or organization in more than one channel. To the user, there is no singular channel experience. An omnichannel user journey factors in the entire customer relationship with a product or service and tells a story of how that user engages with a particular brand. For example, see Figure 4-4 for a visual representation of a customer relationship within omnichannel.

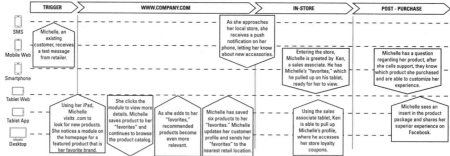

CUSTOMER JOURNEY SAMPLE

Figure 4-4: Customer journey example.

An effective omnichannel user journey must account for the following factors that make it unique from a single-channel user journey.

- ✔ **Entire end-to-end customer journey with a product or service:** Note, this life cycle is not singularly task based; instead it often involves several tasks.

- ✔ **Behaviors across several channels:** In omnichannel experiences, the user jumps from one channel to another, oftentimes expecting optimized experiences per channel (for instance, what a user wants to experience in a store differs from what he wants to experience within a website).

An omnichannel experience accounts for the user experience across all the channels with which a user interacts. Multichannel means that more than one channel is involved, and by definition, an omnichannel experience is multichannel in nature.

The omnichannel strategic framework in Figure 4-5 shows how complex an omnichannel experience becomes. It also demonstrates how a user can easily engage in several interactions across multiple touchpoints or channels.

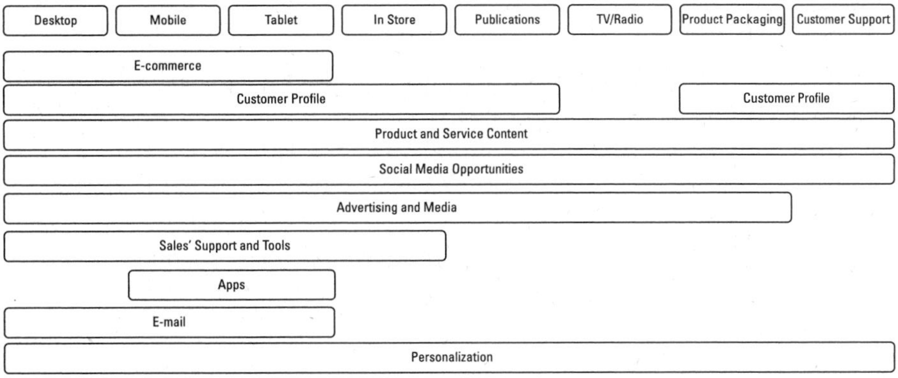

Figure 4-5: Omnichannel strategic framework.

Image courtesy of Kevin P. Nichols, copyright 2013

In using the car example mentioned in the earlier section, "Identifying the tasks for a purchase decision," Figure 4-6 shows how a journey fits within an omnichannel experience.

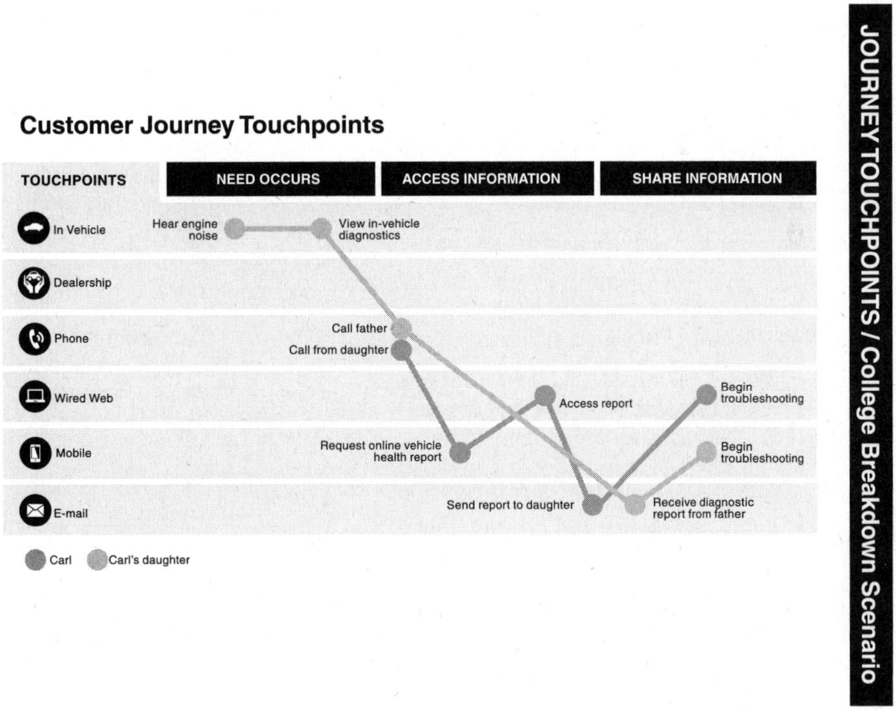

Figure 4-6: Customer journey touchpoints example.

Example omnichannel journey

The following example provides an omnichannel journey and demonstrates the complexity of such experiences. ***Note:*** You most likely won't go to this level of detail until you build out the content experience, but use this customer journey as a source of inspiration for the complexity involved. Also use it to tease out relevant journeys applicable to each point in the omnichannel experience.

1. Ahmad sees an organic insecticide on *America's Most Desperate Landscape* on the DYI TV network.

2. He grabs his iPad, does a search on Bing, and finds that a home-and-garden shop in his area sells the product.

3. On the top search result, he sees that the manufacturer has a page for the products. Curious, he taps the link.

4. He finds a whole product suite on the website and sees a Locate a Store in Your Area module on the page that displays a store near him.

5. Ahmad verifies on the Yelp link provided on the site that the store is reputable, and he notices extremely favorable reviews of the specialty store and the product.

6. He goes to the store, and when he tells the store assistant about his online experience, the assistant offers him an immediate 25 percent discount on all products within the organic line Ahmad seeks.

7. Once home, he notices a coupon affixed to the herbicide, which also contains information about participating in the company's "Help the Earth" community.

8. Ahmad goes to the community website to sign up for a profile, which asks for his Facebook account, Twitter account, and phone number. He opts to provide all three.

9. He "likes" the store's Facebook page, and when he becomes a fan on Facebook, he sees an app that allows him to create a progress library. Every week, he is invited to share a photo and track his "Help the Earth" contributions.

10. While on the "Help the Earth" page, Ahmad sees an ad for birdseed and pet products. His dog, Uli, likes to chew rawhide bones, and Ahmad notices that one of the products uses free-range rawhide.

11. He taps the link that takes him back to the site and places an online order for the free-range rawhide.

12. After he receives the rawhide in the mail, he receives another coupon via e-mail to purchase additional products. He is so impressed that he shares the product with his friends on Facebook and Twitter (using the embedded share functionality) because he knows that many of his friends have pets.

13. Four weeks later, the specialty store that sold him the initial product sends him an e-mail for a coupon on related products.

14. Ahmad notices a syndicated article about ticks and fleas next time he goes to the website.

15. When he goes back to the store, he receives a text notice for an additional 20 percent off of purchases in the product line, with a personalized thank-you note for his loyalty.

The following blueprint provides best practices in completing an omnichannel user journey:

1. **List all user states and channels, and remember that what happens in a store, how a product is packaged, and how e-mails are handled are critical to the experience.**

2. **If building a one-channel experience, consider other channels because these influence single-channel experiences.**

3. **Create an entire end-to-end user life cycle. (Refer to Figure 4-2 to see what this looks like.)**

4. **Review the user goals, but note that the entire life cycle of the user relationship should be accounted for and goals should be contextualized within that life cycle.**

5. **Complete an end-to-end journey for each need.**

Chapter 5

Understanding UX as (R)evolution

In This Chapter

▶ Discovering the power behind a UX strategy

▶ Identifying a model that will withstand evolving technology

▶ Creating an approach that evolves with technology and users

It is not the strongest of the species that survives, nor the most intelligent, but the one most responsive to change.

— Charles Darwin

*E*ffective and meaningful UX starts with a strategy built on the business's objectives and the users' needs. It also responds to technological advances and changes in user behavior.

The world of digital interfaces and technology evolves constantly. New technology continuously emerges, such as in 2013, with the advent of the "smart watch." Also, changes in technology can cause changes in users' behaviors. (Did watch sales go down as people started relying on their smartphones more and more? Will the pendulum swing back the other way now that the hot technology actually *is* a watch?) These changes may also present more channels for users to interact with a store, website, or app.

UX must stay up-to-date with all the rapid change, and to respond to change and evolution, you require a nimble and adaptive UX strategy. This chapter shows how to figure out your strategy, then it moves to what makes a model sustainable. Finally, this chapter looks at how to address changing and emerging technology before looking at how UX processes can advance the future. This chapter reviews the key components of UX strategy, and then explores ways to ensure that whatever you develop, you can guarantee relevancy in the future with a sustainable approach.

Figuring Out Your Strategy

A UX strategy has several building blocks. The first components include your business strategy, user insights, competitive models, and technological constraints. In Figure 5-1, the placement of the blocks and the size of the labels represent how these building blocks interact in terms of priority within the strategy framework.

A brief survey of how these components affect UX strategy proves useful in understanding the unique roles of each:

- ✔ **User Insights:** Includes all the information gleaned about users of the experience. This category includes user research and any tools used — such as personas, user journeys, and testing — to ensure the user point of view is represented within the experience. This research may also include any secondary research articles or marketing insights.

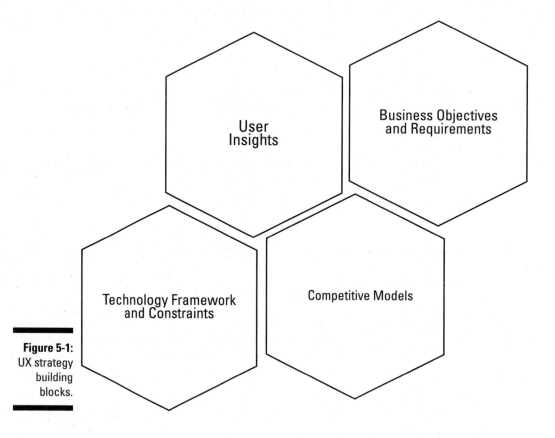

Figure 5-1: UX strategy building blocks.

✔ **Business Objectives and Requirements:** Frames the reason for why the experience exists from a business perspective. What does the UX need to achieve (such as to sell a product, attract new users, promote a service, and so forth)? The requirements include any brand, legal, product, and service requirements that the UX must support.

✔ **Technology Framework and Constraints:** Defines the technology framework in place to support the experience. Included in this category are constraints the technology has upon the experience (for instance, an app created specifically for an iPhone or iPad cannot use Flash technology or play Flash videos because iPhones do not support Flash).

✔ **Competitive Models:** Shows the differentiating factors within competition that you must consider in building out a UX. Competitive benchmarking — identifying which aspects of the competition are desirable and should be a part of your strategy — can drive your UX to a higher standard within your industry.

Each of these inputs is necessary for a holistic UX strategy. But in addition to reflecting each of the preceding inputs, the strategy also requires an effective process. Figure 5-2 represents a typical UX process.

Notice how this process starts with the discovery phase (discussed in other areas of this book) and moves to the define-and-design phase before implementation. After the initial launch of your experience, you use measurements and analytics to determine what is effective and what is not. Then you uncover areas to improve to continuously evolve the experience. The implication with this model is that it is closed-loop and iterative. The UX is never fully completed; instead, it is a process that constantly evolves. This model proves powerful because it relies on constant input from the users: The analytics measure what works and does not for the users so that problematic areas can be resolved.

In addition to the preceding model, a solid strategy also provides a game plan to achieve certain goals over a period of time. Implicit here is that strategy includes the goals, the approach to achieve them, and the period of time for which it takes place. An effective UX strategy answers the following questions:

✔ **What is the strategic intent of the experience?** This question frames an explanation for why the experience (website, Facebook page, app, GPS, or any type of user interaction experience) exists in the first place. For instance, what is the overarching reason or rationale behind it?

✔ **What are the goals and objectives of the experience?** This question can be broken into components:

- What are the objectives of the experience?

- Which user goals must it achieve?

- What are the business objectives that support it?

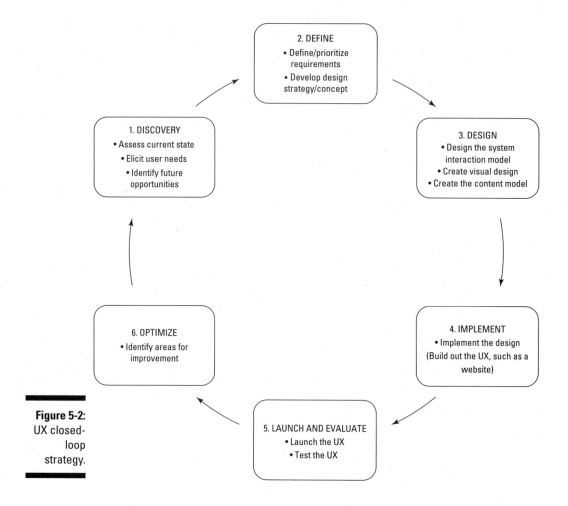

Figure 5-2:
UX closed-
loop
strategy.

For more information on business and user goals, see Chapter 2.

✔ **Which features, functions, and content are necessary to fulfill the goals, and what are its priorities?** This question includes all the components that will go into the UX and be a part of it, prioritized.

If you need to understand how to gather the features, functionality, and requirements, see Chapter 6.

✔ **What demonstrates success?** This question is answered by identifying what it means to be successful, often called *critical success factors*.

✔ **How will you measure it?** The critical success factors drive the analytics and metrics you will use to measure the UX performance.

Before going into the design phase of your solution, you should define the UX strategy by answering the preceding questions. This output should be a final deliverable of the define phase. Note that a strategy is not a singular tool but a series of steps and tools executed when defining your users, their journeys and goals, your business goals, your scope, and what you learn during assessment of your current state and competitive models. A strategic road map is critical to help you define your vision, as well as your long- and short-term goals.

A strategic road map frames what the new UX will contain along with additions you will make in future releases. The road map is iterative in nature, meaning that after you release a first version of your experience, the expectation is that you will also have future releases with enhanced functionality and improvements. Figure 5-3 is a representation of the road map.

Note that this road map captures key decisions made in other UX efforts, such as a prioritized list of features and functionality for the website. The most important features are included in the initial website launch. The second phase rolls out additional features 9 to 12 months following the initial launch. The second release contains some updates to the initial release based upon analytics, user feedback, and trends. Note, in this instance, "social listening" refers to analyzing what users are saying and doing in social networks and media. What are they saying on Yelp, Facebook, Twitter, Instagram, and so forth? Social listening is an important input into websites and many different types of user experiences.

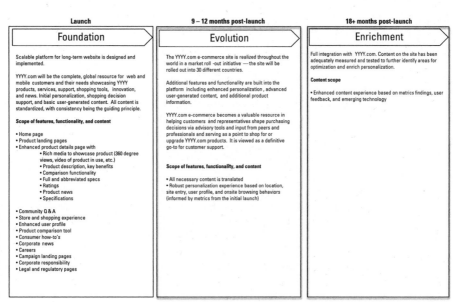

Figure 5-3: Strategic roadmap for a website.

To build a road map, you must first have a prioritized list of features. List the key features you will have at launch and plot them in a category called launch or rollout. Look at a time frame far enough ahead to roll out your next set of features. Generally, it is recommended that you use at least 6 months of testing and analytics before making major decisions around what you previously launched, although 3 months of data can suffice. Ensure you have enough time to complete the desired changes and implement them for the second phase, generally anywhere from 6 to 12 months. The third phase is nearly always after a year past the first launch.

An effective road map typically shows what a UX will evolve toward within the next 18 months. Don't push the phases out too far — say 3 years — because these will affect relevance and accuracy. Also, the further you push out the dates, the more difficult stakeholders within your business may find it to support or buy in. Remember that within each release to allow for the potential changes that analytics, user testing, user surveys and feedback, and other inputs might influence. Thus, don't put so many lower priority features within the second phase that you cannot respond to additional changes that may require more of your attention.

Use a road map as a tool that captures key features of your future UX. Show how it translates over a period of time, generally 18 months to 2 years past the initial release. A road map is a powerful tool to convey significant amounts of important features and present these across a span of time.

Defining a Sustainable Model

Figure 5-2 shows a sustainable model for UX. *Sustainable* means that it is able to evolve and change with the demands of users and emerging technological advances. But how is this entirely possible? If you build your UX around a model of constant testing, and you listen to user inputs and review your UX against the backdrop of your business needs and external technology trends, you can "future-proof" your experience. *Future-proof* means you build an experience that does not quickly become obsolete.

To respond to users' needs, the business needs, competitive models, and technology trends, you should have a team that meets regularly (quarterly, at a minimum) to review user feedback and analytics and metrics, review any changes to business strategy or objectives, discuss changes in competitive models, and address any technological trends. This team should identify any potential changes required within the experience. Consider the following members for this team:

✔ **UX lead:** The chief UX leader within your organization

✔ **Content strategist or lead:** The person who owns content or primary content stakeholder (may be more than one)

✔ **Technology lead:** Technology architect or primary individual who makes technology decisions for the organization

✔ **Brand, legal, and marketing representatives:** Primary individuals responsible for brand, legal, and communications within the company

✔ **Business strategist and business analyst:** Individuals responsible for business strategy as well as a strong business analyst to uncover business requirements

✔ **Important product line stakeholders:** Important stakeholders who represent the product or service lines within a company

A working team that sits underneath this team may be necessary to gather all the inputs and roll out the analysis into a dashboard that everyone can understand. Because this team contains more senior-level employees making more senior decisions, a working team may make recommendations based on the detailed data and analysis. For a smaller company, this team may consist of one or two members, but having UX, technology, and the business represented is a definitive best practice, and generally, each of these roles requires a different set of skills and perspectives.

Figure 5-4 shows a visual representation of the inputs and outputs of a quarterly meeting.

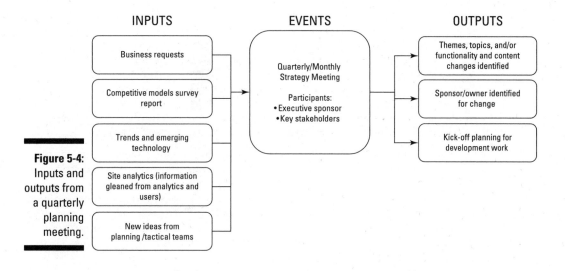

Figure 5-4: Inputs and outputs from a quarterly planning meeting.

INPUTS

- Business requests
- Competitive models survey report
- Trends and emerging technology
- Site analytics (information gleaned from analytics and users)
- New ideas from planning /tactical teams

EVENTS

Quarterly/Monthly Strategy Meeting

Participants:
• Executive sponsor
• Key stakeholders

OUTPUTS

- Themes, topics, and/or functionality and content changes identified
- Sponsor/owner identified for change
- Kick-off planning for development work

A deeper review of each of the areas shows the importance of future-proofing the experience:

- ✔ **User insights:** With a sustainable model, you should understand the following: UX requires continual "seeding and feeding," just like a garden of perennial flowers, and much of this seeding comes from an analysis of user behavior. Before you launch the experience, ensure you have reviewed all existing research, properly tested any prototypes, and completed a thorough round of user testing. After you launch a solution, you should use analytics and metrics to measure how users interact with it. You should also use tools such as user surveys to glean specific information on what is working and what is not. Finally, for areas that you want to test — for example, if you have two different concepts and want to understand which is most versatile — you can use user testing even after an experience is launched. These testing methods are covered in Chapters 12 and 13. It's important to note here that you plan for future measurements to improve your experience.

- ✔ **Business requirements:** Sometimes an experience can take months to create and launch. The needs of the business may change within this time. Also, businesses generally evaluate their strategies and offerings annually, so after an experience is launched, keeping it relevant to the business needs is important. Either way, building in a process to ensure that your experience can account for changing business needs is critical to its success. For example, if you create a website for a small veterinary clinic that initially does not offer pet supplies but does offer them later, then you would want to update the existing website to include this information.

- ✔ **Competitive model:** Ensure you periodically evaluate your known competition, even after you launch your experience. Do your competitors suddenly begin to use features and functions, such as a product comparison tool, which previously did not exist? Keep abreast of your competition: Building this analysis into your UX strategy helps you stay on top of any competitive differentiation that could prove detrimental to your business. It also helps you quickly respond to changes within the competitive environment and have a process in place to implement enhancements for your experience, should it prove necessary.

- ✔ **Technology trends:** UX constantly changes. Today's wearable technology, such as Google Glass, was inconceivable 10 years ago, save for science fiction movies. Tomorrow, technology will seem nearly unrecognizable. Listening for and assessing trends in technology and building this into your UX strategy enables you to report back to other areas of the business what's happening and where things are heading. It can allow you to plan and budget for future enhancements to address technology evolution. This approach keeps you relevant and keeps your experience up to date.

Having the latest bell or whistle and keeping up with the Joneses is not always a good thing in User Experience. Remember WebTV? One of the great things about having a robust UX process is that if you identify future enhancements or potential changes within your experience, you will always test it with users to ensure they want to use it and that it helps them achieve their needs and goals. You should test any major change or assumption you have about a change prior to rolling it out.

Testing plays an important role throughout the UX process. Other chapters, such as Chapter 12, speak to the role of testing as part of the UX strategy. An important user input is the continual user validation of the experience, whether it be from testing a prototype or testing the experience after it is launched. Adapting your UX model to incorporate testing as a necessary cost and input to your process ensures that users' needs and requirements are at the forefront of your experience.

Advancing the Future with a UX Process

Today, if you design a website, a user may visit it from a smartphone, a tablet, a desktop such as a MacBookPro, a smart watch, or an smart TV. These outputs are also known as channels. In most cases, there is often no singular channel experience for a user experience. Furthermore, you no longer have much control for how users access your experience or where and when they do it.

Unless you develop an app or interface that will only render on a specific device (which you may want to do for unique business needs — an interface for a medical device, for example), you need to understand that your experience could end up on multiple types of displays, some of which you know about and others that may exist only in the future.

If you do not give your users control over how they access, use, share, and interact with content, you are severely limiting the viability and effectiveness of your experience. UX evokes emotion, and effective UX can inspire and move users to share their experience with others. Making your solution cross-channel, easy to download, and easy to share means providing much greater exposure to your experience and fulfilling your users' needs to share their experiences.

Enabling your design to be flexible for multiple outputs is another important consideration for UX. For example, a website that looks good on a 32-inch monitor should also display useful and readable information on a smart watch. Two notions that help facilitate this process have recently gained much notoriety in the field of digital UX: *responsive design* and *adaptive design*.

Responsive design

Responsive design is a design technique that allows your design to be responsive to different devices, such as smartphones, desktop websites, and tablets, and displays nicely across multiple mediums. It does not matter whether a user has a large screen or a small one; a responsive design responds to the screen resolution to render an experience optimized and usable for many types of devices. But responsive design has limitations. Responsive design is a design solution and relies on code, such as cascading style sheets (CSS), to determine the resolution of a device and serve up the experience accordingly. Responsive design assumes that the content remains the same regardless of the device (although it may render slightly differently on a smartphone from how it renders on a desktop-based website). If you have a smaller website or content that is going to remain the same regardless of device, and you want a shared experience that renders well across multiple mediums, responsive design is probably the best option for you.

When you have a shared-content experience across devices, then responsive design can prove beneficial to your needs. It can also be quite cost-effective as one code-base is used to support it. However, if you want to share some content across devices but also serve up unique content that is optimized for specific devices then responsive design is not an ideal solution. For example, many retail companies want a longer product description and more detailed product specifications served up on a desktop website than what renders on a mobile site.

Adaptive design

Adaptive design represents a design that easily adapts to devices. It also means that content is designed in a way that a system can serve it up to multiple devices, albeit in slightly different ways. For example, a longer article can be served up to a desktop website, whereas a mobile device might get a summary of the entire article. Adaptive design is predicated upon a technology framework that supports it. It can be more expensive and take longer to develop.

Although it means more upfront coding and work, adaptive design can support multichannel output, meaning your experience can be optimized for many different types of devices. Adaptive design is best for a UX that contains shared content, shared but edited content (content that changes for each device), and unique content per device.

Considering channels

Another important decision that you must make early in the process is how and where you want your UX to live. This decision frames an important piece of your UX strategy. Review Chapters 7 and 8, which discuss how content can be structured in a manner so that it is multi-channel friendly. How you code your experience, structure your content, and identify the channels you think are important for your users impact the future viability of your solution.

As a best practice, a multidisciplinary team with representatives from the technology, content, UX, brand, and legal departments should be present when you look at any forward-thinking UX strategy. Ensure that your technology team members understand the breadth and depth of your vision so that they can plan for the amount of work and technologies required to support your experience.

Code that is more *interoperable,* meaning it can operate on more than one device, such as XML or DITA, can ensure that your UX can live on multiple devices. Also, HTML is predicted to be around for centuries. These types of universal codes and standards can also help prevent your UX from having a definitive shelf-life, but instead, be relevant in the future. Although this work doesn't cover these technologies, work with your technology team members and ask them to use universal standards and code within your experience. It will save you money and costly rework in the future.

Part II
Components of Design

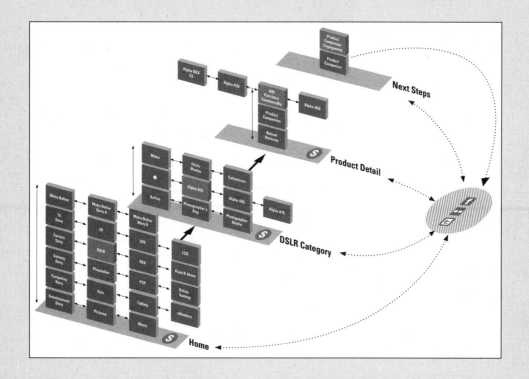

To read more about content strategy and information architecture, visit
www.dummies.com/extras/ux.

In this part . . .

- ✔ Define the core building blocks of UX design, including information architecture, content strategy, and visual design.

- ✔ Assess current experiences and define a plan for improvement.

- ✔ Understand the role of content and content strategy in the success of your UX.

Chapter 6

Taming the Beast: Understanding What You Do and Don't Have

- -

In This Chapter

▶ Understanding the strengths and weaknesses of an existing experience

▶ Identifying which assets can be leveraged from existing sources

▶ Defining new materials and assets you will need

▶ Prioritizing the assets most critical to the ultimate experience

▶ Building a plan for the scope of the project

- -

> *We don't spend enough time up front on projects discussing, assessing,*
> *defining and refining the value of what we make. We jump too quickly*
> *into design and build before applying rigor to what we make.*
>
> — Daniel Szuc

The UX design process centers on the target user and understanding the features, functions, and content that will be the most valuable to her. Yet, after you step back from understanding your target user and modeling her overall experience, you should assess all the other inputs to the design process. This assessment process answers the following questions:

- ✔ If you possess an existing website, mobile application, or related experience, what should you reuse from it? What should you retire?

- ✔ Which competitors have similar experiences, and what can you learn from them?

- ✔ What specific guidance do you have for the rest of the design process, with respect to the design choices that need to be made?

- ✔ What technology considerations should inform the experience?

Defining the critical components and characteristics of the future experience is fundamental for you to start the UX design process. And understanding the strengths and weaknesses of the current state will help you define which assets can be leveraged easily and which need to be created specifically for the project you are designing. This chapter covers the steps to set up the design process for success and to differentiate the ultimate experience from the competition. Within this chapter, steps are outlined to focus the design process on those efforts that will yield the most benefit for the business and, naturally, for the user.

Assessing Your Current and Future States

Chapter 3 outlines the process to define a set of target users, and to prioritize those users that are the most important to the eventual experience. This chapter focuses on the materials the experience will contain: the content, features, functionality, and design choices that will best support your users. The following sections show you different types of assessments and the benefits of each, as well as information on how to effectively execute each.

Understanding UX as an iterative approach

One finds UX design process largely within the world of digital and interactive design. The beauty of that process is that it is typically an iterative process: Most websites, mobile apps, and software packages are enhanced and improved on an ongoing basis. Chapter 5 covers the strategy and approach to ensure a model of success through continual optimization. This process means that many — if not most — UX projects are redesigns, which can begin with assessing the current experience and thinking about some overarching questions:

✔ **What's working?** Identify all the assets that currently are strengths for your system or require minimal improvements for your new design.

- Which parts of the experience seem to be working well, and why?

- Which content is being used or consumed frequently?

- What type of positive feedback do you receive from users?

- What features or functions are not matched by any competitors and help to differentiate the experience?

- How is the experience helping to achieve business objectives?

- In what ways is the current experience an efficient solution to business problems?

✔ **What's not working?** Identifying all the problem areas that you will fix by the new experience.

- Which parts of the experience are underperforming — for the user and for the business?

- What content is not used or consumed frequently?

- For the content and features that are not used frequently, why is this the case? Is the content not used because it is not helpful to the user, or perhaps it is not easily found due to poor design of the experience?

- Where does the experience demonstrate usability and design flaws?

- Have users complained about anything regarding the experience?

- What is the current experience costing the business money to support?

✔ **What's missing?** Identifying what areas you do not currently include but that you should.

- What do your competitors have that you do not have?

- Have your users asked for features, functionality, or content that you currently do not offer?

- What does the design or UX team feel could be added to make the experience better?

Oftentimes, a look at the competitive landscape and other similar experiences can identify content, tools, features, or functionality that is missing from the current experience altogether. Thus, review which features, functions, and content your competitors offer and which they do not. Keep in mind, though, that merely looking at the competition is not the sole source of insight into new features that might differentiate your experience from others' services. Another great source of inspiration for new features is looking deeply at the personas and considering how the experience can help make users' lives a bit easier. Which pain points can be alleviated by the new experience?

Performing an assessment

You have a variety of ways to assess how well a current website or similar experience is performing. Generally, though, the methods fall into two perspectives: assessing how well the current experience supports users' needs (external assessment), and how well the current experience supports the business objectives (internal assessment). Because user experience design focuses on designing interactions between businesses and their users, you may find it challenging to neatly categorize the assessments into either an external or an internal assessment. Both the business and the user perspectives are critical.

The primary objective of all these assessments is to identify a list of potential features, requirements, and design guidelines that will form the scope of the eventual experience, for both the short and long term. As you complete each type of assessment outlined in this chapter, ensure that you continually ask yourself these questions:

- ✔ Does the solution meet the user goals and the user needs?
- ✔ Does the experience meet the needs of the business?
- ✔ Where are the deltas and gaps?

We recommend that you do each assessment outlined in this chapter for a complete analysis of your current state. Should you have no current state to start from, you can evaluate a future-state prototype by completing the assessments, but it will not yield as much information as an assessment of a current state.

Getting an expert opinion: heuristic assessments

As you assess the current state of your experience, you might find the inclination to get an expert's opinion on how well the experience is designed. Getting a third party to audit your experience and provide an assessment is commonly known as a *heuristic assessment.* This mouthful of an expression refers to evaluating the existing experience according to a set of commonly defined best practices in the world of web, mobile app, and software design. Heuristic evaluation is a good method of identifying both major and minor problems with an interface, system, or experience. The best practices are known as *heuristics,* which are the industry standards that are used to design the most common experiences in the world today.

Heuristic assessments are effective at assessing the ease of use and usability of a current experience. These types of assessments do not, however, provide a more comprehensive approach to identifying the features and content that should be included to make the current experience more effective. Furthermore, heuristic assessments typically do not provide detailed recommendations for how to fix problems that are identified. Instead, the assessment is intended as a scorecard for how well an experience is designed.

Common heuristics include

- ✔ **Clarity of flow:** Does the experience provide a simple and clear way to accomplish key tasks, such as purchasing an item or requesting more information? **Note:** If you need help in defining user goals, review Chapter 4.

- ✔ **Flexibility:** Are there multiple ways for the user to accomplish the same task?

- ✔ **Consistency:** Is information, content, and functionality presented in a consistent manner throughout the experience?

- ✔ **Predictability:** Does the experience behave as a user would expect, or are there surprises during a task flow?

- ✔ **Error prevention and handling:** How are errors in the experience handled? Is there clear and understandable guidance for rectifying the problem? Are errors prevented and avoided altogether?

- ✔ **Simplicity:** Is the design easy to understand? Is there a visual system that helps the user focus on the key tasks at hand, while minimizing unnecessary information?

- ✔ **Guidance and help:** Does the experience provide adequate guidance for users throughout the process?

Heuristic assessments are most effective when conducted by external third parties: An unbiased opinion of the current experience is the goal of the audit. Contact your local web developer or design agency to inquire about services for heuristic assessments. Typically these assessments can be purchased independently, without purchasing broader UX design services.

To complete your own assessment, review the UX against the items in the following list. Create a scorecard that measures each bullet on a scale of 1 to 6:

1 — Nonexistent functionality

2 — Bad/lowest performing

3 — Not good/low

4 — Good/medium

5 — Very good/high

6 — Excellent (cannot be improved upon)

You may want to define what each rating means in relation to your existing experience. Use Microsoft Excel or Word to capture the score for each item of content, feature, and functionality evaluated. In general, you should evaluate every unique feature, item, and unique set of content. Thus, you might evaluate a home page and its overall effectiveness on a website and in addition, all components on the home page, such as a navigation system. During the process, capture any rationale for the score, such as, "Certain categories are buried under the See More section, and thus the user cannot easily find major product lines offered by the company." If you do complete a heuristic evaluation, read other sections of this book if you are not well-steeped in UX best practices. A thorough heuristic evaluation assumes you understand and can apply UX best practices.

The final output of the heuristic assessment is a list of tools, features, functionality, and content that need to be added or enhanced for the future-state experience.

Because a heuristic assessment focuses primarily on the UX design of the experience, you should also take a broader perspective in assessing the current state, to understand the strengths and weaknesses of the experience beyond usability and design flaws. Improving the usability of your current experience may improve your business results, but there's a bigger opportunity to look beyond just usability: the overall areas of usefulness and desirability of the experience. The steps to conduct a more comprehensive current state assessment are broken down in the following sections.

Assessing your current-state analytics

A great source of insight into the strengths and weaknesses of any current experience is looking into which parts of the experience are more commonly used, and which are not. This process — called website analytics in the world of website design, but which also extends to mobile apps, software, and kiosks — is enabled by a variety of software tools and packages. For larger enterprises, analytics are provided by a variety of enterprise-level software companies, such as Adobe and IBM. Simple analytics tools from companies like Google and Yahoo!, many of which are free for basic services and insight, are also available and work for less complex applications.

Accessing current website logs or looking at analytics dashboards (if you have them) helps you identify the content, tools, and features that users are most commonly accessing, and the ones that users are least often accessing. This insight can be a great indicator of content that is more useful to users, which is critical to forming the scope of the redesign process. See Chapter 14 for a complete discussion on analytics and metrics.

Understanding what's happening — not why it's happening

Analytics tools are effective at identifying content and features that are viewed less frequently than other content; however, these tools do not answer the question of *why* this content is used so infrequently. It is possible the content is used less often because users have no need for it, and it may be a candidate for removal from the eventual experiences. However, unseen or unused content can also point to design flaws within the current experience. Sometimes the most valuable content can be buried in an area of an experience that is not easily visible to a user. Maybe the search terms that a user would employ to find a page or item are incorrect, and thus the content does not surface appropriately in search results. Analytics tools effectively identify possible problems, but they lack the capability to identify the cause of the problem. Be careful not to make incorrect assumptions about why some content is not used; it's easy to interpret something as not being useful when, in fact, users could be avoiding it simply because it is not easily visible.

Analytics tools can be helpful at providing insight into a variety of areas, including the following:

- **User pathways:** Where are users navigating throughout your current experience? What are the most common journeys throughout the website or application? What are the least common pathways?

- **Source:** For a website, how did the traffic arrive? How many visitors came directly to your site (typing in your URL), compared to how many were referred by search engines (either through paid or natural search)?

- **Landing pages:** What are the most common entry points for a user to land within your experience? For a website, are users coming directly to your home page, or are they coming directly to lower-level product pages? For e-commerce sites, a web search for "cameras" should typically take most users to a landing page devoted to a selection of cameras, not the home page.

- **Referring keywords:** For websites, what term did the users search for that brought them to the site? If "cameras" is referring a significant amount of traffic but most traffic is arriving at a broader electronics department page, it may indicate the need to create a camera-specific landing page to increase effectiveness.

- **New visitors versus repeat visitors:** How many of your users are new to your experience, compared to those who have been there before? A significant number of repeat visitors may indicate the need for more "expert" navigational shortcuts throughout the eventual design.

✔ **Bounce rates:** How many users are leaving immediately after arriving? Higher bounce rates usually indicate a larger problem — users are not seeing the relevance of your experience within the first few moments of their arrival.

✔ **Conversion rate:** For e-commerce related experiences, how many of those visits resulted in an actual purchase? For higher-priced items, users may want to visit the site a number of times before actually making a purchase, but naturally, you want to encourage as high a conversion rate as possible.

✔ **Visit duration:** How long are users spending within your app or experience? Are they spending longer periods of time or shorter periods of time? Short visits can be okay for some kinds of experiences — such as mobile sites for smartphones, where longer visits often indicate a user cannot find what he seeks — but most often you want your visitors to explore the experience. However, very long visit durations can also indicate design flaws that are making the experience time-consuming to navigate.

✔ **Drop-off rate:** How many users drop off without executing key tasks that reflect your business goals — for example, making a purchase or requesting more information? How many visitors leave in the middle of finishing a key task, such as abandoning a shopping cart before the purchase confirmation page?

✔ **Revenue (traffic per transaction):** How much sales is the experience generating in relation to how many visitors come to the experience?

Assessing your search logs for a website or mobile site by using a tool such as Google Analytics provides valuable insight on which content your users seek. You can also find where they enter your site, such as a referral from another site. Looking at what is most interesting to users helps you frame what types of content and experiences to design in the future. You can also gain insight into how the user thinks: Does she search for "cat" or "kitty" toy, for example, and what is she most interested in seeing? For a complete listing of metrics and how to effectively measure your experience, see Chapter 13.

Conducting a visual systems audit

It is also helpful to assess the current experience with respect to the general visual design, called a visual systems audit. Although you may not be a visual designer, you should be able to step back and audit the current experience with respect to the visual design system. This process is helpful and informs the future development of the new visual system.

An audit of the visual systems includes making a comprehensive review of the entire experience and identifying the strengths and weaknesses across the following areas:

- ✔ **Brand consistency:** Is the experience consistent with other forms of brand and marketing materials, such as printed brochures, signage, store design, and corporate identity? Consistency is key in the world of brand communications.

  In addition to evaluating how consistent your experience is branded, it's also helpful to identify how differentiated the experience is: Does this experience stand out uniquely and distinctly from other similar competitive experiences? A simple trick to evaluate this is to cover up the logo on the home page or main application screen. When the logo is covered, does the experience still feel uniquely and distinctly branded? Does the brand come across in the experience in more ways than just the use of the logo?

- ✔ **Visual clarity and simplicity:** Is the design clutter free and easy to visually digest? Does each page, screen, and module of content include ample white space?

- ✔ **Visual elements:** How is the quality of the visual elements in the experience, such as photographs and illustrations? Are they large enough to be legible and clear enough for the user to understand them?? Do they add distinct value to the page, or are they included gratuitously?

All these methods of assessing your current experience — heuristic assessments, analytics, and visual systems audits — are helpful in developing a baseline understanding of some strengths and weaknesses of the current experience. But each of them is taking a business perspective on assessing the current state. The next section focuses the evaluation on how well the current experience meets users' needs.

Using scenario-driven assessment

The initial steps of the UX design process focus primarily on understanding the target user: stepping back from the wide range of users and identifying one or two top-priority user types and turning them into compelling portraits of sample people, called *personas*. You can use these personas to help guide the current state assessment in a focused way: evaluating the experience through the wants, needs, and pain points of the actual users targeted for the experience. Chapters 3 and 4 outline the steps necessary to build a more useful understanding of your target users and the scenarios and journeys for which you should account in designing the experience. You should use this information to evaluate your current experience, such as your website.

The personas help guide a design team to make decisions that are most effective for the user, not just the business. The personas can be used to ensure that the design team really puts itself in the shoes of the target users to evaluate the current state. This is a called a *scenario-driven assessment,* which can be broken down into the following steps:

1. Taking the viewpoint of one of the target personas, identify a common task to use to evaluate the experience. Taking Phyllis, our theater-ticket-buying persona from Chapter 3, the task will be for Phyllis to find ticket pricing for an upcoming Wednesday matinee.

2. Identify how Phyllis might approach the website — via search or directly? Will the search engine refer her to the most appropriate page in the website?

3. Upon arrival in the experience, what does Phyllis really notice? Has she been here before?

4. How easy is it for her to navigate to what she's looking for?

5. Is the information Phyllis is searching for visible?

6. What are her impressions of the experience as she is navigating through it?

7. How long is Phyllis using the website?

8. After she is done, what do you think Phyllis's next action will be, and what will be her next interaction with the website?

This simple process of wearing a user's hat throughout a real-world scenario can be enormously effective in stepping out of the business shoes and stepping into those of the actual user. It helps teams to assess experiences through the eyes of those users who are actually your target users. It also helps to identify the features and requirements to be considered as the scope of the project is defined. In this respect, it is the most important form of current state assessment that can be conducted.

Completing a contextual interview with a user

There is never a substitute for a first-hand understanding of a user's experience. During the process of assessing the current state of an experience, it can be enormously effective to conduct one or two actual research sessions, putting a real-world user in front of the current website, mobile app, or software package.

If time permits, consider finding a couple of actual customers — ones who meet the profile of the target persona — and have them sit in front of the current experience. Ask them to complete a standard task while thinking aloud (sharing their thoughts, reactions, and suggestions). This form of assisted interview, called a *contextual interview* in research terms, helps put the current experience in context of real-world users with real-world needs. It also can be one of the most eye-opening and insightful steps in understanding the strengths and weaknesses of any current experience. Additionally, contextual interviews can be extremely helpful in identifying the gaps in the current experience — content, features, and tools that are missing in the current experience altogether.

To complete the contextual interview, place the user in front of the interface (for existing interfaces). For a new design that has no previous physical interface, you may use paper prototypes. (For more information on paper prototypes, refer to Chapter 12.) Provide the testing participant specific tasks (such as purchase a product or find an item on the website). You should test all user goals you previously identified for the UX. (See Chapter 4 for a quick review on identifying user goals.)

Ask the participant to think aloud and capture her thoughts as well as watch what she does and how she interacts with the site. You should set the expectation that the entire exercise will take than 90 minutes to 2 hours. You may want to record the session digitally. If you do so, you will require a release form from the participant that gives you permission to record her. (You can find release forms online by searching for them on your favorite search engine.) If you do not record the experience using a recorder or digital video camera, you will require two note takers. One note taker captures what the participant says, and the other makes notes and observations about the user's behavior with regard to the following:

- ✔ How long does it take the test participant to complete a task?

- ✔ Is the assumed user journey (the end-to-end click-stream that you assumed when designing the system) the actual user journey? If the actual journey the user takes differs from what you assumed he would take, what is the variation?

- ✔ Which pitfalls prevent the user from accomplishing the task? For example, is he unable to find something within the navigation?

- ✔ What does she like and dislike about the site?

When the interview is complete, review it and pull out the main observations. Create a report that summarizes the following:

- ✔ Issues with the experience.

- ✔ Pain-points or gaps within the experience.

✔ Successful areas of the experience.

✔ Potential features or functions that are uncovered — what's not here that should be?

From this report, extract a list of features, functions, and content that the future-state should include.

Surveying Your Competitors to Build a Better Experience

A competitive assessment means looking at what your competitors do within their user experiences and then comparing and contrasting your current state or future-state vision against what they are doing. A competitive assessment is a power tool within UX design; it enables you to figure out what you are doing vis-à-vis your competitors and how to make your experience better than theirs. For example, you can uncover features they use that you do not and resolve to offer these within your future-state design. You can see where they lack in features, functionality, and content and fill these gaps within your experience. A competitive assessment is your tool to ensure that you have done due diligence in looking at your competitors to improve your ideas around your future-state experience.

Start a competitive assessment by defining a list of known competitors. As a best practice, narrow the primary competitors to four or five. You should also include models that are not directly competitors but are best-in-class models. For example, if you own a small boutique shop and want to market your products online, you should look at a few larger, national chains to see what types of features, content, and functionality they offer. Even if you will never directly compete with those businesses, you can see what types of experiences they offer that your direct competitors may not within their UX designs. Looking at best-in-class and larger companies can inspire you to think about features or functions you previously may never considered.

You may find that some of your competitors offer little or no UX for their users. A small shop may have no online presence, for example. If this is the case then find comparable businesses that do have a strong online presence, even if they are outside your immediate area or are not direct competitors.

The goal of a competitive assessment is to find what others in your industry are doing so you can create a differentiated experience — one that is better and more compelling.

When you have a list of competitors you want to survey, create a list of criteria to use for evaluation. A sample list for a mobile site could include

- **Usability:** How easy is the interface to use?
  - *Can I find what I am looking for?* Can I navigate the site if navigation is contained within it?
  - *Do the labels, buttons, and links make sense?* Do I know where I am going if I select or click on a navigation element?
  - *Is the design consistent?* Or is there a lot of inconsistency in the content, navigation, and/or design?
  - *Does the search function yield desired results?*
  - *Do the pages within the site have clear content priorities?* When I look at the page, does it contain the content its title promises?
- **Innovation:** Does the site employ cutting-edge features and technologies?
- **Functionality:** Does the site have a robust content/feature set?
- **Expectations:** Does the site work as expected?
- **Brand experience:** How well does the site represent the brand and its values?
- **Content:** Does the site offer a rich, meaningful, timely, and relevant content experience?

After you decide upon the evaluation criteria, compose a list of features, functions, and content that your UX contains (or a list of what you think needs to be in the future state). For example, you may have something like this for a small pizza shop website:

- Home Page
- Menu
- Contact Us
- About Us
- Order Online
- Create a Profile
- Shopping Cart
- Coupons and Weekly Deals

Now, place these items in a spreadsheet or within a table and create columns for the competitors. As you go through the competitors' UX, note whether they contain the same features as yours. Table 6-1 shows a completed comparison table.

Table 6-1	Sample Comparison Table		
My Site	*Competitor 1*	*Competitor 2*	*Competitor 3*
Home Page	X	X	X
Menu	X	X	X
	Lunch Menu	Lunch Menu	
	Dinner Menu	Dinner Menu	
About Us	X		X
Order Online	X	X	X
	Track Online Order		
	Your Chef (Name of chef and bio)		

Note that in Table 6-1 that some features captured on the competitive sites are not contained within My Site. For example, Competitor 1 has a feature to track online orders. My Site and Competitors 2 and 3 do not possess this functionality. A matrix such as this captures all the main types of features throughout the entire competitive environment and can provide you with a compelling snapshot of what you don't have — but that you should.

As you complete this exercise, take a second pass to evaluate the competitors based on the criteria you created to use for evaluation. For example, look at the usability of all competitors' sites and rank each one. Ensure you also do the same for your experience. You can create either a scale of 1 to 6, similar to the heuristic design scale, or use a rankings approach, such as one to five stars.

Regardless of which type of ranking you choose, while going through the evaluation process, ensure that you note anything that makes your competitors' experiences better than yours. After you've completed the evaluation, you may want to capture the information in a report, such as a PowerPoint presentation. You can share such a report with other stakeholders on your team, and it can be a powerful tool to make arguments for certain types of functionality or features. Regardless of whether you do a report, ensure that you create a list of all features and functionality that your future-state experience should capture. Add this to what you gleaned from the heuristic analysis and any user interviews.

Look beyond your competitors!

Although a detailed assessment of the competitive landscape will help identify some key features that you should consider including in your experience, it may only help your experience come up to par with competitors' services. For true innovation, it is often helpful to broaden your perspective to identify other types of experiences — although not directly competitive ones — that may help inspire the UX design team to think about new content, features, and design choices that will help your experience stand out from all the rest.

To that end, when your competitive audit is complete, step back and consider other consumer experiences that may provide good inspiration. This practice, called a *best-of-breed assessment,* is common in the UX design process. For example, during the redesign of a hotel site, the team may start by looking at other hotel sites as part of the competitive assessment. Then the team kicks it up a notch by also looking for best-of-breed functionality from a range of other types of travel sites, such as cruise lines, airlines, and theme parks. The team may go further, even, to identify content or functionality found on e-commerce sites that could provide a useful model in making the hotel site one that is unmatched by any competitor.

Defining and Prioritizing Features and Requirements

If you know your personas, your user scenarios and journeys, and your site goals and you have completed an assessment of what you have compared to what your competitors have, you can create a much more robust list of the key features and requirements that will form the scope of your future-state UX. It bears repeating that your detailed understanding of the user should be the focal point to help you make key decisions regarding the scope of what to design and build. You also should use a content inventory and audit (covered in Chapter 7). These tools will define the content your current UX possesses and gaps and issues to address.

One of the primary goals of each of the assessments — including the current state, competitive, and heuristic assessments — is to develop a list of potential features, requirements, and design guidelines for the eventual experience. Naturally, not all features can be built, so identify those features that should be considered requirements, those features that are high priority, and those that may be implemented in a future enhancement after you have the initial version of your UX complete. It is important to be as specific as possible during the process, as well as to move beyond general requirements such as "improve usability" to get to specific and actionable definition of features. The next two sections inform you about how to define and prioritize your requirements.

Ascertaining fundamental requirements

The first step is to identify all the content and functionality that is an absolute requirement for the experience. For a tablet app that focuses on e-commerce, some of those fundamental requirements might be the capability to

- Purchase a product using a credit or debit card
- Manage My Account features
  - View past orders
  - Track an order
  - Change/cancel an order
  - Update personal information (shipping, billing, payment, and personal account details)

For most experience projects, the list of required functionality and content tends to be pretty robust. If you are going to launch a website, mobile app, or similar experience, chances are that you have a sizable list of features and functions that you consider are requirements.

To come up with a list, review the personas, user scenarios and journeys, user goals, business goals, and all the exercises you completed in the current-state assessments. From the prep work you have done, you should already have lists on what you need for the future state. Take these and expand upon them, if necessary. You may want to conduct a workshop with your other stakeholders to define this list. One way to go about it is to bucket the features and functions into logical categories. For example, a typical website may have the following categories:

- Home Page
- About Us or Company section
- Product catalogue (which contains all the products or services on the site)
- Customer Support
- Login or User Profile
- Shopping Cart and Checkout
- FAQs

If you group content, functions, and features in categories such as these, you can then flesh out what needs to go under each area. Again, this approach can prove helpful in uncovering different areas within the experience.

You may also have a list of design guidelines that you consider requirements. For example:

- ✔ The new mobile app must meet WCAG 2.0 accessibility standards for people with disabilities.
- ✔ The new mobile app must support iOS and Android (for business purposes).

Going through the process of identifying these types of requirements ensures that you are designing an experience based upon sound design principles and requirements. If you do not have a list, survey your stakeholders from each line of business and ask them to create a list of requirements or wish lists for the future state. When you merge everything into one wish list or set of requirements, meet with all stakeholders to review that list and agree upon which items are absolutely necessary for the future state.

 When you're asking stakeholders to help compile a list, remember to ask the technology, legal, and compliance teams for suggestions, in addition to product lines and branding teams. These folks can identify requirements that are necessary to ensure industry compliance is met.

Prioritizing features

In addition to the list of required functionalities, you will most likely have a long list of optional features to consider as part of the scope. In fact, many of these features may not feel optional, and yet, not every function needs to be or should be supported. Examples of optional features for the e-commerce tablet app could be the capability to

- ✔ View third-party reviews of a product
- ✔ See physical store inventory online
- ✔ "Wish-list" an item for future purchase
- ✔ Share "wish lists" with other users (similar to a wedding registry)
- ✔ Share product details with other users ("E-mail this page")
- ✔ View which products are currently "hot sellers" with other customers
- ✔ View size and fit guidelines for apparel

Many of these features are worthwhile, but are they really worth the cost and time they will take to develop and to support in the longer term? Furthermore, are these features more important than all the other features that also were identified during the assessment process?

Keeping a list of design principles and agreed upon key features can prove a powerful tool when other members of your team may want to add additional and unnecessary features or functionality to the future-state experience. Bells and whistles or the newest trend may appeal to certain members of your team, but use your work from the current-state assessment and user research and goals to ground your team in reality and perspective if any of its members get sidetracked or start running toward an unrealistic goal.

To provide some guidance to the process of defining the scope of the experience, use a prioritization exercise to evaluate all optional features, content, and functionality. Myriad methods can be used to prioritize requirements, but the process commonly used in UX design focuses on your target user.

Here is a simple prioritization process designed to prioritize all possible features and functionality around the user's needs:

1. **Choose a user goal, overlay it with a target persona, and look toward the scenario and user journey to understand which features are most important.**

2. **Consider each potential feature.**

   On a scale of 1 to 10, how much value will it add to that user's experience? Will it increase the usefulness or enjoyment of the experience? Will it significantly alleviate a pain point? What are the *most important* features that will meet that user's goals?

3. **Evaluate the complexity of that same potential feature.**

   On a scale of 1 to 10, how easy will it be to implement? (10 is very easy; 1 is difficult.) How expensive is the feature?

4. **Plot these items on a simple 2-x-2 matrix or whiteboard.**

   It should be easy to see which enhancements can add the most value with the least amount of effort to implement.

When considering the ease of implementation of each potential feature, also consider the cost of the feature: How much time will it take to design or build? Does the feature require a specific technology or creative asset, such as an original photograph? Online calculators and widgets are more expensive than simple content, for example. Also, don't just take into account the up-front costs; consider the longer-term costs to maintain the feature, if any. For example, some photographs may need to be updated regularly to keep the experience fresh. Online calculators and other tools may need links to syndicated data to work properly.

Use a tool such as that shown in Figure 6-1 to visually represent higher-priority features as well as lower-priority ones.

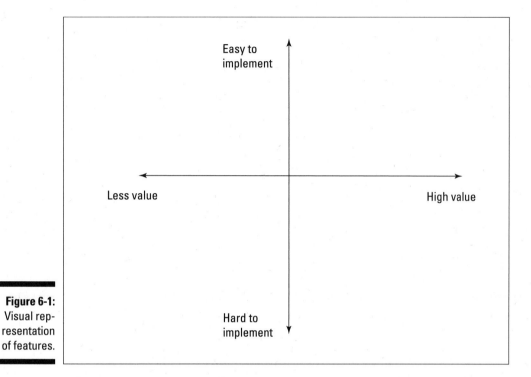

Easy to
implement

Less value

High value

Hard to
implement

Figure 6-1:
Visual rep-
resentation
of features.

Identify which items are in scope for your initial UX design project, and
which items can be slated for possible future enhancements during a
phased approach.

After you define and prioritize your features, you have an initial scope for
the UX design process, based upon the understanding of the current state
and strategy outlined for the experience. Remember this scope may change.
User testing may show that something you originally thought was necessary
actually is not. A deep dive into the content inventory and audit (which
sometimes comes after this effort) may uncover additional content areas
for your site. Furthermore, as you go through the design process, you may
uncover certain areas upon which to expand. Regardless, you have a starting point and a blueprint to kick off the design phase for your future effort.

Chapter 7

Developing Content Strategy

In This Chapter

▶ Understanding the importance of content

▶ Using content efficiently

▶ Seeing how content inventories and audits can influence your future content solutions

▶ Defining your users' information needs

> *Content is king.*
>
> — Bill Gates

ontent strategy is an important discipline within UX. Until recently, however, it did not garner the respect within the digital industry that it does now. Even today, content strategy is sometimes deprioritized in UX solutions. By leveraging best practices of content strategy in your UX effort, you will ensure that your users consume the right type of information, when and how they need to consume it. A solid content strategy framework ensures high-quality, relevant UX for your audience. But before considering the role of content strategy and how this discipline can enhance your ultimate experience, you should first understand the concept of content.

Defining Content and Content Strategy

Simply put, *content* records an idea or piece of information. This definition may seem simplistic and broad, but practitioners use this far-reaching definition intentionally. A cursory survey of different types of content reveals why a strategic approach to how, when, why, and for whom to use content proves critical. Ancient cave paintings in Altamira, Spain; hieroglyphics in the Pyramids at Giza; and carvings in stone unearthed in what was ancient

Assyria are all examples of content. In today's world, the independent science fiction film *Sharknado;* rap music recorded by M.I.A.; the news captured in Arabic on Al-Jeezera's website; a do-it-yourself article in *Martha Stewart Living; Masterpiece Theater* on PBS Network; and *Webster's Dictionary* all exemplify unique types of content.

The preceding examples show information or ideas that are recorded in specific formats. As you might guess, all content has a creator and a consumer. This is true even if no one ever wants to consume it. Good content captures a story that effectively communicates an idea by the person who created it to the person who consumes it. As such, all content embodies a purpose, even if that purpose is at times not clear or easily understood.

Content strategy helps you figure out which stories or pieces of information are necessary for an audience and how to deliver that information to them. This definition embodies three main areas:

- **Content experience:** What types of experience do you need to create for your audience? Which content do you serve up to them?

- **Content life cycle:** What are the end-to-end processes you need in place to acquire, create, publish, and then measure the content before you optimize it or retire it?

- **Content governance:** Which tools and organizational processes are necessary to ensure that the content quality, effectiveness, and usefulness are up to date and maintained?

A content strategy is not a singular process or document but rather a strategy made up of several components. This chapter helps you figure out how to determine which content to create for your UX. The first section shows you how to create the strategic intent for your content, followed by instructions on conducting an audit and inventory. You also find out how to uncover stakeholder requirements with stakeholder interviews, and how to document all the information in an audit report that also extracts recommendations and requirements for the future.

Your users do not come to your experience only to bask in its beauty. UX is not a spa. Users have certain tasks and emotional needs they wish to fulfill. Content offers them the information they need to accomplish their goals. If you invest heavily in the design of the interaction and visual experience and neglect filling that experience with useful, relevant, and timely content, you will fail to meet your users' needs and they may not return to your experience.

Many a UX design and development project has focused on the design and factored in new content as an afterthought. Content can be pricey and require a lot of effort. Successful content requires a solid strategy, planning, and clear goals. Many types of UX require the ongoing development of new content to support it. You must consider all these factors to ensure the success of an experience.

Making Your Content Work

Whether you currently are designing a new UX from scratch or you are redesigning one from an existing experience, content frames the relationship between you and your users. In UX, a visual design and interaction model frames the structure for the experience, but content contains the information. Content provides the substance that a user consumes. This fact makes content a valuable commodity — an asset, actually — for any experience. You should and can measure the performance of the content you create for your UX. Next to the product or service you offer, the content you create around that offering brokers a relationship with your user. The diagram in Figure 7-1 shows the relationship between the user, the business, and the content.

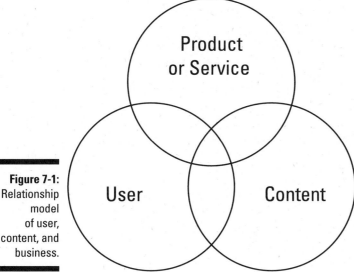

Figure 7-1:
Relationship
model
of user,
content, and
business.

After you realize how valuable content is for your business, assessing how to use it most effectively becomes critical. Before you frame a strategy, you must first create a framework for what you need your content to accomplish at a high level. Often referred to as a *content brief*, this model should answer the questions in Table 7-1.

Table 7-1	Content Brief Exercise
Content Stakeholder	*Focus Area*
Business objective	What is the intent of my content? Why does the experience exist?
Business objective	What are the goals and objectives of the content?
Business objective	How will I demonstrate success?
Audience	Who is the audience?
Audience	What information does the audience need?
Audience	Why are users consuming this information? Which tasks do they need to achieve?
Audience	Where is my audience, and where are they consuming the information?
Audience	When do they need the information?
Audience	How do they consume the information (or which channel is being used)?

You should have the audience information from the work completed by scenarios, personas, and customer journeys. Review it. This will help you frame the strategic intent of the experience. After you frame the strategic intent, create a brief. Figure 7-2 shows a sample brief.

Content Brief

What is the strategic intent of the experience?

- *Differentiate Company X competitively by highlighting unique benefits and showing the value proposition throughout the experience. The value proposition answers the question of "Why X Company" for the consumer*
- *Identify the customers by their personas and needs*
- *Surface key benefits to new customers to drive to them to learn more about our products*
- *Help prospective employees find work with our company*
- *Help investors understand what we do, our annual reports, and our company's goals, mission, and performance*

What are the goals of the content?

- *Highlight key benefits of our products*
- *Drive current customers to new products and provide them support for their existing products*
- *Drive new customers to understand our products to empower their purchase processes*
- *Differentiate our products from our competitors' products*
- *Drive people to learn more about our company and its mission, including our corporate responsibility*
- *Offer differentiated content to existing and current customers*

Content experience required to achieve goals:

- *High level value proposition that answers, "Why Company X and, specifically, why our products?"*
- *High-level brand/product benefits*
- *Timely promotions around products and event content, such as specific content for holidays and events such as "back to school"*
- *People-oriented imagery that demonstrates how to use our products*
- *People-oriented imagery that appeals to emotional and rational triggers to inspire and ultimately drive to purchase*
- *Content that is interesting, fun, and engaging and that the user will want to share socially*

Figure 7-2:
Content
brief
example.

Understanding the Content Inventory and Audit

A content inventory and audit are critical processes and tools to use as you assess your current content and understand where you need to go in the future. You should complete this work before you design the UX: It will inform which content is necessary for the experience. (Chapter 6 explains how to conduct an assessment for the future state.) These activities can run concurrently to those illustrated in Chapter 6.

Even if you do not have an existing experience from which you want to define a new one, you do possess content. Assessing the content helps you determine what new content will support your goals of the future experience. A brief set of definitions is critical to understand the process and tools and how they will affect the future state.

- ✔ **Content inventory:** This tool documents the content in an existing experience. Content strategists use this tool to determine the quantitative value of the content. For an entirely new experience, this tool can capture content in comparable experiences and/or the content an organization possesses internally to describe its service, product, and organization. For a website or app, this document captures each piece of content, how the content is formatted, the volume and scope of the content (for example, 20 press releases or five images of the product). The inventory also helps to determine which types of content exist, how these are labeled and organized, and any type of structure required to support each.

- ✔ **Content audit:** This tool augments the content inventory with additional information to assess the quality of the existing content. This tool captures any issues, gaps, and strengths of the existing content. Content strategists conduct the audit, which is not just about whether content is messaged correctly or effectively, to identify the strengths, gaps, opportunities, and untapped areas (for instance, mobile or multichannel) to consider. But you do not need to be an expert to complete the audit exercise. This section details how to do it.

- ✔ **Stakeholder interviews:** This process uncovers your internal users' needs and requirements. If you have no internal users, you can still use this set of questions to uncover content requirements for other users.

Completing a content inventory

A content inventory requires you to review your current content, document it, and capture details around its author(s), where it lives, which elements comprise it, and how often it is updated. This undertaking can span anywhere from a day to several weeks, depending on how much content you possess. Because a website inventory provides the most robust example (it is the most comprehensive of UX inventories) and because you can apply these principles to any type of UX inventory, this section uses a website inventory to illustrate the approach.

The person who completes the content inventory and audit holds many of the cards to the future success of a UX project. She will know every detail behind which content the organization has, how and why it exists, and what is missing. This wonder woman possesses the power to influence the future. Why, you ask? She can determine much of what is required in the future solution and where each piece of content should reside within the experience.

Your best bet for a tool to document content inventory is Microsoft Excel. If you do not know how to use Excel then get a copy of a book about the version of Excel that you have, such as *Microsoft Excel 2013 All-in-One For Dummies* by Greg Harvey (John Wiley & Sons, Inc.). There really is no better application to complete this exercise, and for more advanced inventories, Excel can help you filter and sort your content.

This section explains how to complete two types of inventories: inventories for a redesign and inventories for an entirely new design (where a current experience does not exist). Regardless of the type of inventory, you should familiarize yourself with both approaches.

A content inventory is not for people with a short attention span. Although it does not demand the attention of a 15th-century cartographer mapping out the coastline of what is now Latin America, a content inventory requires much time and attention to detail. A thorough inventory includes all the content on the site and detailed information about each of the page types (for example, home page, product page, and so on) and what each of those page types contains.

To complete this exercise, start with a template that looks similar to the one shown in Figure 7-3. Meet with your design and development team before completing this exercise; that meeting will help to decide on the level of detail required. If no team is available and it is a small project, err on the side of caution: Capture as much information as possible. In some cases, the technology team may require that specific types of information be captured.

Businesses use a *content management system (CMS)* to publish and manage content on larger websites. This tool uses templates, such as a home page template, a product category template (for a category of products, such as lawnmowers), and a product detail template (for specific products). These templates standardize the way information is presented and which types of content are served up to the end user. Inventories on a CMS may require you to go to a very specific level of detail, capturing each discrete piece of content on a page (such as an image of a product, a product description, or product specifications).

Breaking down the content inventory

In Figure 7-3, the following fields contain specific information:

  ✔ **Top Level:** Captures the first level of the website. For most instances, this information is the home page. This approach works for smaller sites. For larger site inventories, you may want to create a separate worksheet in Excel for each section. Thus, the product category — in this instance, White Wines — would have its own separate spreadsheet, and White Wines would reside in the Top Level. Either approach can work, but for large amounts of content, separating out sections of a website can make it easier to digest the content in each section.

Although you should capture each type of content in the site, you do not need to always include each individual single article (for example, press releases, products that share the same template and types of content but differ slightly [red cellphone case, green cellphone case, blue cellphone case], or reports that share the same type of information). In these cases, you should capture the fact that a press release exists, and then note the number of press releases. You may even want to note which years and how many press releases per year. In such cases, you rarely need to detail each individual document in the inventory. Exceptions are projects requiring content migration — that is, for projects in which you are migrating existing content from an old design into a new design, you may be required to capture each document separately.

✔ **Level 2 Title** (Levels 2–X): Identifies the information under the primary section. There may be several levels within the hierarchy, and your inventory should capture each level that exists and the content within those levels. Some inventories will require page-level information and capture all the pieces of information on a page. Often referred to as the "modules" or "objects" page, specific details are important for an app inventory and for larger sites that are powered by a CMS. Ensure that business analysis and technology team members are present for larger websites to ensure that you capture the correct level of information. The good news is that a content inventory goes from broad to deep in the information it captures, so if a further level of detail is required, you can always add it to the tool.

You may also use a numbering system in your inventory similar to sitemaps. This approach keeps the audit cleaner for deeper sites that may go across several columns in a leveling system. The numbers — 0 for Home page, 1.0 for the first landing page (for example, Products landing page), 2.0 for the second landing page (for example, About Us) shows how deep the site is while keeping all levels in one column.

✔ **Page Title:** Captures the title of the page. On a website, this information is often gleaned from the HTML page title that shows up in the top of the browser. *Note:* In some cases, not every page or template will have a title. A page title may also be the top header of a page and appear within the page.

✔ **Description:** Describes the page in a manner that makes sense to the person conducting the content inventory. In some cases, you may want to list the components of the page. For example, "Devin Dimes home page contains a product carousel that cycles through five pictures with wine of the week, coupons, and monthly deals. This carousel contains images and video and text. Under the carousel, which spans the page width, is a video of how wine is made and how it can be shared socially, and a brief description of the shop. The Devin Dimes site also contains a click to map for directions to its stores." Note that a significant amount of detail is captured for this example.

✔ **URLs:** The URL is the website address. You also may need URLs for every asset or page. Rarely do you need each URL per content type (for instance, do not list each individual press release URL).

Figure 7-3:
Content
inventory
template.

Devin Dimes Wine Shop Content Inventory			
SEO and Metadata			
TOP LEVEL	**HTML PAGE TITLE**	**META DESCRIP**	**META KEYWORDS**
Wine Home	Devin Dimes Wine Shop	Find the best foreign and domestic wine selection at Devin Dimes Wine Shop. Buy Online.	Wines, wine shop, best wine selection, cabernet, pinot, sauvignon, chardonnay, white wine, red wine, french, italian, californian

To complete the exercise for the preceding pieces of information, you may use a content inventory tool to help automate the process. You can find these tools online; in some cases, free versions are available. Such a tool can help to generate a first pass of this spreadsheet. However, note that inventory or spider tools do not always find all information. (A spider tool is an indexing tool that "crawls" a site to capture which pages are within it and sometimes details information about the page.) If you use a tool, you should manually validate that all content is accounted for in larger site inventories. This may mean you need to speak to representatives from the various areas of the business who are responsible for the content creation. Also, if you are inventorying a large site, ensure that after you have an inventory in place that respective stakeholders, who own areas of content on the site, validate the accuracy of that inventory.

Capturing HTML metadata

At this point, you are not finished with the inventory. You may need to capture additional fields. For an existing website, you will also want to capture the HTML metadata fields. To find this information, use the View Source function in your browser; within that page, which generally launches in Notepad, do a search (press Ctrl+F on a PC) for the following:

> <title>
>
> meta name="description"
>
> meta name="keywords"

You can copy and paste the information into the following three fields of your content inventory. Note that a spider or inventory tool will also pull this information into it.

- ✔ **HTML Page Title:** This title appears at the top of a browser. This field may be redundant with the Page Title field mentioned earlier.

- ✔ **META Description:** This information is used for search engines, and thus, is important for a website. The description, which contains a short, keyword-rich description of the page, frequently is used by search engines in the search results to describe the page that is indexed. Thus, a search for "Devin Dimes Wine" might return a link to "Devin Dimes Wine Shop," with the description of the home page underneath. A clear description can influence whether someone will click on the page or not.

✓ **META Keywords:** This is a group of words, generally separated by commas, that describes what is on the page. Figure 7-4 demonstrates what these fields look like with representative data.

Figure 7-4:
Content
inventory
template:
metadata
fields.

Devin Dimes Wine Shop Content Inventory						
TOP LEVEL	LEVEL 2 TITLE	LEVEL 3 TITLE	LEVEL 4 TITLE	PAGE TITLE	DESC	URL
Wine Home				Devin Dimes Wine Shop	Home page for the Wine section of the website	www.devindimeswines.com
Wine Home	White Wines			White Wines Devin Dimes Wines	Secondary level for White Wines	www.devindimeswines.com/white/
Wine Home	White Wines	Pinot Grigio	Pinot Grigio	Pinot Grigio Devin Dimes Wines	Product Category page that lists all the Pinot Grigios	www.devindimeswines.com/white/pinotgrigio/
Wine Home	White Wines	Pinot Grigio	Velentium Manus 2013	Velentium Manus 2013 Pinto Grigio Devin Dimes Wines	Product Detail page for a specific product	www.devindimeswines.com/white/pinotgrigio/VelentiumManus

You may be wondering what metadata is and why you should care about it. *Metadata* literally means "data about data." It is used to describe aspects of content. For example, for the Devin Dimes Wine Shop, the metadata keywords are a group of terms meant to represent the different types of content on the site: wine shop, cabernet, and so forth. Search engines and other types of technologies use metadata for a variety of reasons. The better the metadata, the better chance the website is indexed properly as an internal site search. Good metadata can even lead to an external search engine ranking the site higher than other, similar sites. Also, an internal site search — that is, a search engine within the site itself — also uses metadata to find and retrieve information.

Metadata is critical for search engine optimization (SEO). Chapter 8 describes in great detail the best practices to creating better metadata. SEO is the science behind figuring out how to get a website to perform at its best within search engines, such as Google and Bing. A robust and effective SEO can mean that a website appears at a high rank and displays at or near the top of the search results. Sweet!

Designating content types

But wait: You have more fields to compose. Another piece of information that proves very useful for the future-state design is content type. *Content type* is a term content strategists and technology folks use to represent a piece of content. By definition, a content type captures what type of information is being represented. Here are some examples of content type:

✓ Form pages on a website

✓ User guides for products

- ✔ Home pages

- ✔ Legal disclaimers

- ✔ Product landing pages

- ✔ Product category pages

- ✔ Help or FAQ pages

- ✔ News

- ✔ Warranty statements

- ✔ Press releases

- ✔ Corporate biographies

- ✔ Annual reports

- ✔ Blog posts

- ✔ Videos

- ✔ PDFs

- ✔ Infographics

- ✔ Article pages

You should add a content type field should to the inventory, and you should make an attempt to identify each type of content represented in the inventory. This list will prove quite useful when determining which types of content are required for the future state, as well as determining if content types are missing.

Cataloging other fields for the inventory

Additional fields for the inventory could be as follows:

- ✔ **Notable Functionality:** Captures notable functionality on the website or app. For example: The page has ratings and reviews, user-generated content for comments, RSS feeds for news sources, an embedded video player, and so forth. This field may not be necessary, but some technology teams may want this type of information specifically called out.

- ✔ **Doc Format:** What is the document format? Document format is a fancy way of saying what type of document is being viewed. Remember, a web page is technically a document in a specific format (HTML, JPG, GIF, XLS, DOC, MPEG, and so forth). In addition to text — videos, images, PDF documents, and multimedia files all comprise different types of document formats.

- **Author:** Who created the content? In many cases, content may come from multiple sources if the page contains several different content modules, such as a video, an image, and textual copy. The author may be a line of business rather than an individual contributor (marketing, technical marketing, e-commerce team, and so forth). If this information is not obvious, when the inventory is circulated to other stakeholders, you may ask them to fill in the source detail.

- **Last Updated/Update Frequency:** Capture the date the content was last updated and the update frequency: daily, weekly, monthly, yearly, never, and unknown.

- **CMS Template:** This field captures the template that is used in the CMS to generate the page. This information is useful only for content generated by a CMS, but it can be particularly useful to a technology team. You may use a person on the technology team to help supply this information. This field should be completed after the fields in the preceding list are captured.

After you have completed the necessary fields, you will have an inventory in place. To ensure it is thorough, vet it through any stakeholder who needs to weigh in on its accuracy. If you are building the experience for a client, ensure that your client signs off on the inventory.

 After the inventory is complete, review a few competitors' sites at a high level to see what types of content they possess. You may find that your site is much richer or lighter than that of your competitors. This type of exercise can provide ideas on areas where your future state can expand from a content perspective.

Completing a content audit

The steps to completing an audit are similar to those of the inventory. In fact, the exercise is often completed simultaneously with the inventory. To do this, you must first decide upon your audit criteria. The purpose of an audit is

- Assess the efficacy, richness, relevance, accessibility, measurability, and optimization of the content experience.

- Capture the issues in the current-state content ecosystem — issues that the future state should resolve.

The types of things an audit should evaluate include the following:

- **Content quality regarding brand integrity:** Is the content on brand? Does it reflect the brand well? Is it consistent and is brand positioning clear? Remember, a brand is the essence of the organization. Does the content represent the organization appropriately and effectively?

✔ **Content quality regarding relevance, timeliness, and accuracy:** Is the content correct? Is it relevant? Is it accurate? Does the content contain any errors? Does any content need to be updated?

✔ **Content quality regarding richness and effective messaging:** Is there rich content, with video, imagery, and infographics? Could it be better? Is the messaging effective, meaning, does it drive a user to accomplish the goals the business wants the customer to accomplish? If selling a product or service, is the content compelling and engaging, or is it dry and boring?

✔ **Content structure in terms of how content is labeled and categorized, its taxonomy, and so forth:** Is the content labeled appropriately? When you search for something on the site, can you find it? Is the navigation effective and logical? Is important content buried in the navigation?

✔ **Content prioritization:** What are the content priorities per key pages (priorities on the home page, key landing pages, and so forth)?

✔ **Metadata and SEO quality:** Does the site have page titles and metadata descriptions? Are they well written with the appropriate keywords? From a search engine perspective, is the site optimized so that it competitively ranks?

✔ **Accessibility compliance:** Does the site effectively comply with accessibility guidelines so that visually impaired people can engage with the experience? Do images use ALT text, which describes what the image is and also helps from an SEO perspective? ALT text is HTML or other code that allows you to say what an image is. You will see this in either the HTML code or when you roll your mouse over the image. Image readers for visually impaired readers can then use this text to show what the image communicates. Do images that link to something convey where they are taking the user? Is the site coded in an accessibility-friendly manner?

The World Wide Web Consortium (W3C), an organization devoted to ensuring accessibility-friendly code, has a list of free tools that you can use to test your site for accessibility. The tools tell you if you are compliant with accessibility best practices. Remember, a site that is accessibility friendly is generally better from an SEO perspective, so it should rank better by search engines than a site with poor accessibility. Also, the more accessible your experience is, the more people can use it. Find the W3C website accessibility list at `www.w3.org/WAI/ER/tools/complete`.

You can use the inventory template and add additional fields to it for the audit. As you work through the inventory process, you can capture the issues for each page or template. In many cases, you might create an ongoing list of easy fixes, such as broken links, misspelled words, or writing that needs minor updates. See Figure 7-5 for an example of an audit.

In Figure 7-5, the issues are captured in an Issues field. Following is a quick review of the fields:

Business Rules for Intelligent Content		Qualitative Assessment				
AUDIENCE	**RULES**	**HIGH MED LOW**	**REDNCY**	**QUAL**	**M/D/R**	**ISSUES**
Potential Customers; Returning Customers;	The customer must agree to being over 21 to enter the site since alcohol is sold. Customer must enter birthday and state. Some states do not allow shipping alcohol via post so this functionality will not appear for those states.	High	0	Medium	M	Home page has too much content, clear content priorities are impossible to glean, various voice and tone as opposed to on-brand messaging. The metadata keywords and description appear well written, but there is no alt text used by images.
Potential Customers; Returning Customers;		High	0	High	M	This page is well written, images use alt text, content is prioritized well.
Potential Customers; Returning Customers;		High	2	Low	M	No image alt text, No instructional text; lacks clear content hierarchy. This page contains redundant information to other pages. For example, the wine list for red is repeated on the white wine list.

Figure 7-5: Content audit example with fields.

The fields and columns capture the following information:

- **Audience and Rules:** Capture business rules for which content is served up to whom, as well as any other types of logic or rules necessary to support the content experience. This information is important to capture for personalization. Chapter 8 includes more information on personalization. For experiences that do not build logic into the content, where certain content is served to certain users, then these fields may not be necessary. You may not be able to gather this information without consulting a member of the technology team who built the original experience.

- **High/Med/Low:** Captures the priority of the content. If you specify a high priority, you are stating that the content is very important.

- **Redundancy:** Captures the number of instances of redundancy. How often does this content appear elsewhere? In the Issues column, you can capture the specific URLs or pages.

- **Quality:** Describes the quality of the content. You can use any type of scale, as long as you define the criteria for how you arrive at that scale.

- **M/D/R (migrate, delete, or revise):** Denotes the status of the content with regard to content migration. Again, you should define the criteria. In some cases, migrate can mean migrate as is, without any changes. Revise can mean significantly revise or any type of revision. Note how you want to use these fields.

- **Issues:** Captures any and all issues with the content.

When completing the audit, make sure you look at competitive sites as well as your own site. See what types of content they use in their experiences. Does your content stack up to theirs?

If you are building an entirely new experience, you should still conduct an inventory of all the existing content you have within your organization that will support the new experience. Are you missing content? Does the existing content need to be rewritten for the new experience? Look at product brochures, any public-facing information, and business goals and objectives. If all else fails, look at what others in your industry are doing and make a list of the types of content they provide. Conduct a light inventory of their sites and assess what they are doing and what is effective. An inventory of competitors' sites can prove quite useful in determining what you should build for your future experience. For an effective, free content inventory and audit template, go to www.kevinpnichols.com/enterprise_content_strategy/.

For websites, having a search optimization expert review your audit, particularly the metadata and SEO fields, helps you uncover any issues that might prevent your site or experience from achieving a higher ranking by search engines. If you have no expert on staff, or are doing an experience for a very small site, then check out a guide such as *Search Engine Optimization For Dummies,* by Peter Kent (John Wiley & Sons, Inc.). This book actually has an online cheat sheet, which can help you immensely: www.dummies.com/how-to/content/search-engine-optimization-for-dummies-cheat-sheet.html.

Interviewing Stakeholders for Content Requirements

Stakeholder interviews help you uncover the requirements of content in your organization. This process ensures that you are meeting the needs of even the smallest group of stakeholders, which helps garner their early buy-in of your work. Always review the list of questions in the stakeholder protocol so that you can uncover the types of requirements, issues, and wish lists of the organization.

Start by listing all the stakeholders who deal with content. The point of the interviews is to uncover issues in the current state, including with the content itself, the way the content is published, and any other issues that influence content. You should also use the interview as an opportunity to gather requirements for content for the future-state experience. Types of stakeholders typically represented include authors; content contributors; third-party sources who create content, such as visual design or video agencies; marketing; branding; legal; technology; SEO and analytics; and lines of business responsible for content, such as product lines that require content for their products.

After you develop the list of necessary stakeholders, start the scheduling process immediately. Ask for two hours for each session. Also, ensure you reserve a room and ask the stakeholders if you may record the session. (Notify them prior to asking them to participate.) You will conduct the sessions, but ideally, a note-taker will also be present because it would be difficult for you to ask the questions and take notes simultaneously. In some cases, such as with an entire team (for instance, marketing and technology), you may schedule a workshop with several people and take them through the questions. Start the meeting by asking for complete candor: The more open and transparent the participants, the more likely any issues they have will materialize. Inform participants that by revealing their issues, you can help resolve them in the future-state experience.

The point of the interview is to uncover issues with the current content. Start the interviews by asking each participant the relationship he or she has with the content. Ask the following questions:

- ✔ What is the objective of the content?
- ✔ What needs or requirements do you have with regard to the content?
- ✔ How do you work with it?
- ✔ What will mean success to you in the future experience?
- ✔ What do you think are pain points, choke points, or causes for alarm with regard to the content?
- ✔ Where are the inefficiencies and gaps?
- ✔ What do you consider the ideal future state?
- ✔ What must the UX absolutely contain to meet minimum content requirements?

These questions frame the areas you will probe to uncover the content requirements and understand what, in each stakeholder's mind, the future-state experience should accomplish. Kevin has developed a robust protocol that is seen in the content strategy industry as the definitive guide. The tool is free and places nearly every specific question you would want to ask into sections, based on the stakeholder type (analytics, marketing, and so forth). The template is updated annually to account for changes in the industry. Find that template at `www.kevinpnichols.com/enterprise_content_strategy/`.

One of the areas the preceding protocol dives into is content life cycle. The first section of this chapter introduces the fact that content life cycle is directly tied to content experience. You should make every attempt to uncover any issues and requirements within the current content publishing process. In general, an ideal model uses the following steps:

1. **Identify the need for new content.**

2. **Detail all content.**

   Use either a brief or spec document that lists what new content is required, plus any specifics around its creation (such as whether it contains imagery and whether multiple sources will create it).

3. **Acquire content from various sources.**

4. **Create content.**

    This step may not occur if content is acquired.

5. **Have the legal department, brand managers, and any other necessary stakeholders review content.**

6. **Modify content per review cycles and finalize it.**

7. **Publish content.**

8. **Measure content performance, and then retire it, keep it the same, or optimize it.**

This entire process is closed loop as shown in Figure 7-6. You can use this process to figure out how your organization produces content. If you have never produced content and are building an entirely new experience, use these steps as a baseline for a best approach, even if you are the primary actor in all the steps. For larger organizations, look at what is working within these steps and what is broken.

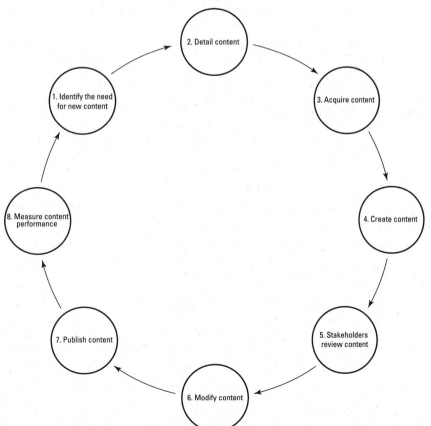

Figure 7-6:
The content
life cycle.

A fragmented content life cycle may adversely affect the quality of the content. It's important to uncover issues and document requirements. The planned future experience should also address any issues that impede the content life cycle process. Your overall UX quality will improve if the content life cycle is optimized. The stakeholder interview protocol in the preceding section provides a list of questions to ask to tease out issues.

Creating the Content Strategy Audit Report and Future-State Point of View (POV)

This report captures all the issues uncovered in the inventory, the audit, and the stakeholder interviews. Because the audit will contain very detailed information, it is important to roll up the primary themes and findings into a report that the larger design team can use for future-state considerations. Also, the stakeholder interviews will also contain very detailed information, and this report helps to summarize the key findings.

The report should be seen as a guide for the future experience in terms of content requirements. A typical table of contents follows:

1. Audit Approach and Methodology Used

2. Audit Findings and Implications (you may use the audit criteria listed in "Completing the content audit," earlier in the chapter, for the groupings)

    a. Content branding (is it on brand?) and quality

    b. Relevance, timeliness, and effectiveness

    c. Personalization

    d. SEO, metadata, and accessibility

    e. Content life cycle

    f. Content governance

    g. Ease of use and readabilty

You can complete this report in Microsoft PowerPoint and Word. As you are going through the issues you uncovered, tie each issue to a recommendation for the future. For example, if you discover that no HTML page titles exist, add the recommendation to create HTML page titles for the future experience, and ensure that the new content creation is accounted for in the plan.

Another piece of the audit report that proves very useful is a list of all known content types and ones that stakeholders feel are necessary for the future experience. This information will help during the future-state design session to ensure that all the appropriate content is accounted for in the future experience. Oftentimes, this content type list also identifies unique types of functionality or features to support it. After your report is complete, meet with the stakeholders you previously interviewed and take them through the findings. Use this opportunity to tweak any recommendations and finalize any specific requirements from each audience member. After the document is complete, review it at the beginning of the design phase with your design team to ensure everyone understands all content requirements.

Chapter 8

Designing the Content Strategy

• •

In This Chapter

▶ Identifying which content types are necessary for your experience

▶ Understanding how to label and organize content

▶ Creating a "content model"

• •

Information is power.

— Robin Morgan

Designing a content strategy for UX requires many different tasks. That is because content strategy is not a discipline where just one or two key activities are performed. Ultimately, many different types of tasks are included in content strategy, and these depend largely on the solution that you are creating. This chapter builds on Chapter 7, which outlines the necessary activities for content strategy in the discovery and define phases of UX work.

Getting Started with Content Strategy

This chapter draws from the deliverables in Chapter 7 to design other elements of content strategy. Given the breadth of the topic, this chapter focuses on key content strategy tasks and deliverables and notes when each is necessary and to which types of work it applies. In general, follow these steps in the design phase of content strategy. Details on how to complete each step are detailed further in the chapter.

1. **Review the audit, inventory, and recommendations to formalize a set of content types. Define each content type.**

   This step assumes that the audit is complete and based on best practices for how users view content and what said users expect.

2. **Map the content types to user needs and journeys and prioritize.**

   This information is gathered via stakeholder interviews, personas and user journeys, and user research and insights — all of which are detailed in previous chapters.

3. **Work with an information architect to ensure the content types are represented within the new design.**

   There may be several meetings whereby you feed the information architect the types of content you uncover during the audit process. These types may evolve in the design phase, meaning you may uncover additional content types as you work through new designs with the UX and design teams.

4. **For each area of the UX, which most frequently is a section of an experience, identify the strategic intent, goals, and objectives of the experience and required content to support each.**

5. **For each area of the experience, extract a rule for the content and capture it within a tool called a *content model*.**

6. **Develop a taxonomy as necessary to label, categorize, and structure content.**

7. **Identify appropriate metadata to support the solution.**

8. **Work with other design team members to flesh out design.**

9. **Create a content production matrix that captures content for new creation and content to be migrated (and identifies where it will go).**

10. **Create any necessary publication workflows for content acquisition, creation, and publication. Account for syndicated, curated, existing, and new content.**

11. **Create an editorial calendar.**

12. **Capture all rules and create a governance structure and model.**

The following sections cover these topics with instructions for how to complete them.

Identifying the Necessary Content Types

Chapter 7 lays out a working definition for content types and then provides some examples. A content type is a logical grouping of content that is based on the essence of that content. It logically defines what the content is. Any effective

UX requires content to support it, and developing a list of content types is the best way to help you figure out, at a high level, which types of content your experience will support and contain. Table 8-1 provides a list of commonly used content types with definitions.

Table 8-1	Content Types and Definitions
Content Type	*Definition*
Annual reports	Chronicles an organization's activities and performance for a preceding year.
Article pages	Spans an array of different themes, but generally is a placeholder for long-form articles that lack heavy formatting. Think of this as a newspaper or magazine article.
Biographies	Captures the biographies of notable people in the organization (typically, the executives and board members).
Blog posts	Accounts for any type of blog post, including user-generated content or executive-level thought leadership blogs.
Company policies	Includes any organizational policy. For example, a privacy policy that is related to the sharing of information and demographics. Privacy policy dictates where a user's rights begin and end with respect to use of a service or experience.
Contact information (as in Contact Us)	Provides physical address, phone and fax numbers, and e-mail and website addresses. Sometimes, contact information is set as a form for a user to submit; generally, it is a best practice to provide some type of e-mail, phone number, or physical mailing address accompanied with a list of key departments a user would want to reach.
FAQ pages	Answers questions that are frequently asked about the experience, a product, a service, and/or the organization.
Form pages	Spans a list of different forms that require user input, such as a contact form, an order form, or a user profile or survey.
Glossary terms and definitions	Lists and defines a set of important terms.
Handbooks	Captures information about the use of a product or service; often a simple user guide.
Help	Includes content designed to troubleshoot problems and aid users in finding solutions and answers. This includes articles or knowledgebase documents to help the user.

(continued)

Table 8-1 *(continued)*

Content Type	Definition
Infographics	Spans an array of different themes, but generally contains an image that diagrams or captures complex information and makes it more accessible through an image and text.
Instructions	Describes step-by-step processes to achieve a task; a description of a means to an end.
Legal disclaimers	States legal responsibilities of an organization and the rights of an experience's user; also addresses liability issues.
Legal notices	Notes issues related to legal matters of liability, responsibility, product or service use, and/or rights of the organization.
Log out	Contains the screen or information necessary for logout and may include a confirmation of the action.
Manuals	Provides information, generally detailed, as it relates to specific use of products or services.
News	Information related to current events.
Newsletters	Reviews current information of an organization, including news and events, presented in a minimal format. Often in the form of a PDF document or e-mail.
Podcasts	Spans an array of themes; includes content captured as an audio podcast; often used to capture a radio program, thought leadership, or a longer organization announcement.
Press releases (news releases)	Spans an array of themes; any release by an organization for a notable event or story. The intent of press releases is to get media to use/pick up the news so it reaches the audience the organization wants to reach en masse.
Product category pages	Captures products belonging to a category, and is the main entrance into a group of products. For example, lawnmowers may be the main category for riding mowers, walk-behind mowers, gas mowers, and electric mowers. A category page is a key, and if a user lands on it from outside the site, he or she has enough information to understand it is a category for a subset of information. Thus, on an online pet toy store, the key category pages for cat toys or dog toys could be considered product landing pages.

Content Type	Definition
Product detail page	Contains details and information about a specific product; often includes product imagery, a description, features and benefits, product specifications, testimonials, or ratings and reviews.
Product user guides	Explains how to use a product or service. Often less robust than a manual that includes detailed instructions for how to use a product.
Reviews	Opinions of other users or industry experts regarding the use of a product or service or interaction with an organization.
Tutorials	Guides that instruct and enhance a user's experience with a product or service.

To figure out which content types your experience requires, you should first look at any content inventory or audit work you have completed. From those efforts, you should have identified content types in your existing UX or within your organization. Ideally, you would have identified preliminary content types during the discovery or define phase. If you have nothing, and you need to start with a list, refer to Table 8-1 to generate ideas and then complete the following steps:

1. **Survey all content in your organization that your future-state experience could offer.**

   Think about what will make the experience the most compelling. Generate a list of content types from that effort. Make sure you also look at what comparable experiences or competitors offer.

2. **Conduct a brainstorming session and generate a list of future-state content types.**

   Use the following techniques for best results:

   - *Create an agenda and bring in a preliminary list of content you think is important to structure the discussion around.* Ensure that it is properly facilitated and have a note-taker capture all decisions. If you have an information architect or creative lead on the team, you may want to work with him or her to generate the preliminary list.

   - *Invite anyone who has a vested interest in which content should go into the experience.* Structure brainstorming activities around a series of questions about which content should be a part of the experience. Good questions to ask are, "What is the best experience you have ever seen similar to this?" and "What items from that experience would you like to see in our experience?"

• *Have the group capture its content types on sticky notes and place them on a whiteboard or wall.* (You can later use the sticky notes in your own session to group, categorize, and prioritize the content types. Also, if you use sticky notes, you can take a picture of the final output instead of re-creating it textually.)

3. **Look at competitive experiences or those of similar organizations to frame a sense of what types of content you should and could provide.**

4. **As you capture the content types, make an attempt to provide a high-level definition of that content type and the function it provides to the user.**

   As you compile the list, start broad. Think of all the different types of content. Even if you don't think your technology will support it, list every type you think may benefit the experience; aspirational content types can often be used to guide future strategic decisions and planning.

5. **After you have completed the list, prioritize it with what is absolutely critical for the launch of the experience.**

   If certain items are important but not critical for launch, note where and when each could fall into future releases. Validate the prioritized list with all necessary stakeholders. These could include brand and marketing teams; technology teams; product line or business lines impacted by the UX; members of the creative, UX, or design teams; legal and compliance teams; and so forth. Another workshop may be useful to pull a larger team together for validation. If you are completing this work for a client, ensure the client signs off on the list.

6. **When you have a complete list of content types, work with an information architect or experience designer to create a sitemap of the new experience.**

   The content types list is a critical component of this process because it informs the types of information the UX must include. Refer to Chapter 9 for more information on how and when to construct a sitemap.

A content type generally has its own publication workflow or content life cycle. A content life cycle involves the overall steps taken to acquire or author, create, design, and publish a piece of content. For example, the creation of a video will be different than the creation of a news release. The section on "Identifying Content Life Cycles for Each Type of Content" in this chapter provides specific details on defining the life cycles of content types.

Your initial list of content types may change as you flesh out your UX design. As the design progresses, you may uncover the need for different content types than what you previously accounted for. The content types list is a dynamic document, which means that it stands the chance of being updated throughout the design process.

Creating Experience-Level, Section-Level, and Page-Level Content Strategy

Effective user experiences always start with a strategy that captures the goals, objectives, and targeted users. When thinking about content, consider these as important inputs. A content inventory and audit, strategy framework, and list of content types can inform you about which types of content your experience should capture. However, you should tie your recommendations for content around a framework or strategy that speaks to the intent and objectives of the experience. Think of this strategy as a content experience strategy. That is, what is the experience of content within your UX design, why does it exist, to whom does it speak, and what does it need to accomplish?

When you first start the design phase, you should work on this approach for the overall experience. You can even include a section in your content strategy framework document that captures it at a high level. As the design progresses, continue to document this strategy as it applies to specific sections and pages within the experience. A content experience strategy provides the following information:

- **Intent of the experience/section/page:** The intent answers the question of why the experience, section, or page exists in the first place. It should conform to the UX strategy and the goals and objectives of the experience, but it should be content-specific. For example, the experience will provide content to the user to sell products, answer questions about the organization, provide up-to-date news, and showcase new products. Ensure that it points or supports the information known about the user such as insights and user research.

- **Users, personas, and customer segments:** Who is the primary audience for the experience? You can point to other documents created, such as personas, but after you start to define this strategy framework at the page level, the audience becomes even more important because it will inform you as to what that specific page or section needs to achieve for a specific audience.

- **Objectives of the experience/section/page:** This should answer what the overall experience, section within it, or specific page type (for instance, the product details page) needs to accomplish. For more information on defining objectives, see Chapter 13.

- **Prioritized list of content and content types required for achieving objectives:** What content do you need to offer up to your audiences to ensure the objectives and intent of the experience are met? You should prioritize this list because objectives for one page will differ from objectives for another page.

Creating a Content Model

A content model represents a series of decisions that are made around content for an experience. If you have worked with content in the past, you may have seen various definitions for what a content model is or is not. These various definitions exist because a content model may represent a lot of different types of decisions around what content in a solution is and how it should function. In general, content models accomplish the following:

- ✔ Document content types that go into the experience.
- ✔ Capture rules for when and how content types are used.
- ✔ Document templates and any rules for when or how they are used.
- ✔ Document modules within templates and specify any particular rules, including logic that is built into the modules, such as intelligent content.

Intelligent content builds logic into content. Examples include personalization, which serves content up to specific individuals based on who they are and how they behave. Also included are *cross-sell* and *up-sell* opportunities. A cross-sell is when a consumer views a product and another product is also recommended, such as a belt and shoes that could coordinate with a suit. An up-sell is when you try to sell a more enhanced product or like-product from the one a user initially selects. Additionally, recommendations are also a type of intelligent content, and these are defined by when a piece of content is viewed and other content is recommended based on what is viewed. All these examples of intelligent content require rules and logic to be served up to a user.

Although a content strategist or content expert generally produces a content model, collaboration with other folks on the UX team is important for this document. A content model captures decisions; as such, it is not complete until the end of the design phase of work. As you flesh out a content model, schedule reviews with other members of the UX and the technology teams to ensure alignment across the effort.

How the design process functions influences the way in which you build a content model. You should start by identifying the basic shell for what you think the content model should capture. The following fields are commonly used in content models and are recommended as a best practice:

- ✔ **Wireframe ID:** Captures the name of the wireframe referenced. The information architect should have a standard approach for naming wireframes, and you should use the same name or number to ensure you can trace what you have identified in this content model back to the information architect's (IA's) work.

✔ **Template:** Generally, a template maps to a structured page type within a content management system, although some UX solutions may use templates without content management. A template is a structure that standardizes the layout and presentation of a page within an experience. It's the shell that can house many different types of content. A template may apply to many different types of content. For example, a news release, news article, and biography of an executive may all share the same template. The shell of a template is populated with or by content modules. As you go through the design phase, work with the information architect to define a set of templates necessary to support the experience. In the content model, capture the templates. You may create a separate worksheet to define or provide descriptions of the templates.

✔ **Module/Component:** A module resides within a template. A module represents a specific type or function of content. For example, a module could be any of the following, but it's not limited to these things: a video, an image, a product description, a carousel with rotating information, a comparison tool. You should capture the module name. You will also capture a description of the module, but you can create a separate worksheet to do so. If you use a separate worksheet to capture modules, entitle that worksheet "module library."

✔ **Content type:** By the time you start the content model, most content types should be identified. If they aren't, refer to the previous section on how to identify content types. Although additional content types may be identified as the design is developed, most content types should be known.

✔ **Character count:** If there is a minimum or maximum character count, note the limit. This type of information is used when you develop sites for mobile devices because you need to limit the amount of characters within the content or have headers or areas on the page such as titles that fit within a certain length.

✔ **Personalization rules:** Note any specific personalization rules that are required. You may note to whom certain content is made available and the circumstances — such as when, where, and what type — under which the content is surfaced. For events-based content, for example, you may create a rule that every time an anniversary occurs, a personalized message to the user is triggered.

✔ **Display rules:** This field is used when you determine on which channel to surface content (for example, a mobile smartphone display, a desktop display, and so forth).

Work with the design team to develop a content model. Capture all decisions around content in this document. As wireframes are designed, the person playing the content strategy role should feed the IA with the content that goes into each template and area. You will collaborate with the IA to determine the rules for content. As you go through this process, ensure that you get technology teams to validate the findings and results. Complete a content model for the overall experience. Then, as you go through the design phase, create one for each section of the experience and page type. This effort should be an input to the information architecture process, and the final page designs should conform to what is called out within this framework.

Creating a Taxonomy

Taxonomy is a term used to denote a hierarchy that categorizes information and provides labels for it. The way groceries are structured in a store is a type of taxonomy. For example, the hierarchy for steak may be: Meats>Beef>Steak>Filet Mignon. In a taxonomy, Meat would be the first category, Beef might fall into Meat type, Steak might fall into the Cut Category, and Filet Mignon might fall under a specific Cut. The categorization scheme structures the information into a hierarchy and makes it easy for someone to find it within a logical category. Taxonomy is used for search, navigation, and intelligent content. It is also used for faceted navigation.

If you have to organize information, such as products, into a hierarchy, a taxonomy may be required. To create a taxonomy, complete the following tasks.

1. **Start with a list of terms that you need to order.**

   For example, for a product hierarchy, use a list of all the products you have. Look for any internally branded categories to represent the information. You can also look to what is used competitively.

2. **Identify the key stakeholders who need to weigh in on the taxonomy.**

   For websites, you will want to engage the SEO (search engine optimization) expert because taxonomies are the fuel for searches. Also ensure that the individuals specializing in brand, product line, or legal or regulatory roles are consulted. Ask them to join a workshop or series of workshops to validate the terms you identify and the category structures throughout the process.

3. **When you collect the list of terms, also ask for any synonyms that you need to consider.**

   For example, "kitty toy" might also be known as "cat toy."

4. **Survey the content inventory and identify any additional content you may need to consider for the taxonomy.**

   A taxonomy categorizes information, so any type of information that requires a hierarchical organization model should be considered.

5. **After all the information and terms are collected, go through an exercise of grouping similar information.**

   For example, if your list includes cats, dogs, horses, and pigs, you may create a category for animals under which the individual animals are grouped. Look at the information and take an initial pass at putting it into categories.

   As you go through this process, think in terms of hierarchy. For example: topic, subtopic, specific topic. A topic could be religion, a subtopic Christianity, and a specific topic Roman Catholicism. In this example, the main nodes in the taxonomy (*node* here means *category*) might be: Books, Religion Category, and Specific Faith. For each high-level category, spend time fleshing out the subcategories. Try to limit the number of categories when possible. First-level categories in a product catalog for a retail store might be Clothing, Electronics, Furniture, and so forth. Under Clothing, you may have women's, men's, children, and subcategories, and then those might break down into even more specific subcategories.

6. **To ensure that you have the correct terms, you may want to use card sorting or tree testing to see how your users actually think of the information.**

   These techniques are excellent to validate the taxonomy and keep it user centric. (Chapter 12 covers testing techniques.) You should also test the labels for how you identify the information. For example, do you use cat, kitty, or feline? Capture any synonyms and make sure you put a field in your taxonomy for related terms.

7. **Plot the terms and categories into a spreadsheet. See Table 8-2 for an example of the taxonomy.**

8. **When the terms are complete, validate with the technology team, SEO team, and any other relevant stakeholders.**

   You will hand this work off to the development team, who will use this document to program the content publishing system and enable search or other types of functionality.

Table 8-2 **Taxonomy Example**

Level 1	Level 2	Level 3	Synonyms	End-User Nomenclature	System Metadata Rules	Content Type	Definition
Legal						Annual Reports	Chronicles an organization's activities and performance for a preceding year.
	Warranty		Certificate of guarantee, warranty promise, guarantee, limited warranty	Warranty		Article Pages	Spans an array of different themes, but generally is a place holder for longer form articles that lack heavy formatting. Think of this as a newspaper or magazine article.
		Complete warranty statement		Complete warranty statement	Inherit all metadata values and Level 2 synonyms	Biographies	Captures the biographies of notable people in the organization, such as executives or board members.

Identifying Content Life Cycles for Each Type of Content

A content life cycle is the end-to-end process for how content is acquired, created, reviewed, managed, published, measured, archived, and/or optimized. Every type of content has a life cycle. Content must be gathered or created, managed, and published. Ideally, content is measured after it is published to determine how well it is performing. Figure 8-1 shows a typical content life cycle process.

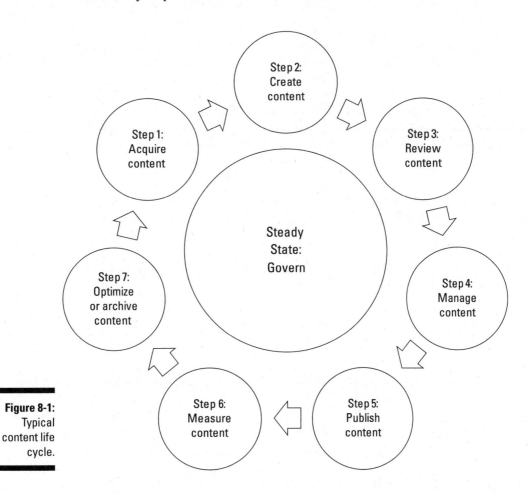

Figure 8-1: Typical content life cycle.

Syndicated content versus curated content

Syndicated content is content that comes from an existing source and is generally paid for with a prearranged agreement with the content provider. Experiences that leverage syndicated content generally have an agreement with a content provider in place to feed specific articles or types of content to an experience. Think of it as subscribing to a specific area of content. Syndicated content is generally entirely written and production ready, meaning that all that is required is to pull it into an existing experience. In many cases, syndicated content is meant to augment or enrich an existing experience. For example, a retail website selling women's fitness clothing might leverage syndicated exercise videos produced by a fitness authority.

Curated content is a term often used in the digital world. It means that a content experience is created from someone identifying specific content to tell a story and pulling it all together, similar to how a curator identifies art for a museum exhibit. Pieces of content are selected and displayed together to tell a larger story or convey an experience. Sometimes, people use the term to apply to content that is pulled into an experience via an automated means, such as an RSS feed. However, curating cannot be entirely automated. An entirely automated process of pulling content into an experience is called *aggregation* and has little to do with curating.

Notice that in this example there is a closed circle of repeatable steps, which are described here:

- ✔ **Step 1 — Acquire Content:** Content acquisition is generally reserved for two types of content. Content that is physically acquired from another source and content that is created after specific requirements are gathered. In the latter case, the gathering of content inputs and requirements is the acquisition process. Acquisition is therefore the first step in most content life cycles. In some cases, the content is already created from another source, such as with syndicated and curated content.

- ✔ **Step 2 — Create Content:** Content creation is the step in the process where content is actually created. In the case of copy, it is what an author writes; in the case of video, it might involve several steps, including storyboarding, scripting, actor selection, shooting, editing, and finalizing. Images might require a different set of steps. The three types of content — copy, video, and images — require very different substeps within the creation process. Thus, each of these content types has a unique life cycle.

- ✔ **Step 3 — Review Content:** Content reviews can include several steps and processes relative to reviewing and finalizing content. In larger organizations, typical review processes include a review from the brand team, legal teams, and a member of the UX design team to ensure the finalized content appears as it should.

✔ **Step 4 — Manage Content:** Content management generally applies to the method used to enter content into a system, such as a content management system or a publishing engine. This includes the entry of the content into the system, the review of the content within it, and the management of changes.

✔ **Step 5 — Publish Content:** Publishing is the series of steps required to actually publish the content within an experience. In some cases, the content may be hard coded into the experience; this step is reserved for when the experience is actually launched. In the case of a website where content is frequently updated, this includes the series of steps content must undergo to get it to a live site after the content is ready for publication. In these cases, several of these steps may be technical in nature.

✔ **Step 6 — Measure Content:** Content measurement includes the actual steps to, well, measure content. In many cases, some of these are automated after a metrics strategy and process is defined. These steps also include the organizational steps required to measure, report the findings, and act on those findings.

✔ **Step 7 — Optimize or Archive Content:** After the performance of the content is evaluated, these are the final stages in the life cycle. If the content requires optimization or changes, you might kick off the life cycle again. If new content opportunities are identified after content performance is evaluated, the life cycle will need to start again as well. Archiving content is the process of retiring content from the experience. In many cases, content may be left as is, meaning you leave it on the site or within the experienced unchanged.

You should understand that a content life cycle is rarely as methodical and black and white as the preceding steps might make it seem. Many of these steps may be in parallel and some may occur in a different order. For example, if a content management system (CMS) is used, you may have authors create their content within the actual CMS as opposed to creating and finalizing it and then having it entered within the system. Content reviews may occur throughout several of these steps all the way to publication. However, the preceding steps communicate most typical processes at a high level required for most types of content.

Defining content life cycles for content is an important step in the content strategy process, because if the delivery method is broken, then the content experience will most likely have issues. To define content life cycles, complete the following steps.

1. **From the list of content types, create a spreadsheet that lists the content types and then each step in the process to acquire, create, and author them.**

   You may have to consult authors, producers, visual designers, and technology folks to glean this information. Start with the preceding life cycle, and then use these large steps to create substeps. For example, to create a video, capture all steps necessary for the video creation. If you are using other companies that specialize in videography to create content, it may not be necessary to capture all the steps they go through to create the actual content, but you should understand these steps at a high level, and know the additional steps that are necessary after the content is handed off to you.

2. **As you flesh out the steps, capture the timing required for each step.**

   Does it take one week to write an article? Does it take three weeks to review it? Knowing how long it takes for each step helps to plan the overall duration of the process.

3. **Consult the stakeholder interviews during the process and use them to validate each life cycle.**

   Chapter 7 discusses stakeholder interviews. One of the areas you should dive into during discovery is how each content life cycle functions within your current processes. If you have that information, you also should have uncovered any gaps, issues, pain points, and requirements for each content life cycle. Having this information enables you to plot out updated content life cycles. If you don't have this information, you may have to take a stab at creating an initial pass and then vetting it through each member who touches the content or should touch it to ensure you have correctly documented the life cycle and not left out any necessary steps.

   Many content types share the same workflow. For example, the steps to write a long-form article may be the same as writing short copy for a news article. It's okay for similar types of content to share the same workflows.

4. **Capture any necessary reviews in the process.**

   Remember that after content is entered into a system, it should be viewed again to assess its look and feel before it is officially published.

5. **For acquired content, such as syndicated or curated content, ensure that the content is in fact reviewed prior to publication.**

   Acquired content may not necessarily meet your requirements or support your brand the way you want it to. For aggregated content, be careful with your sources. Manually spot-check aggregated content. In some cases, such as with syndicated content or content from other sources, you may not be able to modify it. Regardless, ensure that you manually review all content or have a process in place to ensure that the content aligns with your brand and organizational standards.

6. **If you have user-generated content, such as comments, ensure you build a process to manually review the content prior to it being published.**

7. **When you are finished with the content life cycles, you can document them in a diagram called a *swim lane* to illustrate the overall workflow and process.**

   An application such as Microsoft Visio is good for creating a swim lane. You can also use something like Microsoft Word, PowerPoint, or Excel to build these types of diagrams. See Figure 8-2 for a representative life cycle.

Managing user-generated content

User-generated content is content that your users create and submit a site. User-generated content refers to any type of content that is created by a user of your experience and generally communicates a user viewpoint concerning her experience with your organization, brand, product, service, or the UX itself. User-generated content is important; it helps you stay in touch with what your users say about you. You should encourage such content by offering ratings, reviews, and comments within your experience.

Some user-generated content may include comments that are inappropriate, unethical,

or hostile. Ensure you build into your life cycle a mechanism to moderate all user-generated content. You can create a policy that clearly outlines which types of content you will allow. Any content that doesn't violate your policy — including content that might be negative or critical of your brand — should be allowed and published. By publishing it, you show transparency and authenticity. You can respond to negative feedback directly as opposed to censoring it.

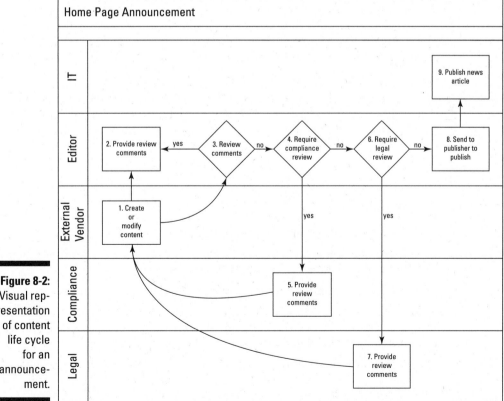

Figure 8-2: Visual representation of content life cycle for an announcement.

8. **Ensure that you vet the final workflows with all necessary stakeholders and make any final changes.**

   You also supply these changes to a member of your technology team. A workflow can be used by a CMS, and the technology team may want to automate the workflow as much as possible. For example, if authors enter the content into a CMS in the creation process then the reviews can be tracked and managed and the entire publishing process contained within one system. When a task is complete, a CMS can be set up to trigger an e-mail for the next person in the process. For example, after an author finishes an article, a CMS can e-mail the brand reviewer to let him know he has a new task to review the content. When he is finished, an e-mail can let a legal reviewer know she needs to look at the content.

Creating a Governance Model

Content governance creates a process and system to govern and guide the content development process and ensure that a mechanism is in place for future content creation and production. It encompasses procedures, processes, people, and tools needed to successfully run content publication. A comprehensive model includes a committee with defined roles, content guidelines, and a workflow.

There are two types of content governance: governance by committee and governance by tools. For example, a content style guide that provides guidance and rules on how to write content and when and where it should be used is an example of a tool that provides governance. A content life cycle that is documented and enforced is another tool that can help with the process.

A governance committee, in contrast to a tool, has a variety of responsibilities, including

- Managing the quality of content throughout the organization
- Recommending changes based on metrics, trends, user feedback, and future content needs (such as new products or services)
- Reviewing, approving, and overseeing changes in the content
- Providing oversight and making any changes to tools for content, such as content style guides, content life cycles, content processes, and even weighing in on technology issues
- Communicating any changes in standards and policies to the larger teams

Content governance has many benefits. It ensures that a mechanism is in place to regulate content and make future decisions around it. A successful governance model can streamline decision-making throughout the content life cycle.

Table 8-3 compares governance functions by tools versus by committee:

Table 8-3   Governance by Tools versus Governance by Committee

Governance Tools	*Committee Responsibilities*
Templates (such as wireframes, comps, and system-coded CMS templates and modules)	Committee definition (governance model)
Content life cycle processes (enforced in part by CMS)	Charter definition (which is the charter for the committee)
Editorial standards	Necessary meetings and decision-making process
Content and visual style guides	
Editorial calendar	
Content matrix/model	

Governance tools such as editorial calendar or content matrix, are discussed throughout this chapter, so further clarification is not necessary. A governance committee should be formed around decisions concerning content. There are three different models for governance structures. Figure 8-3 shows the different types to consider.

There is no one-size-fits-all for governance. In some cases, a centralized model works best. In centralized models, one group of people sits on a single committee and makes all decisions that affect content organizationally. This does not always work for large or global businesses. For example, if your company operates in many different countries or in several regions, each region may want to have a certain amount of control over standards, policies, and guidance of content. In that case, you may need to use a federated or decentralized approach (see Figure 8-3). The key to governance is to work with the stakeholders who have a vested interest in content to ensure a model works for everyone. After you have come up with a model, ensure that it has appropriate members. Figure 8-4 shows what a typical governance committee looks like.

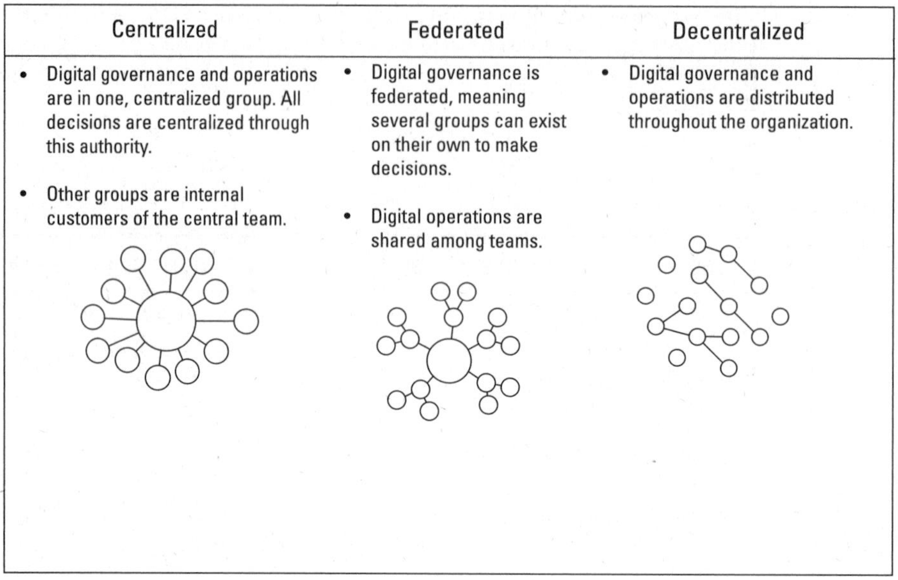
Centralized
Federated
Decentralized
• Digital governance and operations are in one, centralized group. All decisions are centralized through this authority.
• Other groups are internal customers of the central team.
• Digital governance is federated, meaning several groups can exist on their own to make decisions.
• Digital operations are shared among teams.
• Digital governance and operations are distributed throughout the organization.

Figure 8-3: Three types of governance structures.

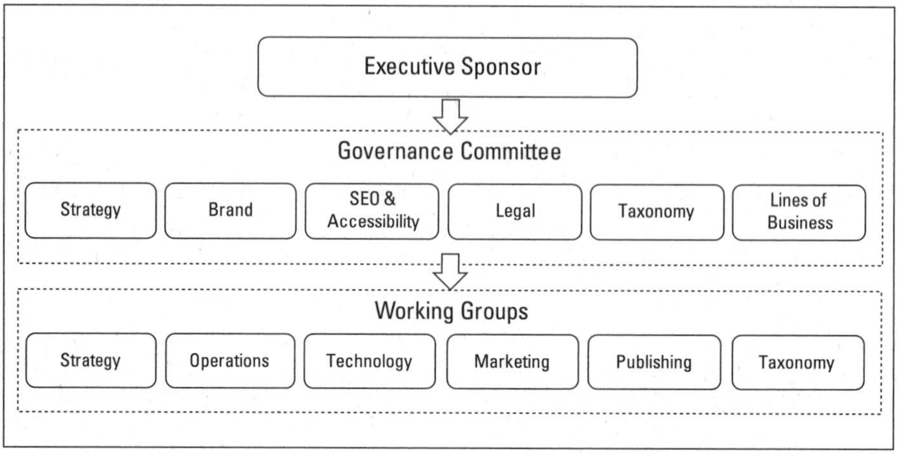
Executive Sponsor
Governance Committee
Strategy
Brand
SEO & Accessibility
Legal
Taxonomy
Lines of Business
Working Groups
Strategy
Operations
Technology
Marketing
Publishing
Taxonomy

Figure 8-4: Typical governance model.

After you decide on a model, you should have a governance charter. A governance charter typically includes the following components:

- **Purpose of the charter:** The purpose of the charter sets the overall goals of the governance committee. Why does it exist? What does it govern? What are the business goals and objectives that are specific or applicable to the charter?

✔ **Functions:** These are what the committee is responsible for. In general, the committee is responsible for the following:

- Ensuring compliance with any and all content standards and rules.

- Identification of optimization changes and new content.

- Managing effective change, which means that when new processes and policies are identified they are rolled out in a way in which they will be adopted by the larger organization.

- Managing risks and performance, meaning that metrics and analytics and the findings should be reviewed by this committee, to inform future changes.

- Setting strategy, polices, and providing oversight of all tools used by and for content. This means providing a list of all tools the committee oversees.

✔ **Roles and responsibilities:** This defines who owns what with regard to content and what the responsibilities are for said ownership. This might include an organizational matrix as well as job descriptions.

It's a good idea to have a workshop with all committee members to flesh out the areas in the preceding list. After a committee is in place, you should meet monthly to ensure that everything is on track. On a quarterly basis, you will also want to assess the findings from metrics and make recommendations for the future. Figures 8-5, 8-6, and 8-7 show how governance can work in action to maintain the UX solution:

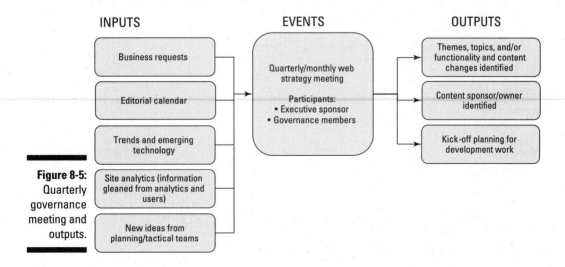

Figure 8-5: Quarterly governance meeting and outputs.

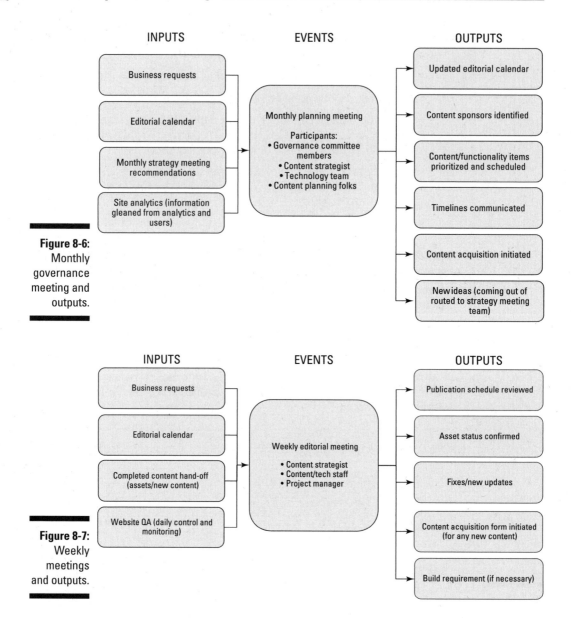

Figure 8-6:
Monthly governance meeting and outputs.

Figure 8-7:
Weekly meetings and outputs.

Creating an Editorial Calendar and Production Tools

An editorial calendar helps you know which content is necessary to support an experience. An editorial calendar should be created at the annual level, and then evaluated quarterly using the previously described governance processes, looking at metrics, business needs, trends, and user feedback to identify new content opportunities. An editorial calendar plots out all the content across an annual calendar and shows what is getting released in which months. This includes content for new products and events such as anniversaries and holidays, as well as any steady-state content that is ongoing in the content process. Steady-state content is content that you always produce to keep the experience fresh. Examples are news stories or weekly articles.

To create a calendar, plot a series of dates — monthly, weekly, or daily — across an annual calendar. Use a spreadsheet. If you have weekly or daily content, you may want to create separate worksheets for each quarter or month. See Figure 8-8 for an illustration of a calendar.

Figure 8-8: Editorial calendar example.

						Q2 Editorial Calendar		
	APRIL					**MAY**		
	1	8	15	22	29	6	13	20
	Company Announcements	Company Announcements	Company Announcements	Company Announcements	Company Announcements	Company Announcements	Company Announcements	Company Announcements
Marketing Content	Content for Easter holiday	Content for Easter holiday	Content for Easter holiday	Content for Easter holiday	Content for Easter holiday			
	New Product Content							
	Annual Report Release		Quarterly Earnings Report					
Investor Relations								

Update your calendar after the monthly and quarterly governance meetings with any newly identified content.

For content production tools, you can track the content in a detailed matrix in Excel or another spreadsheet program. To do this, list all the content that you have and use the content life cycles to map each step in the process. See Figure 8-9 for an example of how to do this.

Figure 8-9: Content production matrix.

Article Title	Content Requested	Copy Version 1	Edit Review	Copy Version 2	Edit Review	Images Requested	Images Created	Metadata Tags	SEO Review	Legal Review	Brand Review	Final Edits	Entered into CMS	Tagged	Q/Ad	Published
Strength Training For Women	Complete	Complete	Complete	Complete	Complete	Complete	Complete	Complete	Complete	Complete	Complete	Complete	Complete	Complete	Complete	Complete
Critical Vitamins for Women	Complete	In process	Not Started	Not Started	Not Started	Not Started	Not Started	Not Started	Not Started	Not Started	Not Started	Not Started	Not Started	Not Started	Not Started	Not Started
Knowing Your Body: A Doctor's Advice	Complete	Complete	Complete	Complete	Complete	Complete	Complete	Complete	Complete	In process	In process	Not Started	Not Started	Not Started	Not Started	Not Started
Comfortable Workout Attire	Complete	Complete	Complete	Complete	Complete	Complete	Complete	Complete	Complete	Complete	Complete	Complete	Complete	Complete	Complete	Queued
Yoga Versus running	Complete	Complete	Complete	Complete	Complete	Complete	Complete	Complete	Complete	Complete	Complete	Complete	Complete	Complete	Complete	Queued

Chapter 9

Building the Information Architecture

- -

In This Chapter

▶ Defining the core components of information architecture

▶ Understanding why information architecture is critical to the UX process

▶ Using assets to illustrate the future experience

- -

Architecture starts when you carefully put two bricks together. There it begins.

— Mies van Der Rohe

Good information architecture enables people to find and do what they came for. Great information architecture takes 'find' out of the equation: The site behaves as the user expects.

— Jeffrey Zeldman

Information architecture (IA) is one of the most fundamental and critical components within UX. The information architecture of an experience defines how the content is structured and how a user can navigate through the experience. It also defines the hierarchy of all features, functions, and content. Similar to physical architecture, the IA outlines the underlying structure of an experience, combining form and function into one cohesive whole. And also similar to physical architecture, the process for defining information architecture involves blueprinting the experience in the form of wireframes, sitemaps, annotations, specifications, and illustrations.

Information architecture concerns both the art and science of designing and structuring information in a way that makes the most sense for the user, for the business, and for longer term maintenance of the experience. The process of defining and designing an effective information architecture is one of the components of the design process that is most often identified with UX design overall. Simply put, to many people, "UX equals information architecture" (combined with a good understanding of users). Although there is a lot more to UX design than just information architecture, if a UX experience has a weak underlying information architecture, the overarching user experience will most certainly fail. Your user experience is only as strong as your information architecture.

Benefits of Good Information Architecture

Investing the time to develop an effective information architecture results in many benefits:

- ✔ **Usability:** Good information architecture ensures that users can find easily and quickly the most frequently used (and most useful) content and features within an experience. It ensures that the most important content is given a higher priority than less important content, which also helps ensure that navigating through the experience makes rational sense to a user. Good information architecture ensures that an experience behaves the way a user expects it to behave. On the flip side, bad information architecture always leads to poor usability.

- ✔ **Efficiency in the UX design process:** Defining an effective architecture of information can help separate form from the function, and thereby focus the overall design effort on the areas that matter the most to the user and to the business. It can also help break down a user experience into a series of reusable components, such as wireframes and modules, which can be reused effectively throughout the experience, bringing consistency to the experience and reducing the level of effort required for design.

- ✔ **Cost to maintain the experience:** Given that information architecture breaks the experience into reusable components and helps to separate form from function, good IA helps reduce the cost to update the experience by allowing updates to specific reusable components of the system rather than to every page.

- ✔ **Satisfaction:** Improving clarity, consistency, and usability of an experience directly leads to how satisfying an experience will be to a user.

Creating a Sitemap as the Framework of Your Experience

Like a map of a city, a sitemap has a many uses. First, it is the highest level illustration of the major points of interest in the experience: in this case, the major content areas. Second, it helps to illustrate the general proximity of one content area to another, similarly to how maps show the closeness of one building to another. In this instance, a sitemap can also illustrate the hierarchies in information showing where one category of content fits within the larger experience. For example, for a website featuring music, the category of punk rock music can break into subsections such as era (1970s, '80s, and so on) and artists. Finally, the sitemap can illustrate basic pathways: how a user can get from one place in the experience to another, much like maps show how you can travel from point A to point B.

Sitemaps are very useful tools for illustrating the core components of any user experience, whether it is a website, mobile application, kiosk, or software package.

Don't take a sitemap too literally. Although there are many parallels between actual maps and sitemaps for digital experiences, there are also a number of fundamental differences. The digital nature of a sitemap means that the map itself is merely a representation of the experience, and in this representation are features and details that cannot be expressed. For example, although a sitemap can show possible navigational paths between two areas of a site, it typically cannot show every possible navigational path. Keep in mind that the sitemap is a general representation of the experience, not a definitive blueprint of every aspect or detail of how the ultimate experience will behave.

Assessing your content

All possible content and functionality for the experience is analyzed and prioritized during the content audit, which is covered in Chapter 7. It is now time to step back and identify the categories of content that will form the core components of the eventual experience. Fundamentally, you want to identify content that falls across these three categories:

- ✔ **Primary content:** What content is most critical to the user? What content is critical for the business to promote? Where are the deepest categories of content, compared to categories that are superficial? In short, what content deserves to be highlighted persistently and consistently throughout the experience?

- ✔ **Secondary content:** What content is important to the experience, but not necessarily critical to all types of users, or all moments in the customer journey? Secondary content typically plays a supporting role in the user's journey: It's helpful in making a decision but is not necessarily the reason a user visits the website (or mobile app) in the first place.

- ✔ **Tertiary and contextual content:** What content is necessary to include, but not mission-critical to the user or the business? Content that fits this description can often be background company information (although on corporate websites this may be primary), legal disclaimers, and content that is related to a specific moment in the experience.

After you have identified the most important content types, the next task is to look at the inter-relationships of content types. What content, features, and functionality belong together, and which do not? For example, in an e-commerce website, product availability and product reviews belong along-side product information. In contrast, warranty and return policies most likely belong with customer service information.

Don't make blind guesses at your content prioritization and categorization! If you aren't sure what type of content is most important to users — or how to group similar content elements together — there is an easy solution: Ask your users! Many simple user research methods can answer core questions about which content is most important and how to group content to create a meaningful information architecture for your users. Chapter 12 highlights some of these techniques.

As you identify which content is high priority for the experience overall, the primary criteria should be which content is most important to users. Many corporate websites suffer from the problem of taking an organizational view of their companies and using it as the underlying structure for their digital experiences. In other words, they are making the mistake of using company divisions and departments as way to organize the content in an experience. What may work for structuring the organization of a business, however, may not be how a user thinks of navigating through content. As a rule, always view the experience from the user's viewpoint. Kerry Bodine and Harley Manning, analysts at Forrester Consulting, call this "Outside In" thinking: viewing the business from the customer's eyes. (If you want to read more about this, check out Bodine and Harley's book *Outside In: The Power of Putting Customers at the Center of Your Business* from New Harvest Books.) This type of perspective is absolutely critical during the information architecture process.

Creating a high-level sitemap

After you have identified the primary content areas of the site, it's helpful to illustrate it in a simple illustration that shows the core content buckets. Figure 9-1 shows an example. This illustration is called a high-level sitemap because it typically includes only the primary content areas, called Level 1 categories, and doesn't show other details, such as the lower-level content (Level 2+), tertiary content, or detailed annotations. Furthermore, the words used to describe each of the content buckets are merely placeholders. They are most likely not the final copy that will appear on the eventual experience. Although you will create additional details during the design process to show all levels, the high-level sitemap is the initial task at this time.

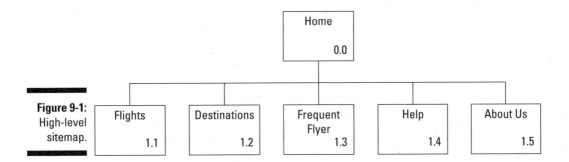

Figure 9-1:
High-level
sitemap.

This sitemap represents the core content buckets for a website for a new regional airline in the United States. The design team that approached this project chose five primary content buckets to be Level 1 categories:

- ✔ **Flights:** Naturally, for an airline, the most critical and frequently accessed content will most likely be focused around flights: flight search, booking, schedules, check-in, flight status, and so forth.

- ✔ **Destinations:** Because this is a new airline, the business stakeholders and the project team felt that content associated with the destinations the airline serves was also important. Content in this area doesn't go very deep, but includes a destination map, location information about airports, and hotel partners. Although this information is tightly associated with flight information, highlighting the destinations the airline serves (and does not serve) was worth highlighting in its own Level 1 content category.

- ✔ **Frequent Flyer:** Like most businesses, this airline cultivates and rewards repeat customers. This section of the website contains all relevant information on how to sign up for the frequent flyer program, benefits, checking mileage balance, and instructions on how to redeem miles for free flights.

- ✔ **Help:** One of the value propositions for this new airline is providing great customer service. Therefore, the business stakeholders felt it was critical to highlight "Help" very visibly in the site, rather than including it merely as a tertiary navigational element, as many other airlines do.

- ✔ **About Us:** Finally, because this is a brand-new airline, many users to the site are not going to be familiar with it, what to expect onboard, and why they should fly with it. Although it is common practice that most corporate-related content is treated as secondary or tertiary content in other web experiences, given the start-up nature of this airline, the project team felt users should have a clearly visible area of the site to introduce the differentiating characteristics of the airline.

After you have defined a high-level sitemap, you have begun the process of creating the information architecture. The next step is to flesh out each of the primary content areas (Level 1 categories) in greater detail.

Creating a sample browse path

A sample browse path requires that you take a user's journey through one of the primary content areas and identify

- ✔ **Sample content:** What might the user be looking for?

- ✔ **Page type:** What type of page is it: high-level content, or greatly detailed content? These page types will form the basis of the page inventory you create in the next step.

- ✔ **User mode:** What mode is the user in, at each step of the process? Browse mode (surfing) or highly engaged (such as product purchase), or something else entirely?

Figure 9-2 highlights the user's path through one area of a corporate website and contains some very useful information to help complete the next stage of the information architecture:

- ✔ **Browse path:** This user is browsing through four levels of the site below the home page.

- ✔ **Sample content:** This user is exploring a range of content within the content category of "Corporate Responsibility." Content explored includes pages focused on a list of topics associated with corporate responsibility, such as "Sustainability," and a detailed article on the "Future."

- ✔ **Content depth:** Given this user's flow through this section, the site looks to be four levels deep (the home page is typically considered Level 0).

- ✔ **User modes:** At the bottom of the browse path illustration, the design team highlighted how a user may be navigating through this journey. This is illustrated by identifying the possible "User Modes" — the primary mindset the user is in — which includes "Exploring," "Digging/Browsing," and "Consuming."

- ✔ **Page type/template:** Finally, the browse path helps to identify the types of pages that will help support the user at each step, given the user mode and the type of content at each level within the site. These page types will help you create an underlying system of pages to support your experience.

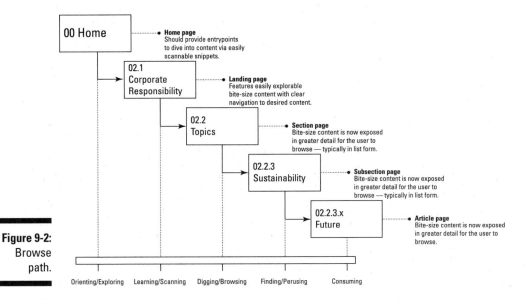

Templates versus pages

One of the benefits of the UX design process is that UX design aims to create an underlying system to support the overall experience: a system where pages that are similar to one another in content and function can be supported by the same underlying system, called a template. Developing an experience that leverages a templated system of pages will reduce the level of complexity in the design and production process (not every page will need to be created uniquely). It also will help ensure a greater consistency in how the user experience behaves for the user (similar pages have a similar structure). In short, the time you take to create an effective system of page templates will pay off exponentially later by saving time in the design and production processes, and by improving usability for the user.

Templates are a simple way of defining a consistent underlying structure for all the pages within an experience. During the later stages of the UX design process, templates are used over and over again, as the site is populated with a variety of different content.

The development of templates is a process unto itself! First a template starts with a wireframe that is based on a page type (for example, a product details page or a home page) with inputs from a content strategist on which types of content reside within it. Second, a visual designer creates a comp of the wireframe. Third, the process is vetted with the larger team, including technology team members, to ensure it can be built and supported by the technology, such as a content management system (CMS). Finally, rules are created for which content is served up within it and how in the form of a content model. Read more about templates in Chapters 7 and 8.

To see template design in action, check out your favorite website, such as Amazon.com or Target.com. Take a look at the layout of two similar but different product pages (different TVs, for example). You will probably notice that the two pages are quite similar in structure, including product placement, use of photographs, navigational placement, rating and reviews, and so forth. Although each of these pages highlights a different product, they use the same underlying page template. Understanding the basics of a page template is a core skill in UX design. To see more templates in action, use browser-based tools, such as Wirify (www.wirify.com), which enable you to see the templated versions of any page on a live site — something that's very useful as you learn the importance of page templates.

Every page can be broken down into a series of underlying components that serve a specific purpose for the overall UX. This is basic framework for understanding information architecture at a page-template level. In its most simplistic form, a page template can include the following components, which are shown in Figure 9-3.

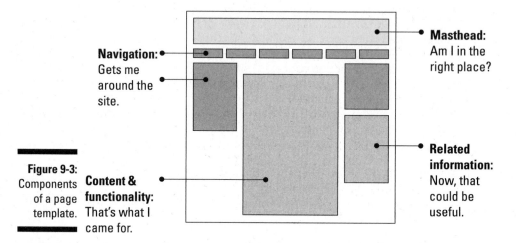

Figure 9-3:
Components of a page template.

Navigation: Gets me around the site.

Masthead: Am I in the right place?

Content & functionality: That's what I came for.

Related information: Now, that could be useful.

✔ **Masthead:** Typically, at the top of a website or software application (but in different places for mobile apps), the masthead serves to orient the user within the overall experience at any point, as well as to visibly brand the experience.

✔ **Navigation:** Navigation is typically categorized into primary and secondary navigation, with primary navigation focusing on primary Level 1 categories, and secondary navigation enabling the user to move within a category.

✔ **Content:** The main content of the page. This can be written copy, images, video, or other content.

✔ **Related information:** Typically, this includes content or links to content that may often be associated in a tangential way.

Figures 9-4 and 9-5, respectively, show a very simplified template approach for a home page and an article page. Each box in these illustrations is considered a "module" of content.

Template: **Home**

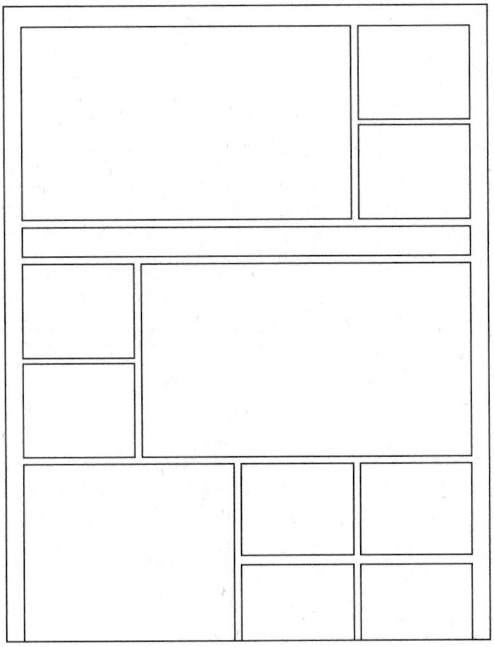

Figure 9-4:
Home page
template
(high-level).

Template: Article page

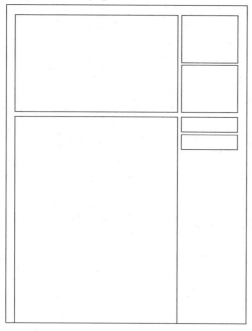

Figure 9-5:
Article
template.

> ✒ **Home page template:** Most home pages in any user experience serve
> a variety of purposes. First, the home page must support a diverse set
> of users, who might include potential customers, existing customers,
> members of the press, job seekers, and others. As such, the home page
> template contains a wider variety of content elements, such as naviga-
> tion, a large home page "Hero" (typically a large image with simple head-
> line and content), content modules that may show a variety of featured
> content, and more. Most users who arrive at the home page of a site are
> in "browse and scan" mode, looking for links to the lower-level and more
> detailed content that they are searching for.
>
> ✒ **Article template:** Pages like the article template serve a more focused
> and singular set of needs: This page is intended to deliver detailed con-
> tent in the form of an article. As such, this template most likely contains
> a far less diverse set of content, but the content is in a greater level of
> detail. Therefore, the simple template illustration in Figure 9-5 contains
> many fewer modules of content. Most users who visit this level of a site
> are in "consuming mode."

Templates as part of the design system

The preceding illustrations and explanations help bring to life the components of a page in template form. Designing your experience using this
approach is called a modular design system (see Figure 9-6), where the

experience is composed of a series of assets that are used and reused throughout the design to enable consistency and efficiency. See Chapter 8 for more details on modules and how they are used in the design process.

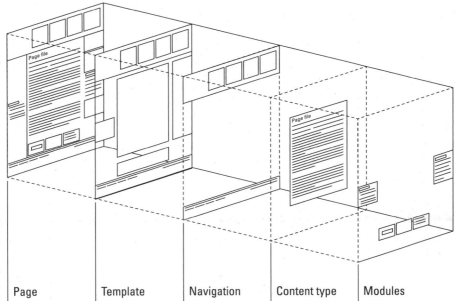

Figure 9-6:
Modular
design
system.

| Page | Template | Navigation | Content type | Modules |

Template inventory

Modular design systems require you to define and design your experience at a component level, where the experience is enabled using a template-driven approach. After you have defined your sitemap, and defined a few core browse paths within each primary content area, you will have a preliminary list of the types of templates that you need to create. The illustration in Figure 9-6 highlights a few templates that often are included in any template inventory:

- ✔ **Home page template:** Provides quick access to a variety of areas within the site. Contains only high-level content.

- ✔ **Section page (Level 1):** Overview pages for core content areas, often called *landing pages*. (For big box retailers, a common section page is the Electronics category.) This type of page allows further refinement of choices of content.

- ✔ **Subsection page (Levels 2 and 3):** Similar to a section page, for those content areas that have a wide depth and breadth of content, the sub-section page allows further refinement of content selection. For the retailer example, within Electronics this could be Cameras as well as Camera Accessories.

✔ **Article page/product page (Level 4 or 5):** A core part of the template inventory, this is typically a destination for the user. It is the point at which she reviews a detailed product listing or reads an article, job listing, or similar content type.

✔ **Search listing (Level 1):** This type of template shows a variety of product options with faceted navigation to help the user refine her choices. Search listing templates commonly replace subsection templates on many sites.

A variety of other types of commonly used templates are included in different types of user experiences. E-commerce sites typically have a set of standard product checkout templates (purchase and payment, review, confirmation, and so forth). News and media sites usually have standardized rich media templates (photo and video galleries). As you step back from the experience you are designing, it's critical to think of all the different styles of pages you will be creating, and then to identify the similarities and differences between them.

Keep your template inventory as small as possible. Every new template requires increased time, effort, and cost during the design, production, and maintenance processes. In addition, each new template style requires the user to think more consciously about how the experience is behaving as she uses it. In most cases, you want her to focus on the content of the experience, not on the design system. Some of the best user experiences have a very limited set of templates that are reused in creative ways.

Constructing a Blueprint with Wireframes

Within the process of building a website, wireframing is where thinking becomes tangible.

— Christina Wodtke and Austin Govella

Now that you have a preliminary inventory of page types and templates, it's time to start designing them, bringing each template to life in the form of a wireframe. A *wireframe* is just a schematic representation of a page, intended to illustrate page contents, functionality, and features. The main focus is on functionality and hierarchy of content, not on the look and feel. The look and feel will be brought to life in the visual design process.

Wireframes typically focus on

✔ The kinds of information and content displayed

✔ The range of functions available

> ✔ The relative priorities and hierarchy of the page content
>
> ✔ The rules for displaying certain kinds of information, in the form of annotations

A wireframe primarily focuses on the information, interface, and navigation of the experience. Wireframing is critically important because it enables the designer to plan the layout and interaction of an experience without being distracted by colors, typeface choices, or precise content and copy. The content, look and feel, and style of the page are of secondary or even tertiary consideration to the general functioning of the experience.

 You have many ways to create wireframes. The simplest is with pencil and paper, or even a whiteboard. Simple hand-drawn schematics, although limited in their reuse, are the most basic form of a wireframe. For more robust solutions a variety of tools are useful and very popular, including Axure, Visio, InDesign, and OmniGraffle. Some software packages can be used purely for simple wireframing, whereas others enable you to create a working, clickable prototype. More tools than the ones mentioned here are available, including some specifically for developing smartphone apps, for hand sketching, and for software. What's best for you depends on the complexity of the experience you are designing, your desire to learn robust applications, and whether or not you will be creating wireframes repeatedly in the future.

Examining components of a wireframe

All the important components of an experience should be represented in your page wireframe. Use simple shapes instead of actual graphics, copy, or text, and label them. These elements include

> ✔ **Navigation and masthead:** These links and buttons enable users to visit the main sections of your site. Consider both primary navigation (for Level 1 categories) and secondary navigation (to navigate with a Level 1 category).
>
> ✔ **Branding elements and company logo:** In its simplest form, the logo must be represented by a box.
>
> ✔ **Content modules:** Where will your different sections of copy, content, and functionality appear?
>
> ✔ **Search boxes, user login areas, and other utilities:** These are any tools the user would use such as a search engine, user profile, or tools such as online calculators (such as, to calculate a mortgage rate).

Figure 9-7 is a simple, high-level wireframe for a smartphone application. A number of page components are visible:

> ✔ **Masthead:** Shows the My Home App branding and Log In link.
>
> ✔ **Primary navigation:** Highlights Our Products, Inspiration, and Find a Store content categories.

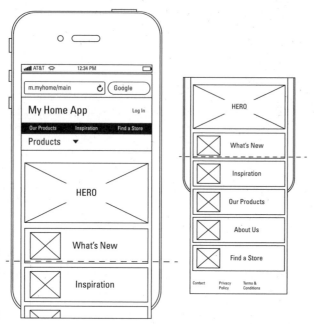

Figure 9-7:
High-level
wireframe.

> ✔ **Products section page:** Shows sample content for the product landing page, including a Hero, which is used to define rotating content that the app wants to feature, such as new products or rotating promotions.

> ✔ **Below-the-fold content:** Shows some of the content that is visible only to the user when she scrolls down the page. This content is typically called *below-the-fold* content because it typically is visible only when the user scrolls down below what was visible as the page loaded.

> ✔ **Footer:** Below the fold at the bottom of the wireframe is the footer navigation, including Contact, Privacy Policy, and Terms & Conditions.

Figure 9-8 is another example of a simple, high-level wireframe for an iPad application. This example nicely illustrates an Electronics section page within an e-commerce application. Global navigation is visibly present, as is the secondary navigation within the Electronics category (showing new products in Electronics). This wireframe is a great illustration of how page contents are represented by abstract modules, such as <Product Name> and <Module 1>, which keep the focus on how the page elements come together to function as a system, but not on the specific content elements (the camera products, for example) themselves.

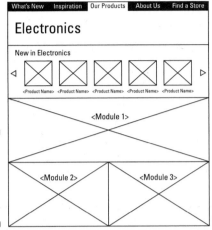

Figure 9-8:
High-level
wireframe
for an iPad
application.

Annotating your wireframes

There are typically five audiences for wireframes: clients (internal or external), developers, visual designers, copywriters, and, most importantly, your future self.

— Dan Saffer

One of the uses of wireframes is to document how the experience will be constructed and how key features and functionality will come to life. To this end, wireframes provide a critical bridge between the design and technology development processes. Much like blueprints for a new house act as a bridge between the architect who designs the house and the contractor who will build it, wireframes provide the bridge between the UX designer and the technology developer. Every piece of functionality that requires technology development should be documented and defined within the wireframing process.

That functionality is defined through annotations on low-level, or detailed, wireframes. Annotations are quite simply footnotes and call-outs on the wireframes, defining how the experience will react and behave for the user. Annotations are most typically located to the right of any wireframe, are numbered numerically, and serve a variety of functions:

- ✔ Identify any interactive functionality.
- ✔ Define any technology dependencies on underlying systems.
- ✔ Provide a rationale for design decisions, or any other design commentary that is necessary.

✔ Call out variables that may affect key modules (for example, logged-in versus not-logged-in states).

✔ Provide needed contextual information for any of the key template components or modules that remain abstract on the wireframe (for example, explaining what "Hero1" is on a key wireframe).

Annotating your wireframes can be a time-consuming process, so only annotate those elements that need an explanation, or justification, or have more involved technical requirements and dependencies.

Figure 9-9 shows a wireframe from a transactional website, and it contains four key annotations. The first annotation (01) identifies a module of content that relates to a pending flight that is to be modified. Annotation (02) identifies the dependency on the underlying flight booking system. And finally, annotations (03) and (04) identify the key actions a user may take (either cancel or modify the existing flight).

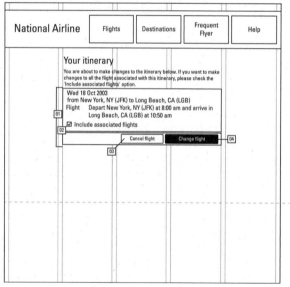

Figure 9-9:
Annotated
wireframe.

In this example, the annotations on the wireframe provide an excellent explanation of the technology requirements to any team members who may be responsible for developing the code necessary for the "change" and "cancel" functions.

You don't have to use real text in your wireframe. Instead, you can use "lorem ipsum" text as a placeholder where actual text will reside within the page. Lorem ipsum has been used in typesetting and visual and information design for centuries. It allows a designer to use placeholder text where copy will go when the experience is complete. You use this text when the actual copy is not finalized or where copy will change repeatedly within the final experience. Visit www.lipsum.com for actual block copy of the lorem ipsum text as well as guidance for its use.

Maintaining sitemaps and wireframes

As time progresses and you update your experience, adding, deleting, and modifying content, it's important to keep your documentation up to date. As you make changes to key templates, also update the wireframes that contain the key functional and technical requirements contained within those pages. As you add and delete pages within the experience, update the sitemap that supports it. This may feel like an unnecessary task, but remember that your wireframes and sitemap are like the owner's manual to the experience you have designed. They will be very useful for future team members in under-standing the underlying design system that supports the experience. In addition, they may be very helpful to you as time goes on because they con-tain the rationale behind design and functional decisions that you may not remember when you make future changes.

You do not need to update your wireframes and sitemaps every time you make a singular change to your experience. Instead, define a process where you make updates to the documentation after every five or so changes made to the experience. This way, you are keeping the documentation up to date without creating a constant task of updating these assets.

Wireframing navigation

The last major step in defining the information architecture for any experi-ence is defining the primary interaction: the navigation. Navigation involves both defining where a user can travel to through the experience (the starting point and the destination), as well as how to get there (clicking a link, expanding a drop-down menu, and so on). How the navigation is designed is highly dependent on the medium in which you are designing. Websites can be vastly different than smartphone applications in how the navigation is implemented. This section focuses primarily on designing the fundamentals of an underlying navigational system, but doesn't delve into platform-specific navigational paradigms.

Navigation systems in UX generally fall across four areas:

- ✔ **Primary:** Navigation across primary content areas of the experience. Primary navigation is typically present throughout the experience in the masthead or header. Also called main navigation or global navigation.

- ✔ **Secondary:** Navigation within each primary content area, specific and distinct to that content area.

- ✔ **Tertiary/contextual:** Alternative ways to navigate across the experience. This type of navigation, often used for Related Content or Utilities, does not contain duplicative navigation from the primary or secondary navigation choices. Tertiary navigation is used to navigate from one lower-level point in an experience directly to another lower-level point in the experience, too.

- ✔ **Footer:** Utility and related navigation, typically at the very bottom of the page.

One of the best methods for helping to flesh out the navigational system is the creation of a few sample browse paths, covered earlier in this chapter. From the scenarios and journeys you created earlier in the project, define a few sample pathways through your experience, identifying which pages within the experience the user must navigate to. Identify a navigational system that will require the fewest number of clicks for a user, and, the greatest flexibility in accessing your content.

In Figure 9-10, from a website, the navigational system that has been defined has been brought to life in a wireframe showing the fly-out behavior of the drop-down navigation. In this example, the primary navigation includes these choices: What's New, Inspiration, Products, About Us, and Find a Store. The Products content area has a secondary navigational system that includes three ways for a user to navigate:

- ✔ **Ways to Shop:** Includes common ways shoppers want to browse product selections.

- ✔ **Brands:** Filters products by the retailer's key brands for Electronics.

- ✔ **Browse by Category:** Enables a user to filter product selection by product categories, such as TVs or Cameras.

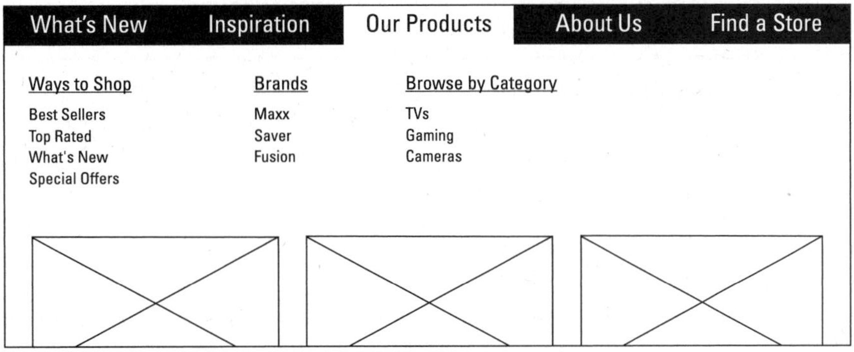

Figure 9-10: Navigational wireframe.

Limitations of wireframing

Although the process of wireframing an experience is enormously helpful to the UX process overall, it's also important to recognize some of its limitations. Wireframes can convey an enormous amount of information about the experience, but they are limited in giving a true sense of the "look and feel" of the experience. In this respect, it's important to know when to use — and when not to use — wireframes during your UX project. Take a look at Table 9-1.

Table 9-1	Strengths and Weaknesses of Wireframing
Wireframes Can	*Wireframes Cannot*
Convey sample page contents in the form of content buckets or modules.	Accurately convey all actual content, including written copy (for tone), images, video, and other assets. Particularly for marketing-heavy experiences, wireframes can be limiting in conveying a differentiating experience.
Illustrate the hierarchy of page elements: which content is more important than others.	Illustrate exactly how visible some content is — that happens during the visual design process.
Define key functional and technical requirements.	Define every requirement covered for the project. There is a limit to how much you can document on each wireframe.

(continued)

Table 9-1 *(continued)*

Wireframes Can	*Wireframes Cannot*
Give a sense of the interaction of the experience.	Precisely convey the interactivity and response. You need a clickable prototype or other solution to convey interactivity.
Allow you and any stakeholders to get a sense of the experience. Without being distracted by final content.	Give a sense of the eventual experience in its finished form.
Identify problems in usability, such as confusing navigation or information overload, while they are still easy to fix.	Foresee all usability problems. You still want to test your solution before you take it live.
Make a complex experience simple — if designed correctly, with the right number of annotations and page content	Make a simple experience too complex or noncompelling, given the black-and-white and abstract nature of the wireframe.
Be created quickly and easily.	Be annotated and maintained without a level of commitment.

Now that you have defined a basic sitemap, sample browse paths, wireframes, and navigational structures for your experience, you have completed the basic building blocks of your UX. These elements, along with the content strategy defined earlier in the process, form the backbone of any UX. The remaining steps involve bringing the system to life through visual design, content, and copy, and testing the solution to minimize any problems.

Chapter 10

Designing for Specific Channels

• •

In This Chapter

▶ Understanding channels

▶ Leveraging channels

▶ Examining channel-specific features

▶ Uncovering opportunities in social networks

▶ Examining unique channel-specific features and how they impact your UX

▶ Uncovering potential social opportunities you may not have known existed

• •

The message is the medium.

— Marshall McLuhan

*T*o implement an effective UX, it is increasingly important that the experience operates on more than one channel — a smartphone, a tablet, a website, and even a smart watch. In most cases, you no longer can afford to design for a singular channel experience, unless you are designing a UX for a specific device, such as an interface for a screen attached to a treadmill. In many cases, the experience you develop could surface in a variety of technologies, which means the screen size and even the way a user interacts with it could change per device. For example, a user might swipe navigation to browse a site on a smartphone, whereas he would click a navigation menu with a mouse if experiencing it on a desktop computer. In the not-so-distant future, swiping likely will involve gesturing with a hand in the air instead of on a physical surface. All this flux should translate to a hyper-awareness of how a user interacts and engages with the experience you have or are creating.

More channels than ever exist today. By channel, we mean the platforms or devices that present information. These include TVs (including smart TVs), mobile phones, tablets, desktop computers, smart watches, UI interfaces such as GPS, and interfaces in cars. Tomorrow, these could even be things such as augmented reality; think interaction with a hologram!

This chapter explores how to prepare your design for multiple channels, and highlights design considerations for specific channels, including: home desktop, laptops and large screens; mobile phone and tablet experiences; and other digital channels such as e-mail, SMS, and print. It concludes with a discussion about the role of social media within UX.

Keep in mind that entire books have been written on the design considerations for creating experiences for specific channels, such as *Mobile Web Design For Dummies* by Janine Warner and David LaFontaine (John Wiley & Sons, Inc.). Our goal in this chapter is to profile some of the most fundamental considerations of designing a UX for specific channel, and even more importantly, to highlight UX process evolves from channel to channel, and from experience to experience.

Changing Trends in UX

In the early 2000s, the "below the fold" concept could not be ignored in website and interface development. This concept meant that any information that a user had to scroll to see was significantly deprioritized over what a user could see without scrolling. The "fold" is the bottom of the user's screen; anything below the fold can be viewed only if the user scrolls down. In traditional website design best practices, many UX experts called for information to not be placed below the fold. In fact, unless the web page contained a long-form article such as a newspaper story that would require several pages, many websites at one point preferred to not have users scroll at all.

Evolution of technology means designing for tomorrow

In today's world, more and more technologies continue to emerge. Twenty years ago, people probably never thought that a pair of glasses could capture an image or video of something upon which they were gazing, or that they could incorporate such a technology into their everyday wardrobes. A few years back, the only time we saw such gadgets were in science fiction films. But today, this technology is not only possible — it is on the market.

In the mid 1970s, Pulsar and Hewlett Packard introduced the calculator watch and the advent of wearable technology was born (http://en.wikipedia.org/wiki/ Calculator_watch). In 2013, the smart watch emerged with functionality of a smartphone and the capability to measure biometrics such as heart rate and even track the distance a person walks. Mobile technology (mobile phones, tablets, and so forth) that enables a person to interact with information and connect to others anywhere and at any time continues to evolve. You can use mobile phones to control your house alarm systems, your cars, your home heating and lights; function as your wallet; and track your health and fitness regimens. This all adds up to significant implications and considerations for UX.

Today, page real estate, or the space the information occupies, is still very important, so the information above the fold continues to hold a position of the highest priority, but attitudes are changing about how much content can be on one page. Most common websites include content below the fold, but the designers know that any above-the-fold content is more likely to be seen.

Often, you can't control which screen size users employ to consume your experience, which makes the challenge of creating a robust UX solution more difficult. Google Insights reports that the time spent during a typical user interaction goes down significantly with screen size. (Visit www.google.com/ think/research-studies/the-new-multi-screen-world-study.html to read the report.) This means that with large screens, such as smart TVs, users spend a lot more time within an interaction than they do on a mobile device. Thus, the smaller the device, the less information users will likely consume on a particular web page or app. Also, the actual screen size on smaller devices limits how much information can be easily displayed.

To make matters even more complex, significant research and our experience suggests that users are no longer using one device to accomplish a task; users tend to jump from one device to the next to a complete task. For example, to purchase a new computer, a user may go from watching an ad on a television to finding the product on a tablet — which sits on his lap as he watches TV — to a desktop to read and view detailed specs and product comparisons, to a mobile device in the store where he pulls up a coupon or scans a QR code. While in the store, the user may see packages of several different computers or see multiple computers displayed on a shelf. Thus, your UX may require a multichannel approach, even if you initially planned to design a simple website or app.

On one hand, certain design principles will always remain the same with UX, regardless of how or where users experience it. For example, the experience should always meet user needs and put the user at the center of the experience. But much of what was traditionally thought about users, even five years ago, is changing. As technology changes, so do user behaviors and the ways with which users interact with experiences.

Preparing Your Design for Multichannel

"For desktop or mobile?" — that is the question. Well, for UX, this question fails on many levels. In the not-so-distant future, new channels will surface and so will new types of technologies. Notwithstanding, user considerations will evolve. Twenty years ago, no one thought she could talk to a computer. Today, many experiences embed natural-language user-interface technology so that voice interaction replaces a display interface. An example of this technology is Apple's Siri.

And just when you thought it was safe to dive into the water, there are even more factors beyond just expanding channels. Semantic technology is getting smarter; *semantic* is a fancy term for "meaning," and in technology this term signifies that a machine can understand the meaning of something. Search engines, such as Google, offer a good example of this. Semantic search technology can anticipate what a user is looking for based on previous searches and patterns in previous behaviors. In essence, the search engine can derive what is meant when a user searches on a particular term and serve up results that are tailored to that user. This technology is evolving and will continue to surprise us in the future with how it will meet and anticipate our specific needs.

In 1962, Marshall McLuhan wrote about how the globe called Earth became a village via mass media and communication in *The Gutenberg Galaxy: The Making of Typographic Man* (University of Toronto Press). In the early 1990s, this concept was actualized with the advent of the World Wide Web. Today, the global nature of the Internet and the evolution of universal translators — technology that translates a web page from English into Chinese, for example — means that a website created in Vancouver, Canada, featuring the habits of Maine Coon cats could end up translated into Mandarin Chinese and viewed in a house in Nanning, China. The global village is more than an idea; today it is reality.

All these challenges may make the task of designing sustainable user experiences seem daunting. But you can leverage certain best practices to ensure your experience is relevant and usable by multiple users. Applying some existing rules and best practices may help you future-proof your work and ensure it can be captured in multiple channels.

Chapter 4 covers the role the user journey has vis-à-vis different channels. That chapter introduces the concept of omnichannel. While you complete your user journeys, you should uncover and map the different types of content you want to serve up to the users within the experience. This effort helps you determine how to build a truly optimized content solution for your users against all the different channels they use. But it won't necessarily address all your concerns if you want to build one experience across multiple channels. The next two sections explore how to position content so it is successful in multichannel environments and apply best practices for multichannel UX.

Future-proofing a UX means designing it so that it can evolve with technological, user, and business advances in the future. A future-proofed solution means that the experience is optimized and kept relevant through repeatable actions that don't require an entire overhaul in a year or two.

Considering content for multichannel

Delivering meaningful, relevant, timely, and channel-optimized content is a key component of effective UX. Enterprise content strategy expert Ann Rockley has devoted her career to developing the concept of intelligent content. Intelligent content is content that is conceived and structured in a way in which it can adapt to multiple platforms and environments, be easily updated and reused, and support logic such as personalization. To ensure that content can easily interact and adapt to various channels and platforms, Ann states that content should conform to the following characteristics:

- **Structured:** Structured content means that content lives within a system where it can be easily identified, labeled, created, and repeated but is not dependent on the presentation or format. Thus, it can be reused in more than one place or channel.

- **Modular:** Modules live within a system, such as a template, and can be easily updated and repurposed. An example of a module is a carousel on a web page that shows images, videos, and featured content. Content is updated within the module as needed. Thus, instead of updating an entire page, a module can be updated and all instances of it will retain the update. Modules can also be tagged with metadata so that they serve up content based on who the user is or what his needs are. For example, for a 40-year-old man who has a profile with an eyeglass company and has previously purchased glasses with the company, a module might serve up content to remind him of his annual eye exam or feature frames that are for men that fit the type of prescription he has.

- **Reusable:** Content that is reusable is structured or modularized in a way where it can be reused regardless of the output channel or format. For example, a website can pull an image of a product from the same source from which a product brochure procures it.

- **Metadata:** Metadata, or *data about data* as it is known in technology, is critical to facilitate search and the discovery of information. It is also critical to helping machines talk to each other. So, when a PDF file is downloaded or a video is shared, metadata is a critical component of that process. Ensure your development team uses metadata judiciously. Although a deep exploration of metadata is not a part of this guide, metadata will help ensure your experience is shareable and findable. It helps identify where and how to publish content to multiple channels. For example, metadata can tag a long product description to go exclusively to a desktop website and a short product description to go to a mobile device.

✔ **Format free:** Format-free content means that the presentation layer controls how the content is formatted, and the content is not hardcoded or bound to a specific format limiting it to a single channel or experience. Format-free content separates content from the presentation layer so that it can surface in multiple types of formats.

Following these best practices that Ann puts forth will ensure that content is flexible and adaptable to multiple channels and experiences. (You can read more in *Managing Enterprise Content: A Unified Content Strategy* by Ann Rockley and Charles Cooper from New Riders.)

Ensuring a multichannel approach

When you understand that your UX may live in different channels — that your UX can adapt and live in more than one channel — it's multichannel. Many an organization creating websites have thought only about a singular use of its UX and where and how it should live. Such an approach limits usability and reduces the number of users who will actually use the experience. The following steps for multichannel UX help you ensure success:

1. **Ensure you understand your user journeys and which channels require optimized content to serve their needs.**

   Keep in mind that regardless of channel needs, your users may view or interact with your experience in a multitude of channels. Refer to Chapter 4 to understand how to create user journeys across multiple channels.

2. **Structure your experience in a modular fashion, so that some modules can be served up depending on the device and context for which the user engages.**

   Work with your technology team to ensure that your experience contains the structure and modules to support it. Identify with this team which modules need to go to which channels and have the team code the experience responsively and/or adaptively. See Chapter 9 for more information on templates and modules.

3. **Use adaptive approaches to multichannel.**

   Adaptive approaches mean that you structure your UX so that it can easily adapt to multiple channels. In many cases, one size does not fit all. For example, you may not be able to build one website and expect it to populate all channels. You may need to build one experience and tailor specific aspects of it to singular channel experiences. For example, a mobile smartphone website may not contain all of the sections that a desktop website would contain.

4. **Determine which content and features are global across channels, global but edited, and channel specific.**

   - **Global content:** This content remains the same across the channels (for example, a company logo image or a product image).

   - **Global but edited content:** This content is shared but edited per channel (for example, a long product title for a desktop website, and a short product title for a mobile experience).

   - **Unique content:** This content is unique per channel (for example, scanning for a QR code with a mobile experience or a long job application that is only for a desktop experience).

A responsive design works on multiple devices by optimizing its presentation to a device regardless of the device (for example, a website renders nicely on a smartphone as well as a desktop). Responsive design is a visual design solution and translates a visual design to fit a device based on screen size. Responsive design is not a content solution that accounts for when different content surfaces on a mobile website than on a desktop. Responsive design works best when you have a reason to have the same content surface across multiple channels and where the same content can and should surface in all channels. For larger and more complicated websites where user needs differ based upon the device, responsive design may not be ideal. Instead, an adaptive approach, which considers the device and serves up content accordingly, is more appropriate. For example, you would use an adaptive approach to serve up a long article for a desktop website but a summary of the article for a smartphone. In many cases, you may combine the two approaches and use responsive for shared content. See Chapter 5 for further discussion on responsive and adaptive.

5. **Conduct user tests to see how users engage in each channel and which features and content they use in each.**

   Look at not only how the user interacts with one experience but how the user jumps from one channel to the next. For example, examine when a user goes from a desktop experience to a tablet to a smartphone. Why does he do it? What types of features does he expect to see in each interaction? Read Chapter 12 for additional information on user testing best practices.

6. **Incrementally measure the performance of the experience so that you can optimize it continuously.**

   Build a process to evaluate and measure how users engage with the channels, measuring which content, features, and functionality help you to determine how to evolve your experience for future needs as well as to consider technological advancements you may not have taken into account.

7. **Test your experience with various devices to ensure it renders appropriately.**

   Emulators are tools that enable you to use one device to replicate others while viewing an experience. In other words, you can see how your experience will render on an Android, iPhone, and tablet by using an emulator on your PC. You can do a web search for *emulator* to find downloadable tools you can use.

   If you can afford the investment, nothing beats testing in the actual environment in which the experience will be used, but emulators do a sufficient job if it isn't practical to test in every possible environment. You can also use translation technology to see how your experience will render in languages such as Arabic, Chinese, or Cyrillic script languages, which have specific design requirements. Make sure to test to ensure the experience renders appropriately in the various channels.

8. **Use standardized coding languages such as HTML, CSS, XHTML, and XML.**

   Note: This book does not cover coding languages. Refer to a book such as Sue Jensen's *Web Design All-In-One For Dummies,* also published by John Wiley & Sons, Inc. The rule of thumb for coding a user experience is to use a universally understood and relevant coding language. HTML, CSS, and XML are not going away anytime soon; machines, browsers, and interfaces will understand these languages for a long time. Ensure that your developers validate their code against a standard, such as W3C standards. Also test for accessibility to guarantee that all users, including those who are visually impaired, can interact with the experience. Accessible UX solutions are ones that are built so that people who are visually impaired and deaf can still interact with the experiences.

W3C is devoted to relevant and standardized HTML and other markup languages. The validator can be found here: `http://validator.w3.org/`. Using W3C ensures the code is compliant to industry standards and is clean. This will help mitigate any bugs or issues with how a website is read from one browser or operating system to the next. Using clean code is good usability because it helps ensure a consistent display across different channels and browsers.

Support accessibility whenever possible. Many countries require a certain level of accessibility compliance with products, services, digital information, and user interaction experiences. If you are developing a website or using markup language such as HTML, W3C provides a list of validator tools at `www.w3.org/WAI/ER/tools/complete`. W3C also includes information about accessibility best practices in general.

Designing for Home Desktop, Laptop, and Large-Screen Computers

Desktop computers are personal computers with a monitor that sits on top of a desk. Technically, a laptop is not a desktop computer, and it fits within the category of mobile devices because a user can easily transport it from one place to another. That said, user tasks on desktop and laptop computers are similar. Both types of devices possess larger screens than smartphones and tablets, and both have larger keyboards. Desktops and laptops support the capability to use a mouse; because both have good-size screens, users can easily point a cursor and click small icons, buttons, or text links. Equally important is the idea that a user completes a task while remaining stationary while using a desktop or laptop computer. Consequently, design considerations for both desktop PCs and laptop experiences can be grouped in one category.

Screen size for desktops is a primary driver in optimizing UX for the device. Larger screens allow for more space to display information. Because such screens require a user to remain largely stationary (even though a laptop can be moved from one place to the next, a user generally sits and works on a laptop in a specific space), when designing UX for desktops and laptops, you can assume the user will be engaged and focused. Consequently, you can offer more detailed information with the expectation of longer engagement periods.

With respect to websites, many users want to read longer stories or articles on a larger screen and expect that such content will be offered. Although in many cases, readers may prefer to print longer articles. When testing for a larger screen, attempt to see what types of tasks a user wants to complete within the environment for your experience. Does she use the larger desktop to read longer articles, such as a report on deforestation in the Amazon or to view specific technical details of a sound system to troubleshoot an issue she encounters? Maybe she wants to watch a longer video than she would on her tablet or mobile phone because the picture is larger.

Here is a brief list of types of content that a user might prefer to engage with in a larger screen format:

✔ **Complex images or infographics:** An *infographic* is an image that conveys a story or representation of multiple data. For images that contain detailed information or infographics, such experiences are often best consumed on a larger screen.

✔ **Product guides or instructions:** Product instructions or technical information often contain several detailed pages of information. Sometimes infographics contain detailed instructions for product assembly (a piece of furniture, for example).

✔ **Long-form editorial content:** This includes longer videos (anything more than three minutes) and long-form editorial articles, such as feature newspaper or magazine articles. This category also includes financial reports and research reports on any topic.

✔ **Long forms:** Long forms request detailed information from a user. Examples include job or college applications, user profiles, detailed surveys, and different types of financial forms, such as mortgage applications.

✔ **Involved tasks:** Tasks like completed tax forms, things that take a while to complete, such as filling out a spreadsheet or manipulating graphics or images in a visual design application, are often easier with a larger screen or desktop experience.

✔ **Detailed product information:** Detailed product information includes lengthy product descriptions; 360-degree videos of a product; interactive product modules that allow a user to interact with a product, such as viewing the inside of a car; detailed specifications; and technical information about a product.

✔ **Product comparison tools:** These tools compare detailed information about multiple products. Such a tool could compare a product or service, such as different fund types offered by an investment firm.

Optimizing your UX too much around one channel can lead you to make incorrect assumptions about your users' behavior. Many websites were designed around the assumption that users would access them from a desktop or laptop computer. However, as mobile phone usage increased, many UX teams discovered that a large percentage of users were accessing it from a mobile phone, where the experience was sub-optimal. The earlier versions of Facebook were a great example of this: robust functionality on the desktop version, but sub-optimal experiences on a mobile phone. Keep in mind that your users will decide which channel is most important, and your UX needs to support them all.

More content can fit on a page that's displayed on a desktop or laptop screen than on mobile device screens or smaller interfaces. Furthermore, clicks for links or calls to action are done with a cursor that is maneuvered by mouse or touchpad, both of which offer the user greater control than using a finger on a touchscreen. Thus, inline text (within an article or experience) can be hyperlinked, without fear that the user won't be able to easily select or click it See the United Nations desktop home page example in Figure 10-1 for an example of large amounts of information fitting nicely into a desktop website experience. Note that although much information is presented, it is still logically grouped into categories and is visually grouped using color and boxes.

Figure 10-1:
UN.org
desktop
website.

Designing for Mobile Phones

The first key consideration for mobile phones is the fact that currently these devices are grouped into two categories: feature phones and mobile smartphones. A feature phone does not have a touchable screen with which to interact. A smartphone includes a screen that allows for interaction. The usage of both types of phones varies dramatically depending on which region of the world you reside in. In the United States and Western Europe, smartphones are quite prevalent, whereas in many areas in Asia, Africa, and South America, feature phones have the widest use. If you assume that a global mobile experience should not really consider feature phones, you will miss the UX mark significantly. The vast majority of mobile phones in the world are feature phones, not smartphones.

If you expect your UX to have a global audience, then remember that feature phones may be the only way that millions of your users can connect with it. Feature phones are also not going to go away soon; many countries have high feature phone use because the countries' network bandwidth does not adequately support smartphones. Statistics show that many households in these countries do not own a desktop PC or laptop, but do own a feature phone. Facebook, for example, has optimized its site and has factored in these statistics in its multichannel approach (`www.insidefacebook.com/2013/07/30/ facebook-achieving-worldwide-growth-through-feature-phones/`).

Feature phones and smartphone share some characteristics that are important to note for usability:

- **Mobility:** The fact that a user can take a mobile phone nearly anywhere at any time and interact with it means that you must consider such tasks when designing for it. Given that a majority of mobile website searches result in click-to-map actions, meaning the user looks up a website and then clicks to find the physical site location (oftentimes en route to the store), ignoring this critical functionality within a design means a lost opportunity for any type of brick-and-mortar business. Also, mobility means a user can interact with your experience in a store, or your product within various locations.

- **Phone functionality:** After nearly 140 years, Alexander Graham Bell remains relevant. A mobile phone may have all sorts of shiny bells (no pun intended) and whistles, but the fact remains that it is still a telephone, and a telephone provides one primary function: to dial and speak to another person. A recent study revealed that a consumer is 15 times more likely to buy a product from a phone call than he is from browsing to it on a website. Another statistic noted that next to click-to-map, clicking-to-call is the second most widely used function from website searches on mobile devices. If you ignore the functionality to click to call then you most likely will cut off an important connection point between you and your consumer. (Visit `www.mobilecommercedaily.com/4-myths-of-mobile- metrics` to read the full "4 myths of mobile metrics" article.)

- **Smaller and variable screen sizes** — Mobile phones have smaller screen sizes than monitors or many other types of LCD screens. The amount of information that can fit on the actual screen is significantly less than what can fit on most laptop or desktop screens. Furthermore, there are many different variations of screen sizes. Screens from one brand or product type vary significantly.

Mobile website design best practices

For mobile phone UX, use the following mobile website best practices. These guidelines can easily be extrapolated as general rules and best practices for UX development for smaller screens in general.

✔ For smartphones, account for the fact that finger sizes vary, and use larger hands as the standard to determine the sizes for buttons and swiping features. For testing purposes, ensure that a user can use a thumb to tap the navigation and buttons.

✔ The font size should be large enough for the user to read the text on a small screen. One simple test to see if the experience is easy to read is to hold the device at arm's length and see if the text can be read with 20/20 vision.

✔ Limit use of large file sizes for images. These take longer to download and increase the amount of time for a site to render.

Bandwidth consideration is always important for mobile use because most mobile service companies provide limited amounts of data use with less expensive service plans. Large file sizes from nonoptimized images and content-heavy sites require more bandwidth to support the experience. Bandwidth is less of an issue for desktop experiences whereas it is a major issue for mobile site. You don't want to be responsible for your users incurring overage charges because your mobile website is too large!

✔ Use one column to display information rather than using tables with several columns. For optimized content display, stack features vertically instead of displaying information horizontally. For example, place a picture of the product at the top of the screen, put a short description below it, and then list key features and benefits below the description. The U.S. National Aeronautics Space Agency (NASA) mobile site offers an excellent example of an optimized mobile display. (See Figure 10-2.)

Notice the minimalist approach to the overall page design used in Figure 10-2. Compare the difference between the mobile NASA site with the desktop version shown in Figure 10-3.

In Figure 10-2, the information is vertical, whereas in Figure 10-3, a horizontal placement allows many different content modules to appear on the screen. For best practices, consider the following:

✔ Go through an exercise that determines the most important content based on user needs. Validate the assumptions with user testing. Prioritize the most important content and features and place these at the top of the experience. Even though some users don't mind scrolling, limit endless amounts of scrolling and don't place important information that requires several scrolls down a page.

✔ Limit content and features on mobile devices to what is most important and needed for the user. In Figures 10-2 and 10-3, respectively, compare how NASA treats information for its mobile site versus its desktop experience, which contains much more content and many more links.

Figure 10-2:
NASA.gov
mobile site.

Figure 10-3:
NASA.gov
desktop
website.

✔ Leverage user testing to determine which content and features are the most critical for mobile use. You should also stay abreast of insights and research as user behaviors continue to evolve with regard to the use of mobile devices. Your user testing should account for mobile separately from desktop: You should test users on both mobile devices and desktop devices because users have different needs and expectations for each experience.

✔ Navigation should be flattened so that a user can find information easily. A complex navigation system for a desktop does not render well on mobile phones. Simplify the navigation and optimize it for mobile use. Keep the site hierarchy to three or fewer levels: for example, Mowers⇨Riding Mowers⇨Specific Product. Six or fewer levels in a navigation menu is preferable. Limit the number of overall navigation links on the page; strive for ten or fewer. Mobile users do not spend as much time on a site as do desktop users, so overwhelming mobile users with too many options oftentimes results in the user leaving the site without completing a task.

✔ For larger sites, use collapsible navigation or nested navigation for complex product catalogues. Collapsible navigation allows a user to expand the navigation menu by tapping it; users can hide the navigation when it is not in use. In Figure 10-2, you can see an icon with three lines at the top-right corner of the screen. After the user taps this icon, the navigation menu is expanded, as shown in Figure 10-4. This navigation module is global, meaning that it displays on all pages. So the user can easily navigate to other sections regardless of where she is on the site, but she also does not need to view the navigation unless she selects it. This form of navigation allows only the most important content and information to surface on the actual screen the user views and the control to either view or hide the navigation as she requires it.

✔ Allow the user to see the full desktop web experience by providing a link to it. This is critical if your desktop website contains a lot more information and details than the optimized mobile site. For a responsive design, this is not necessary because the site is the same across devices. See Figure 10-5 for how NASA uses this feature.

Figure 10-4:
NASA.
gov mobile
site nested
navigation.

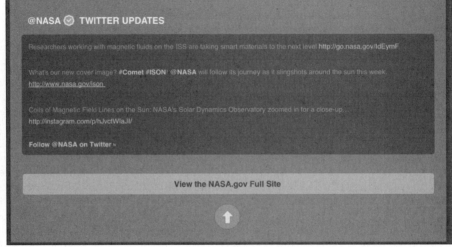

Figure 10-5:
NASA.gov
mobile site
desktop
experience
feature.

✔ If you use form fields, such as a search box or text input boxes, ensure that they are large enough for the user to interact with. Long forms are not easy to use on many phones, so an ideal approach is to use an adaptive form and limit the amount of information a user is required to input.

✔ Allow a user to go back; ensure that a Back button is operational. In many types of smartphones, this feature is a part of the actual browser, but this is not always the case, and you should make sure to include it as part of your experience for those times when it is not available in the browser.

✔ Text links are not easy to use if the font is small, but icons for links take up more bandwidth and longer to download. Use larger font sizes for textual hyperlinks when possible.

✔ Pop-ups can be frustrating and can prove difficult to interact with (or make it difficult to return to the previous site), so limit their use unless user testing shows the need for such functionality.

✔ The site should be viewable in a variety of different lighting situations. For example, a site with a black background and white text can be difficult to view when in direct sunlight, so your designs needs to be usable under a variety of lighting conditions.

✔ Some technologies work only on certain phones. For the most part, iPhones and Apple devices do not support Adobe Flash and this precludes Flash apps and videos from being accessible on iPhones.

✔ Try not to force a user to adjust the screen from horizontal to vertical to view information, unless the specific functionality warrants it, such as when the user is viewing a video.

- ✔ Breadcrumbs or long lists of links are unnecessary on mobile sites, and difficult for users to interact with.

- ✔ Be cautious about using icons to visually represent information. An image of one to four stars for user reviews is understood by most users, but many other types of icons may present challenges or may be misunderstood. Although you may find it tempting to use a lot of icons in lieu of text due to space constraints, do so only if you adequately test with users to ensure they understand the icons. Even then, use icons sparingly.

- ✔ Remember that rollover buttons — buttons that change color or state when you hover the mouse over them — do not work well in mobile sites and are unnecessary. They also take up more bandwidth.

Special functionality for mobile sites

Use the mobility of the phone as a primary consideration to determine features. The following features are examples of functionality that mobile sites can use effectively:

- ✔ **Click-to-call functionality:** For mobile sites for businesses, this functionality is critical and should communicate an actual phone number that the user can tap to make the call.

- ✔ **Click-to-map:** Allows a user to tap an address to find the geographical location of a store. Click-to-map should engage the user's map app, Google Maps, MapQuest, or relevant GPS maps to provide the user with directions to the address.

- ✔ **Wayfinding — inside/indoor maps:** For when users are in your actual store or building. These types of functions allow users to see where they are within a store and which items or products are within their immediate range.

- ✔ **Coupons and featured deals:** Coupons on mobile should be friendly to the device and allow the user to scan the coupon at purchase. (Do not require the user to print these.)

- ✔ **Shopping lists functionality:** Allows a user to generate a list and then interact with it while in the store, such as marking items as she procures them.

- ✔ **Loyalty programs and digital loyalty cards:** A loyalty card is what a consumer signs up for that is specific to the store. Loyalty programs track purchases and reward customers on how much they spend, as well as offer unique promotional opportunities.

✔ **Reviews of product and services:** These reviews enable your users to read how previous customers weigh into the product or service to make an informed decision to purchase. Providing review functionality within your experience and making it mobile friendly allows a user to engage with the experience. Using the mobile phone's camera, shoppers can scan bar codes and link to relevant product information, including competitive pricing and user reviews.

✔ **Product comparison tools optimized for mobile phones:** These should not contain the same amount of detail as desktop websites. Leverage clearly readable icons such as check marks and Xs to indicate whether a feature is or is not in a product. Stick to key features of the product. See Table 10-1 for an example of an effective comparison chart for mobile devices.

Table 10-1	Mobile Site Product Comparison Sample		
Product	*Calories*	*100% Natural*	*Price*
Food Brand X	1000	X	$2.00
Food Brand Y	500	✓	$5.60
Food Brand Z	250	✓	$2.24

✔ **Price comparisons functionality:** Allows a user to compare prices of a product with other products. Refer to Table 10-1 for an example.

✔ **Purchasing decision-making tools:** These are tools that help a user decide which product or service is best for him — for example, a tool that shows which computer is best for the user based on his needs.

Don't forget to include practical information that a user would want to see. For example, if you have a physical business or organization, include your hours of operation. These should be easily accessible and findable (for example, "Open 9:00 a.m. – 5:00 p.m. Sun – Sat.").

Accounting for feature phones

Although smartphone sales continue to grow throughout the world, more users still rely on feature phones than smartphones, and this trend will continue into the near future.

Many countries do not have the network bandwidth to support smartphones, but the networks can support feature phones. In addition, feature phones still require significantly less electricity for power and have longer battery life.

The primary consideration for feature phone sites is bandwidth. As you design with feature phones in mind, opt for text over image-heavy sites, use the features listed earlier for click to call and click to map, and simplify the experience with only the most important content. For navigation on feature phones, remember that many feature phones support smart key logic, so build these into the navigation.

Designing for Tablet Experiences

Tablets are mobile devices that can be taken nearly anywhere and generally have a smaller screen than laptops and desktops. Users interact with tablets by swiping and tapping on a touchscreen. For the most part, the interaction experience is limited to a touchscreen, although a user can add an external keyboard to interact with most tablets. Nearly all tablets have cameras built into the hardware. *Phablets,* which combine the size of a tablet with the phone capabilities of a smartphone, are another type of tablet-like device, although the market share for these devices is relatively low.

Tablets have also shown some unique advantages over smartphones and desktop computers. Consider the following: Tablets have impacted populations that often go unrecognized. Within the past two years, programs that work with individuals with autism spectrum disorder and developmental disabilities have used touchscreen tablets to enhance communication and other developmental skills in a way that was not available in the past. The touch-and-swipe aspect of the screen appears to play a key role in this process. Moreover, tablets are being used in more and more schools as a learning resource.

But tablets do have constraints when compared to desktop or laptop computers, including

- ✔ Tablets do not support the number of computer functions or applications of a desktop computer.
- ✔ The smaller screen means less information can be presented.
- ✔ Tablets do not generally possess the processing strength of desktop or laptop computer memory.
- ✔ Some applications such as Microsoft Word and Excel are not entirely tablet compatible.
- ✔ Interacting with a tablet means interacting with only the screen, so when the on-screen keyboard is engaged, it generally covers half the screen.

Despite constraints, a tablet has unique features that a desktop computer lacks, such as the following:

✓ A user can take it nearly anywhere, and many tablets come with wireless service plans to make Internet and data access easy regardless of location.

✓ Users can use the web-browsing features while shopping in stores.

✓ The touchscreen functionality allows a user to engage with experiences in real-time regardless of where they are.

Tablet UX design considerations are similar to the considerations for smartphones. The following presents a list of key considerations:

✓ **Social network friendly:** Tablet users tend to be highly engaged in social networks, such as Facebook and Twitter, so thinking about how to create experiences to accommodate this need and adding features where users can share your content with social networks can greatly increase user engagement with your experience. For more information on best practices with regard to social networks, see the "Considering the Role of Social Networks" section later in this chapter.

✓ **Location and contextual features:** As with all mobile devices, location is an important consideration. Where is the user and what is she doing? Is she sitting in front of a TV watching an ad that leads her to your experience? Is she in a park capturing images of birds where she wants to learn which bird seed is ecofriendly for use in public places? Depending on what your experience offers and how and where your user is, you can design experiences and feature content relevant to the tablet experience. A growing amount of research suggests that tablets are particularly important in how customers engage with brands (`http://services.google.com/fh/files/misc/multiscreenworld_final.pdf`). Users tend to multitask with tablets, such as when they watch TV and use a tablet simultaneously, and they will use them to obtain more information about a product or service both at home and in a store.

✓ **Touchscreen features:** Similar to the smartphone, users can swipe and touch the screen, which allows them to interact with content on the screen. Swiping can mean left to right and up and down, so interactive carousels can provide ways to display multiple pieces of information within an experience. Because more content can fit into a tablet experience, in general, larger navigation elements are preferred. The National Cancer Institute site shown in Figure 10-6 shows an effective approach to an optimized mobile experience. Note how the navigation modules account for larger fingers. The content on the page is simplified, and only the more important content features are listed.

✔ **Data visualization:** Tablets are excellent devices to show interactive data visualization apps. The United Nations Country Stats app shown in Figure 10-7 allows users to compare different types of data, such as gross domestic product (GDP) across different countries. Notice how the information is contained within one screen; navigation supports finger touch; and a large amount of data is consolidated within the interactive experience.

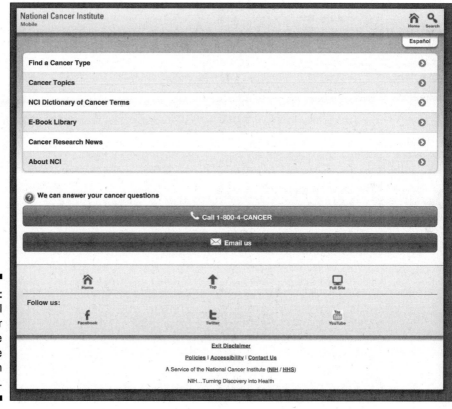

Figure 10-6: National Cancer Institute mobile website on a tablet.

Figure 10-7:
Data
visualization
on a tablet.

Designing UX for Other Channels

New screen interfaces emerge nearly every day. Refrigerators and kitchen appliances appear to be getting "smarter," and many possess interactive LCD screens. Exercise equipment in gyms, interfaces in cars (with self-driving cars, this will only evolve further), kiosks in stores — digital appears to be everywhere and anywhere. There are also nondigital channels that require consideration because they are part of the overall customer journey with a brand or organization. The next four sections consider other types of digital interfaces, in-store kiosks, e-mail, and SMS and nondigital channels.

Other digital experiences

Given the multitude of digital experiences and combinations thereof, there is no accounting for specific direction for how to design UX for all digital interfaces. Also, many of these interfaces have not been around long enough for us to have gathered large amounts of data on use and user engagement. The best practice of user testing and following other recommendations in this guide offer a solid approach to ensuring the user needs are met, and that user satisfaction can be achieved. Additionally, there are some other key recommendations:

✔ **Interoperability:** Interoperability means the device can interact with other devices. For example, if a user engages with a digital screen in a gym on a treadmill, can she use a memory stick or some other device to capture workout information? Can she download the information at home and track her results? The more interoperable you keep the device, the more opportunities you allow the user to engage with the experience, whether while using it or after the fact.

✔ **Tracking features for user data:** Ensure that you build in features to track how users use the interface, which features they ignore, and which content within the experience they consume. If possible, you may even want to provide a source for user feedback for the user to provide information on desired features or functionality.

✔ **Social sharing features:** Build social sharing features into the experience. For example, for a treadmill, have an app to enable users to download their results and workouts to share them on social networks. The more a user shares his experience with others, the more recognition your product or service will receive.

In-store kiosks

In-store kiosks present a user with many different options for engaging with a product or service. In a fashion store, a user might try on a product, take a picture of the experience, and share it with her friends using an in-store kiosk. A user might use an interface to take a picture of herself and then virtually try on different types of clothes to see how she looks. She might then share the experience with friends in her social network so that they can weigh in on what looks good. Or perhaps a user shopping for groceries wants to scan a bar code to compare prices of other products. In-store kiosks offer a variety of ways for users to engage with a brand. Additionally, user testing and understanding what user needs are should drive design decisions for the UX.

E-mail and SMS

E-mail and SMS present ways to interact with existing customers in a tailored and effective format. Although neither e-mail nor SMS requires sophisticated UX design considerations, each requires an understanding of what a user would like to read or what features would be useful. Following are some best practices for e-mail and SMS messages:

- **Self-selection:** Always allow a user to opt in for both e-mail and SMS. The user should say that he does not mind receiving either e-mails or SMS messages. Do not require a lengthy opt-in process, and incentivize the user with coupons, promotional content, or special offers as an impetus to sign up for a message service. Provide functionality that the user can use on the spot to prevent e-mails from being spammed rather than waiting for him to receive an e-mail and specify it is not spam. If the user opts in for SMS, ask for permission to capture geographical location; this will allow contextual targeting (for example, "Jenny, you are near our store; buy one coffee, and get another free.").

- **Judicious use:** The user should not be bombarded with e-mails or SMS messages. Figure out a strategy to target users and give them only content that they asked for or that is useful to them.

- **Personalization:** Think of ways to personalize content for the user. Use the person's first name when addressing her.

  - Are there events such as birthdays or product anniversaries that you know are important for the user? For example, "Jenny, you bought X a year ago. Here is a 30% off coupon on your next purchase."

  - Do you have information about the user's profile to highlight your service? For instance, "Jenny, your last hair cut was six weeks ago. Would you like to make another appointment?"

  - Send confirmation e-mails when appropriate. For example, "We shipped your product; did you receive it?"

  - Consider any types of event-triggered e-mails you think are relevant (such as Valentine's Day, back-to-school, Black Friday, and so on).

  - If the customer has been absent and you know it, are there e-mail opportunities to entice him back? If doing so, provide the user the chance to offer any feedback that may have prevented him from returning to your organization.

Print materials

Print materials are still an important part of user interaction and engagement. Print materials span anything from manuals, brochures, guides, and packaging.

Much has been written on best practices for print materials, but the following are two key considerations:

✔ **Channel engagement:** Are there ways to drive the user from print to other channels, such as a website? Are digital copies of the information also supported? Many users will expect limited print materials, and, as more people become green friendly, this trend will only increase. Are there social prompts to engage the experience to share the experience socially?

✔ **Personalization:** Product inserts and packaging can be personalized if shipped to the user. Do you include a brief note thanking him? Do you mention him by name?

Considering the Role of Social Networks

Social networks are user-created networks on social media sites such as Facebook, Twitter, LinkedIn, and so on. Although they're technically not channels — channel implies a technology platform — they have unique features that are an important aspect of UX engagement and warrant some discussion. To not consider social networks as an impact to your UX, or to limit engagement with social networks altogether, severely limits your ability to promote your experience relatively inexpensively. The two primary benefits of social network engagement are

✔ Social networks can promote you and your experience. For example, someone shares what she thinks about your experience because you provided her an easy way to do so. Her social network peers weigh in on it and promote it further. They decide to try your experience for themselves. If you are afraid of social media, you should note that a user may share her involvement with your experience whether you want her to or not. It is going to happen and by being part of the experience, you can appease your users and also track what they are saying or how they are engaging with you.

✔ Social listening is a powerful tool to see what others are saying about you and your experience. If you have a social network site on Facebook and Twitter, for example, social listening tools can provide valuable opportunities see what others say about their experience with you. You can see what is working and what is not. You can figure out types of content, features, or functionality to invest in for the future. For example, if you make your content on a website easily shareable, social listening can tell you which content your users are sharing and why, which can inform you about what types of content experience to invest in.

Following are some best practices regarding social networks:

- ✔ **Integrate social sharing opportunities:** Most types of UX provide opportunities to integrate with social networks. For content, the more nimble and shareable you make it (for example, features to share a video, a product, a website page, an image, an article, or a report), the more exposure opportunities you provide for your content. Commercial applications such as Gigya (www.gigya.com/) and ShareThis (www.sharethis.com) provide functionality to easily share your content, features, or functionality within your UX.

- ✔ **Create a social presence:** Although different social networks exist internationally, in Western Europe and North America, the key networks to engage with include Facebook, Twitter, Google+, and LinkedIn. Use these networks to post valuable information about your organization or business, updates, news, and anything relevant you feel your users would value. If your users engage with you, engage with them by responding to their tweets or comments.

- ✔ **Authenticity:** Do not censor what your users say about you (unless it is inappropriate or illegal, such as racist comments, swearing, or threats). Censoring what users say even if you do not like it presents your identity as unauthentic. Besides, if a user has a negative interaction with you he will tell others about it using other social sites, such as Yelp.com, or within his other social networks. Negative responses provide the perfect opportunity to respond with an explanation or even service offer.

- ✔ **User-generated content:** Encourage user-generated content, which is content that a user creates and then shares with you digitally. These could be ratings and reviews of various aspects of your UX (such as ranking a feature, function, or piece of content). User-generated content presents the opportunity for your users to assess your product, service, or experience and then provide their reactions to it. You can see what they like and what they do not. Additionally, other users will see what has been said and use the information in their own decision making.

Chapter 11

Diving into Visual Design

In This Chapter

▶ Understanding the visual design process

▶ Identifying the core components of the visual solution

▶ Getting started on the visual design

▶ Documenting the visual system in a style guide

Good design is a lot like clear thinking made visual.

— Edward Tufte

*V*isual design is the process that takes your UX solution to new levels, by giving it color, photos, and a customized look and feel. Although the wireframes you create in the previous phase (see Chapter 9) start to illustrate your UX solution with respect to basic functions and general layout, the visual design process gives the UX solution true meaningful form in the eyes of users. Think of it like this: The information architecture (IA) solution provides the newly constructed house, but the house doesn't take shape until the people move in, furnish the place with their personal belongings, and give the house a life of its own by turning it to a home.

The visual design process involves far more than just adding colors to a wireframe. During this process you consider the entirety of the UX, and you focus on how the form will meet the function. Whereas a wireframe outlines the layout for the page and for the experience overall, the visual design considers all aspects of the look and feel of the experience. To illustrate this example, consider the following: If a wireframe illustrates a primary navigation in a header across the top of a page, the visual design can take that model and identify a range of visual solutions for how that navigation is realized. The visual designer may reconsider the horizontal navigation and opt to display it vertically, along the left-side column of the page (to better support web and mobile experiences). Simply put, whereas the main objective of the wireframing process is to illustrate functionality and information hierarchy, the visual design process may reconceive all visual expression of the experience. In short, for maximum benefit, you should keep an open mind about the design of the experience during the visual design process.

Wearing a UX Hat for Visual Design

The process of visual design for UX solutions is borne out of the field of graphic design. Graphic design (also known as communication design) is both an art and a science: typically combining an underlying system to all things visual (the science part) with what people will find compelling or even beautiful (the art part). The visual design process, though, is not focused solely on making things visually beautiful, although visual appeal is always welcome. Visual design is all about making an interactive UX truly engaging.

Mastering the field of graphic design is not something that can typically be picked up quickly. Myriad undergraduate and graduate programs focus on training people in graphic design. Different types of graphic design exist for advertising, physical packaging, and UX, as well as different styles of design that are popular in different geographies and cultures across the world.

Given the deep nature of the field of graphic design, this chapter's intent is not to turn you into a graphic design virtuoso after one read. Rather, it covers the basics of the visual design process within a UX project, and explains how the visual elements come together with the rest of the components to create a successful UX. Learning the basics of visual design for UX also will help you collaborate with professional visual designers on your team.

If you think you need an expert when it comes to the visual design challenge within your UX, call one! If your UX is highly visual in nature — say, a marketing-oriented or uniquely branded UX — enlist the help of a properly trained design professional. Even the best thought-out UX cannot survive poor visual design treatment, so a good visual design component of any UX is typically well worth the investment. Visual design is a popular industry for freelancers and contractors, so check local resources to find the right person for the task, should you think you need help.

Layout: Information architecture versus visual design

Ten years ago, in the early development of the practice of UX, the information architecture and visual design processes were much more clearly distinguished than they are today. Now, on many UX projects, separating the IA process neatly from visual design can be a challenge. Many teams who create wireframes are including more visual elements, such as sample images, logos, copy, gradients, and even color and copy. Although this greatly helps integrate the two processes, it also can complicate the objective of the IA process: IA aims to separate form from function by focusing on the process of defining the core components of the underlying information architecture. In reality, both processes are conducted in parallel to each other and inform one another. How visual you make your wireframes is a matter of personal choice: The less visual they are, the greater the room to explore visual styles in the visual design process.

Defining the benchmark based on screen sizes and platforms

Before you get started with the detailed visual design task, it is critical that you have a clear understanding of the technology requirements of your eventual experience. The visual design process is highly dependent on the technology environment of your experience. Desktop websites, smartphone apps, tablet apps, and software applications all have very different capabilities with respect to screen size, image rendering, size of buttons, and navigation, and screen resolution. Before you begin the visual design process, you need to clearly define some parameters that will affect all visual design decisions.

- ✔ **Screen resolution:** One of the most important parameters is screen size/resolution. Smartphones have very different screen resolutions and sizes than desktop or laptop computers. Within the category of smartphones, Android phones have different sizes and resolutions than iOS phones. The screen size and resolution are dependent on both your user's hardware (type of phone or screen manufacturer) and their software operating system. For your experience, defining the overall screen resolution determines the size of the page that you have to work with, similar to a painter choosing the size of his canvas before he begins his painting. Today, most laptop users have a screen size and resolution of 1024 x 768 pixels or higher for viewing websites.

- ✔ **Color depth:** How many colors can your user's screen display? Defining the color depth helps determine how many colors you have to work with, much like a painter choosing the number of paints she will use during her work.

- ✔ **Mouse or touch-enabled interaction:** How will a user interact with your UX? Are you designing a standard website intended for use on a laptop or desktop, or should you design for touch by a user's fingers? Tablet and mobile phones are all touch-enabled, which means button sizes and navigation choices should be larger than in mouse-centric solutions.

- ✔ **Other elements:** Consider use of technologies such as JavaScript and other plug-ins, HTML features, supported browsers, and even download times.

The World Wide Web Consortium (W3C) provides an up-to-date analysis of current technology platform adoption and the most prevalent screen sizes and resolution that are in use. W3C (http://www.w3.org/) is a great online resource to use when you are defining the benchmarks for your design.

Deciding on your target benchmark is not purely a decision based upon your business objectives: You should base it on your target user! Different types of users frequently use different technologies, and technology adoption can vary by country or geographic region, too. Always consider your target personas as you define the design benchmark. (Read Chapter 3 for more information on personas.) Don't make decisions in isolation from your target users. In addition, Chapter 10 provides a great overview of the UX considerations for each specific channel.

Starting with brand guidelines

If your UX is a new product or service, you may have a clean slate with respect to defining the visual system. However, if you are working on a UX project for an existing company or an established brand, or redesigning an existing UX, you should begin the visual design process by understanding what guidelines already exist for the visual system. Larger companies typically have brand guidelines intended to ensure consistency in all customer-facing experiences. These brand guidelines typically include specifications regarding logo usage, primary and secondary color palettes, fonts and type styles, photographic treatment, and content and tone.

These brand guidelines and your wireframes are the two most important inputs of the visual design process, as they define key requirements and standards that influence the design process. Think of the brand guidelines as a core set of ingredients for a baking exercise, where you can decide how you want to mix and combine each to bake a cake, cupcakes, or another dessert entirely. Just as ingredients create specific opportunities for recipes, brand guidelines provide guardrails for just how wide you can take your UX.

Understanding the Basics of Visual Design

Before you begin the visual design process, your best bet is to be sure you understand the core components that make up the visual system of any UX. Those components include the underlying grid, master template, color palette (primary and secondary), typography, and use of photographs.

Master template and grid

The master template and grid system collectively form the chassis of any modular design system. Using a grid ensures that all the templates you create have an underlying consistency in structure, feel, and behavior. The grid and the master template are the backbone of your UX. The grid consists of guides to which type and graphic elements are aligned. The guides imply a number of fixed vertical columns and variable horizontal layout within the columns. Some modules can be placed only within specific vertical columns, and some modules may stretch across two or more vertical columns.

The master template defines the position of mandatory page elements and defines a grid that is used to provide consistent positioning and layout of additional page elements. The top of the master template is typically reserved for main global navigation and identity elements, and the bottom is reserved for the additional global navigation and copyright.

Figure 11-1 represents the foundation of all pages: grid structure and global navigation. Grids are in use in all types of experiences, including printed newspapers, websites, software packages, smartphones, and tablets. The underlying grid helps ground a user. For example, as a user navigates through an experience, he is subconsciously grounded as to where on each page the navigation will be consistently located.

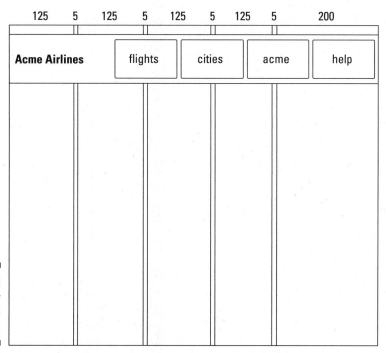

Figure 11-1:
Master
template
and grid.

Most grid systems are based on three, four, or five columns. Modules can span across columns, but the underlying columns provide a consistency in dimension of page elements.

The design of the modular system for the website shown in Figure 11-1 assumes a benchmark based on a screen resolution of 800 pixels wide by 600 pixels high. Taking into account browser scroll bars and browser controls, the viewable page area should be 760 pixels wide by 480 pixels high. For purposes of consistent page layout, the design allows vertical scrolling but not horizontal scrolling; that is, the design is constrained to a width of 760 pixels, but it is not constrained vertically.

The design grid enforces the horizontal space constraint and provides logical spacing between page-level elements. The grid is composed of four 125-pixel columns and one 200-pixel separated by four 5-pixel gutters.

The grid lines define beginning and ending positions for modules. All module columns fall between 5-pixel gutters. A module may not be smaller than one column; if content occupies less than one column, problems with readability and wrapping occur.

Grids in action

Figure 11-2 shows how the master template and grid system provide a consistent place for all types of navigation, including primary, secondary, contextual, and tertiary navigation. All templates can be designed with these requirements in mind, which will help consistency, predictability, and usability of the eventual experience, as well as reduce the level of effort needed to create new templates and modules.

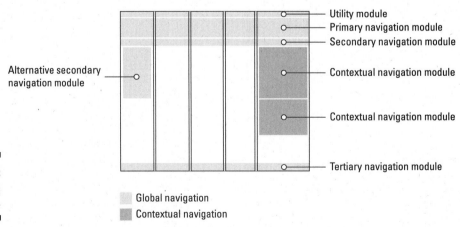

Figure 11-2: Navigation overview.

Using color appropriately

The proper use of color enhances the effectiveness of any UX. Color affects us all psychologically, physiologically, and perhaps even emotionally. Color helps define how users perceive information. Using color appropriately throughout the UX offers many benefits, such as engaging the user with a more immersive and compelling experience. In contrast, using color inappropriately can also create problems, including usability problems, brand inconsistency, and general aesthetic issues. To add to the complexity, many judgments that people make about any UX design are subconscious. A user may not provide any feedback about the use of color within your UX, but he's likely thinking about it. The goal is to create an effective color palette that includes a select number of complementary colors that support core UX functionality and helps to accommodate future needs. Color usage needs to be defined for navigation, text links, marketing, promotional advertisements, and all graphical elements.

During the visual design process, you define a select number of primary colors for key template elements. If you are working with an existing brand, color guidelines likely already exist. Primary colors are most often associated with core brand and logo elements (for example, the blue in IBM's logo, or the red in Coke's). All other colors are secondary and should be used in conjunction with the primary colors. Secondary colors also typically are included in existing brand guidelines. Secondary colors should never dominate the composition of the page; instead they should be used to highlight areas of interest, such as promotions, buttons, and graphical elements.

It's also important to remember the digital nature of UX design. Digital experiences have a different method of expressing colors than print mediums do and that the digital equivalents and formats are also dependent on your target user's hardware and browser, so keep in mind that you need to define your print color palette in digital equivalents, if appropriate.

Leveraging the power of type

Across your UX, you want to define a standard use of fonts, font sizes, and overall type treatments. Page headings should all be consistent, as should subheadings and written content. Brand guidelines normally include specifications for all common typefaces, some of which can be proprietary to the brand. Similar to the use of color, though, the use of fonts and typefaces across different platforms can vary greatly: Be sure to understand which fonts are supported by the platforms used by your target users. For example, web browsers have collections of fonts integrated into their code, and using fonts outside these collections will cause degradation of the design you are creating.

Other key components of the visual system

Because visual design encompasses the entire look and feel of an experience, you should consider how to use a wide array of elements to enhance your solution. The more visual you make your experience, the more engaging it may become to your user. The following is a list of a few key elements that can greatly enrich your experience.

- **Photographs and illustrations:** Defining standards for how you use images and illustrations across the experience is critical. Standards can include the image sizes (images that are too small can just create visual noise, and often prove not useful for the user, and images that are too large can take too long to load), image cropping, use of black and white versus color, and other specifications. You have heard it before: An image can be worth a thousand words. And so it is just as true for a bad image: Poorly chosen or inadequate images can say a lot about the quality (or should we say lack thereof?) of your UX. Ultimately bad images can also affect a user's perception of the brand, as each image you chose is a reflection of who and what you are communicating. Finally, respect copyrights and laws that govern them. Be sure that you have the rights to use all images you choose.

    Public domain images are images that you can use freely, or without many restrictions, within your experience. Most images produced by the U.S. government and many international organizations, such as the United Nations, are public domain. Sites such as Nasa.gov have image libraries where you can conduct searches. In most cases, proper attribution and citation is required. Also, services such as Creative Commons offer public domain images (`https://creativecommons.org`). If you are on a shoestring budget or cannot afford to create your own images, these sources can provide you with a large selection of image collateral from which to choose.

- **Button styles:** Interactivity is a key part of UX design, and the design of buttons and other interactive elements is critical. Button styles can help convey messages to users. Green buttons often imply moving forward or "go"; red buttons imply "stop" or cancel. In addition, button styles should take into account how a user will interact with them. For UX solutions that are tablet or smartphone based, make your button styles and other navigational choices large enough for a user's fingers, not a mouse or other digital pointer.

- **Iconography:** Icons can be great visual shortcuts for the user. If you choose to use icons in your visual system, be sure they are consistent with each other, clear, and intuitive.

Consistency is key. In creating a visual system for your UX, remember the goal is always to work from a consistent set of standards. Consistency in visual elements brings uniformity across the eventual experience, and that uniformity, in turn, aids in usability and overall perception of the UX.

Conceptualizing Visual Design

After you understand the basic components that make up the visual system, you can begin the overall visual design process. Visual design can occur in parallel with the IA process, but typically you want to get a bit of a head start on your sitemap and wireframes before you get too involved in the visual process. The reason for this is based upon the fact that you will find it easier to focus on the components of the visual solution when you already have something work with. In most cases, a wireframe. As a best practice, you should try to develop wireframes before visual designs and get your primary stakeholders to approve them. This step can help you avoid costly rework and allow your visual designer to focus on the visual representation of the information.

The visual design process of any UX project tends to be where the creativity in the process is most visible. Visual design decisions have a huge impact in bringing the UX solution to life. However, you should undertake this process with systematic thinking and careful methodology that focuses on making the core decisions, the ones that matter the most.

Mood boarding

One of the more abstract exercises that are commonly used in the visual design process is called mood boarding. Developing a mood board is typically the task of a trained visual designer or art director. However, understanding the goals and objectives of mood boarding is helpful to everyone involved in the UX process.

Simply put, a mood board and visual exercise aims to identify a high-level "mood" for the visual look and feel of the site. Much like elements on a collage or scrapbook, various visual elements are collected and consolidated around key visual themes. Items that are typically included in a mood board are photographs (capturing a style of photography), color swatches, headline text, printed advertisements, and possibly button styles. The mood boarding process typically involves creating two or three boards, each one capturing and identifying a distinct mood or tone.

The objective behind this process is to find an appropriate starting point for the visual process. Whereas one board might feel futuristic, another might feel down-to-earth and lifestyle oriented. Both may be appropriate to consider for the eventual UX, but the team needs to decide which one might be more in line with the brand and business goals. Mixing the two divergent styles to produce a final design may give it a "Frankenstein's monster" feel.

Mood boards can be particularly helpful if third-party stakeholders are involved in the UX process. Why? Because mood boars can help to align those stakeholders with a common vision for the mood or tone of the eventual UX. In this sense, this tool can get the visual process off to a good starting point. Used properly, mood boards set the stage for a visual solution providing a clear set of visual inputs to begin the creative exploration.

Creating a page comp

The next step in the visual design process is to create some initial designs, called page comps. The objective is to identify a core wireframe or two; in a website, these are typically a home page and another key page from the sitemap. Each wireframe is reconceived in the page comp as the wireframe would be experienced by an actual user; in other words, you bring the wireframes to life with example visual elements. The extent to which the wireframe is reconceived is entirely up to the visual design goals; in many cases, the page comps have a lot of similarity to the original wireframes on which they were based. In other cases, however, page comps can be a comprehensive rethinking of the content and functionality included in the original wireframe. For example, primary navigation that was included as a top header in the wireframe may be explored as persistent navigation along the right-hand column: The functionality remains the same, but how it is expressed to the user is entirely different.

Most design processes explore a variety of directions, taking two or three core wireframes and developing a limited number of distinct conceptual directions in parallel with one another. Three conceptual directions are common in the visual process. It gives the team (and any other stakeholders) a range of choices of visual styles from which to choose. Frequently, a designer mixes and matches elements from one conceptual direction to another, although good designers know that preserving the integrity of the original visual concept is critical.

With a visual direction chosen, your UX process achieves a critical milestone: the creation of what's commonly called a design direction. The design direction conveys high-level information on the visual style for the eventual experience. From this collection of two or three page comps, many additional decisions can be made regarding color, typography, images, icons, button styles, navigational treatment, and many other characteristics. The remainder of the visual design process becomes an exercise of a interpreting the original design direction and extending the core visual styles into different types of pages, modules, and templates.

As a general rule, do not overload your designs with too much content. White space in a visual design can be enormously effective in UX. *White space* is term used to described empty space within a screen or page. This empty space often provides an important function to the user: The empty space draws a user's attention to the elements of the page that matter the most. White space gives the design room to breathe, and can greatly aid in a user's ability to process the information on the screen. It is a common mistake in UX design to overload pages with too much content or functionality. Less is sometimes more! Think carefully about where you can provide some visual breathing room in the form of white space.

Validating the Visual Design

After considering all of the above, you are now ready to put the finishing touches on the visual design. One of the critical components in completing visual design is exploring how the design direction looks and feels with actual written content and copy.

Replacing placeholder text with actual content and copy

One of the techniques many visual designers use during the creation of visual solutions is to use Latin text, known as "lorem ipsum," as placeholder text. Using placeholder text allows the focus to be drawn to the treatment of graphic elements, such as typography, layout, and style, rather than to the actual content. In order to finalize the visual design, however, you must, of course, populate the page comps with actual meaningful content, such as images, product descriptions, full-length written content, and other elements.

The goal of populating the designs with actual content is to show how the completed experience will look and feel in the real e-world. The actual copy gives a voice and tone to the overall UX, something that is not possible with placeholder content. Adding actual content into your design is a great way to further validate it. By seeing how actual content resonates within the design, you will know it actually works. The following section discusses additional validation of your design.

In populating the visual design samples with real content, in many cases, the goal should be to choose "worst-case" scenarios — such as examples in which the content and descriptions are the longest. This strategy ensures that the design system will hold up under maximum worst-case scenarios. Visual designs that hold together under these circumstances can be considered validated from a content perspective.

Validating visual designs with stakeholders

Many a UX project has gone wrong during the visual design process. If myriad stakeholders are involved with developing a UX solution, you must tightly manage the visual design process, including the careful management of stakeholder input and approval. Visual design can be a subjective process. You will often find yourself subjected to multiple viewpoints on all aspects of the design, from which colors to use to the size of an image on a particular page. Focusing the feedback on meaningful, objective direction is critical. Purple may be a favorite color of one of your stakeholders (subjective input), but if it's not included in the brand palette, it may not be a useful ingredient in the visual design (objective requirement). Minimizing these impacts from subjective criticism can become a full-time job. But since you ultimately want to develop the visual system according to carefully defined business goals and actually complete an experience, you can likely achieve both — with your sanity intact — by observing some key best practices:

✔ Defining which key stakeholders need to be actively involved in making any visual design decisions, and which stakeholders are part of a broader team of building consensus.

✔ Minimizing the stakeholders who are involved in more abstract exercises, such as mood boarding, to those who appreciate visual language, brand, and marketing. Too many opinions during abstract exercises reduce the effectiveness of the exercise.

✔ Using objective criteria to evaluate designs. Visual decisions should be focused less on what looks good to a stakeholder and more on what feels aligned with business objectives and brand guidelines. You can harken back to your goals, objectives, and design principles that you outlined earlier in the project to keep everyone honest about the intent and reason for the design.

✔ Identifying what works with the conceptual design and what does not without trying to solve the problem during a stakeholder review.

Holding frequent reviews with stakeholders avoids problems that can require time-consuming rework in later stages. When you hold these reviews, try to get sign-off on each stage of the visual design process and ask that sign-off mean that previous decisions are not re-examined later. At each step of the visual design process, you should explain to stakeholders the overall process, and the type of feedback that is most useful at that stage of development.

Creating and Using Style Guides

Now that you have created the visual system, you can complete the final task in the visual design process: the creation of the style guide. The style guide is the documentation of all visual elements — most of them very detailed — that comprise the visual system of your UX.

The style guide is a document or an online resource that illustrates the design system that was developed through careful consideration of customer needs, business objectives, and any brand standards. It provides a set of rules designed to maintain consistency and simplicity through the experience while still allowing for flexibility, growth, and evolution. The document's goal is simply to establish a set of guidelines that follow a set of aesthetic, brand, business, interactivity, and usability principles. The style guide is especially useful when new team members are asked to maintain the experience in the future, and as a way to record the design decisions that were made during the UX process.

Style guides are only effective, however, if you keep them up to date as the experience continues to evolve. Just like wireframes and sitemaps need to be updated as changes are made, so too does the style guide.

Common components of a style guide

Style guides come in many different forms. Some may be short and high level, but most are very detailed — documenting every component of the visual system and providing ample illustrations along the way. In larger organizations, it is common practice to turn a printed style guide into an online resource — a website that can be used by team members in different departments, geographies, outside agencies, at any given moment. One of the more famous style guides is the BBC's. The BBC has made its "Global Experience Language" resource openly available to the public. You can view it at `http://bbc.co.uk/gel`, and it is worth a visit to see just how robust a style guide can be.

Components frequently documented within a UX style guide include the following:

- ✔ **Grid:** Defines overall page size, grid system, and measurements in pixels for each.

- ✔ **Page structure and page types:** Gives an overview of the key templates to be used throughout the UX, with definitions for how to use them.

- ✔ **Typography:** An overview of all fonts to be used, and where to use them. This typically includes headlines, subheadings, and copy text, but also other components, such as footer text, graphically treated text, and additional elements.

- ✔ **Link styles:** Details regarding how to treat linked text within the body of copy.

- ✔ **Color:** Detailed specifications for all primary and secondary colors in use, with their appropriate web-safe hexadecimal values; specifications for how and where to use color (in what instances); and examples of how not to use color.

- ✔ **Logo:** Guidelines for how to treat any brand elements that are part of the overall logo. This is particularly critical if any revisions to branding elements are needed as part of the UX process and extending the logo to new devices or platforms (like smartphones).

- ✔ **Button styles:** Guidelines for how to treat buttons, including size (pixel dimensions), shape, gradients, shading, and interactivity. See Figure 12-3 for an example.

- ✔ **Ad or promotional space:** For experiences that will contain advertisements or internal company promotions, specifications for where promotions should be placed within the templates, and what size ad units are supported.

- ✔ **Images and photographs:** Specifications for how and where to use images, including color treatment, size of image, cropping instructions, and other design details. Image guidelines typically include examples of both good and bad usage of images to help illustrate what is appropriate and inappropriate.

- ✔ **Icons:** Visual shortcuts or cues for commonly used functions. You should ensure that your icons are clearly understood and consistent in look and feel. Guidelines can ensure that all icon elements feel like they are part of a consistent family, and in addition, can provide specifications for how and where to use an icon.

- ✔ **Additional guidelines:** Additional guidelines to help address components like animation, spacing, error message dialog boxes, lightboxes, tables, carousels, and styles.

> ✔ **Template examples:** Style guides contain examples of final versions of some of the key templates and page comps created throughout the UX process.
>
> ✔ **Embedded video specifications:** These include requirements for any embedded videos, such as which player, resolution, and so on.

Figure 11-3 illustrates the details for button styles. You can see that the specifications included the HEX value of the color of the button text, the font and font size, shadowing, highlighting, and background color of the button. Standardizing the appearance of other buttons similar in function ensures the entire experience will be consistent for the user. The user will be able to quickly and subconsciously identify other similar buttons across the experience, allowing her to concentrate on the actual content of the experience, not how to navigate through it.

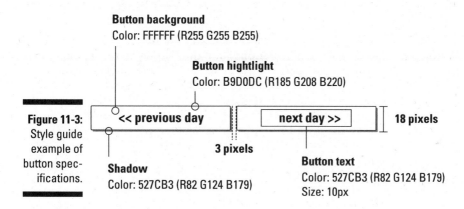

Button background
Color: FFFFFF (R255 G255 B255)

Button hightlight
Color: B9D0DC (R185 G208 B220)

Figure 11-3:
Style guide
example of
button spec-
ifications.

<< previous day   next day >>   18 pixels

3 pixels

Shadow
Color: 527CB3 (R82 G124 B179)

Button text
Color: 527CB3 (R82 G124 B179)
Size: 10px

Guidelines for voice and tone within content and copy

Although much of the focus of style guides is around visual elements, many style guides provide specifications and a framework for effectively conveying the distinct brand personality (the voice and tone) to be expressed in the experience. These voice and tone guidelines comprise a set of principles for how copy should be written to adequately express the brand's personality. For example, some brands are formal in tone; other brands are casual. Applying these voice and tone principles as the experience is continually maintained and updated ensures a consistent and unique experience for users.

The content voice and tone guidelines serve a number of purposes. Conceptually, they

- Define the tone of the experience
- Inform language practices
- Provide a point of correlation for the experience's visual language

In practice, the voice guidelines serve as a reference for development of

- **Nomenclature and navigational elements:** Naming system and style for content categories, buttons, and links.
- **Headlines and captions:** Specifications for page headlines, and photo and image captions.
- **Feature stories and images:** Descriptive copy for articles that accompany images or illustrations.
- **Instructional copy:** Instructional copy is an essential part of any experience. It is the invisible, informational text that supports the usability and business objectives. It exists only to help users to complete a process. Instructional copy guidelines include directions for answering questions, answer choices, error messages, help text, and commands for inputting information or choices into a form. It should be used to explain a section or a function, guide users through a process, or confirm an event.

The bigger picture

Finally, in addition to documenting all the detailed design specifications, the style guide is also a great vehicle for documenting the higher-level design strategy for the experience. A style guide can continue to be used for years after an experience has been designed. Future designers may pick up the style guide to learn about the standards that were defined as part of the UX design process, so it can be useful to also include some key objectives of the design overall, such as the overarching strategy for the experience, the mission, or the broader experience pillars as defined by the goals, objectives, and intent of the experience that define the overall UX strategy.

The completion of the visual design process is a critical milestone in the UX process. It means that the majority of all creative decisions have been made — decisions that are fundamental and wide-reaching across the UX, as well as the small details. The remainder of the UX process largely focuses on the build-out of the design with real content, images, and functionality, as well as the technology development process that brings the experience to life. As you complete the visual design and production process, however, understand that it is critical that you test your UX with actual users before the design process is complete.

Part III
Your UX in Action

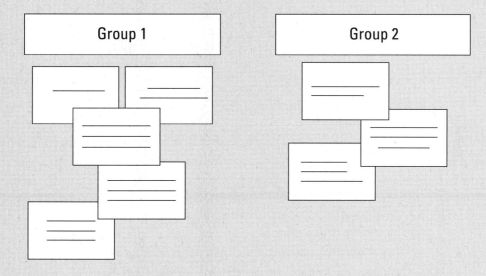

web extras

Visit www.dummies.com/extras/ux to check out information on ways to future-proof your UX.

In this part . . .

- ✔ Understand the role that user testing plays in creating success-ful experiences.

- ✔ Define a plan for testing that will work with your project.

- ✔ Create a plan for ongoing measurement and monitoring of your UX to guarantee that the experience will always be relevant for your users and your business.

Chapter 12

Testing: How It Can Save Your UX

In This Chapter

▶ Defining the basic methods of user testing

▶ Understanding the value of testing in the UX process

▶ Creating a plan for testing your UX solution

Design isn't finished until somebody is using it.

— Brenda Laurel

It is no secret that the world of UX is commonly associated with the practice of usability testing. Although UX is a broader practice beyond the field of usability, drawing a parallel between UX and usability is valid. The world of UX focuses on designing solutions with the user at the center and ensuring that the final experience is useful, usable, and compelling. In order to ensure these three criteria are met for any UX solution, the user needs to be included in the process, and the solution needs to be tested.

Many a digital experience has failed in the market because of ineffective user testing — or the lack of testing altogether — during the design process. Yet creating an effective testing plan can feel like a formidable challenge for anyone who is new to the world of UX. To make matters more challenging, there is a constant evolution in popular testing approaches, with online testing software packages on the rise. Deciding on what technique to use and when to use it are key success criteria for your UX process.

Not testing your UX is arguably the single greatest way to invite failure of your UX solution. On the converse, the best way to ensure success of your solution is to test early and test frequently. For example, the sooner you put your new website in front of some actual users, the sooner the website becomes an actual user experience. You don't need to have polished artifacts, such as pixel-perfect screen comps or clickable prototypes, to begin the testing process; you just need to get some sample users and form a plan for how to engage them.

Eight Common Testing Myths in UX

Any cursory review of UX testing best practices can seem daunting for those new to the process. Because of the amount of information that exists on whom, how, where, and when to test, and because you should not feel overwhelmed to the point where you cannot execute an effective testing strategy, we will start by debunking some commonly held myths on UX testing. After this section, the chapter covers the variety of techniques and approaches you can employ to ensure success. The eight most erroneous assumptions that you should avoid are

- ✔ **You need a user testing professional.** Although the market research field is filled with some very experienced research and testing professionals, testing a UX solution does not always require a trained professional researcher or research team. In many cases, you can effectively test a solution with minimal guidance and experience.

- ✔ **User testing requires a full-scale clickable prototype.** When many project teams and stakeholders consider user testing, it is frequently assumed that a formal, polished "real-world" prototype is required for testing. This is simply not the case: Many forms of effective testing can be accomplished with simpler assets such as paper sketches, wireframes, and static screens.

- ✔ **User testing means usability testing.** A variety of testing methodologies beyond straight usability can be used to ensure your solution is useful, usable, and compelling. Usability testing is simply the most popular technique, and the one that is most commonly understood. However, this chapter highlights some alternative testing techniques beyond usability.

- ✔ **Usability testing requires a lab environment.** Many folks commonly believe that usability testing requires a formal lab-like setting to be effective. This is not true: Usability can be measured and evaluated in a variety of environments and settings, including remote testing where online participants engage with moderators who are in entirely different locations.

- ✔ **Effective testing approaches require large samples of users.** You do not need a lot of users for many types of user testing of a UX solution. In fact, the most commonly used testing methods for UX solutions are qualitative in nature, where a small number of participants give detailed contextual feedback on a solution.

- ✔ **User testing solutions are expensive.** Certainly, user testing can be expensive, but it doesn't have to be. You can create an approach to testing so that the overall cost is minimal, and yet the value can be enormous. Furthermore, the cost of not catching problems that can be identified in user testing and corrected before a project launches to the public can far outweigh the actual cost of testing itself.

✔ **User testing will slow project schedules.** Similar to the myth around the cost of user testing, it's often believed that user testing will take significant time and will slow an overall project schedule. However, many testing approaches are quick and agile in nature, and can be conducted in parallel with other tasks on the project schedule.

✔ **Problems can be fixed easily post-launch.** The digital nature of most UX solutions encourages many project team members to believe that most design problems can be addressed and fixed post-launch, after the solution has gone to market. Although this may be partly true because many UX solutions undergo a series of ongoing enhancements after they have launched, the complexity of "fixing" a solution after it has been built into the overall design may be significant. In addition, if the problems are fundamental, they may have a significant impact with respect to users successfully adopting the solution in the first place.

The Power of Prototypes

Creating a prototype of your UX solution is a great way to explore the effectiveness of your solution. In simplest terms, a *prototype* is a representation of your final experience — similar to how architects commonly create small-scale models of buildings before they are constructed.

In UX, however, prototypes can take many different forms. The most common form of a prototype in the UX process is a clickable, on-screen example of the final experience. This can be a simple black-and-white prototype, constructed from the wireframes created during the information architecture process. Alternatively, a prototype can be a full-color illustration that has been built out with sample content, copy, images, and functionality. The higher resolution the prototype, the more effort required to create it. However, the benefits of higher-resolution prototypes are that they can more accurately reflect what the final experience will look and feel like to a prospective user.

When you develop your prototype, remember to use all the inputs from earlier phases of work. Prototypes work best when informed by user insights, as well as user research. In addition to clickable prototypes, however, prototypes can also be simple, paper-based illustrations — either digitally created (wireframes) or hand-sketched — that are used to convey the general functionality of the eventual experience.

Don't assume that in order to test your UX solution effectively you will need a higher-resolution clickable prototype. Many methods of conducting user testing use simple, low-resolution prototypes that you can create quickly, easily, and cheaply. These simple prototypes can be enormously effective at quickly gathering user input into the design process.

Deciding on Your Testing Strategy

You can choose from many user testing methods during the life cycle of your UX project. Some methods are more exploratory and open-ended in nature, whereas others are less open-ended and focus on evaluating whether specific components or details of a solution are useful, intuitive, or in line with what a user might expect. Still other testing methods focus on ensuring the quality of a solution before the UX process is deemed complete. Whatever method you choose to test your UX, make sure you test your solution with users as part of the design or build phases.

The following list provides an overview of the most commonly used testing solutions. Some of these techniques are explained in greater detail later in this chapter.

- **Participatory design testing:** Completed during the design phase. Participatory design testing refers to a range of testing methods that are used during the design phase (for example, card sorting). The objective behind using participatory design techniques is to ensure that the design team does not just design for users, but instead designs *with* users. The name refers to bringing sample users into the design process to give feedback directly to design teams, as well as refers to the strategy of getting members of the design process directly involved with the testing itself (instead of having a third party moderate the testing). This type of testing technique provides an opportunity to make quick and easy changes to designs because the testing is so tightly integrated with the design process.

- **Card sorting:** Completed during the define phase and early phases or the design phase. Card sorting is a simple participatory design technique in which users help define content categories and UX nomenclature through the sorting of index cards.

- **Tree testing:** Tree testing is often referred to as "reverse card sorting." It is completed to test a site map, taxonomy, and/or navigation system. The user is provided a hierarchy (or site map) to navigate and given a task to complete. The user then drills down through a navigation, usually in the format of a list, and not the actual finished site itself. This form of testing validates navigation and hierarchies.

- **Concept testing:** Completed during the design phase. Concept testing asks sample users for feedback on any number of characteristics of the design, including reactions to the overall creative strategy or feedback on the visual design.

- ✔ **Guerrilla testing:** Completed during the design phase. Guerrilla testing refers to a category of testing techniques that are conducted in the field or in context of typical user environments. For example, the design team for a hotel website may ask hotel guests in a local hotel lobby to give feedback on a UX design.

- ✔ **A/B testing:** Used during design and build phases, but also used after an experience is launched. A/B testing involves testing two different concepts, whether two different navigation buttons (option A or B), images, or even product descriptions. Each option is tested with a wide set of users (some users may receive option A and others option B). The administrator of the test determines which option is most effective based on which options yield the best results. A/B testing is very commonly used to test variations for online banner ads or other simple experiences. Many A/B tests are conducted with automated software.

- ✔ **Heat mapping:** Completed during the design and build phases. Heat mapping is an automated testing technique that involves tracking where users focus the most attention on the screen. This can be measured by tracking where the mouse moves throughout the page or through more advanced camera-based eye-tracking systems.

- ✔ **Usability:** Completed during the design and build phases. Usability testing is the most common and widely referenced form of testing during the UX process. It tracks the ease by which users can accomplish key tasks using a prototype of the UX solution, as well as the critical problems that should be corrected before a project launches to the public.

- ✔ **Beta testing:** Completed during the test and launch phases. Beta testing is a form of quality assurance testing and is used in a closed environment with an invited set of users before a UX solution launches to the public. Beta testing is used to identify a variety of problems that need to be addressed before launch, such as technical performance errors and remaining usability flaws.

- ✔ **Accessibility testing:** Completed during the test and launch phases. Accessibility testing ensures that a solution complies with the W3C standards for people with physical or other types of challenges.

- ✔ **Browser testing:** Completed during the test and launch phases. Browser testing ensures that a solution works across the defined set of technology platforms, such as web browsers or mobile operating systems.

- ✔ **User acceptance testing:** Completed during the test and launch phases. User acceptance testing (UAT), a form of quality assurance testing, is used in larger scale projects where solutions are developed for third-party stakeholders or clients. UAT asks that representatives of key stakeholders spend time testing the overall quality of a solution to ensure that the solution meets any previously agreed upon standards for functionality, performance, and quality.

Deciding on an effective strategy for user testing can be broken down into four key steps:

1. Identify what to test.
2. Choose a testing method.
3. Identify research participants.
4. Select a location for testing.

Each of these decisions is explained in the following sections.

Identifying what to test

Before you choose which testing method you should use, you have to determine a few key factors — namely, are you looking for more open-ended input on your UX design, or are you looking for more focused and detailed feedback on specific components and characteristics of the design itself? If you are looking for open-ended input, choose one of the testing methods described earlier, such as participatory design, concept testing, or card sorting. These methods tend to be more wide-reaching in the types of topics they explore, and are most useful in the earlier stages of the UX design process. If you are interested in more specific detailed feedback, choose from a range of testing methods that explore specific components of the design, including usability testing, A/B testing, or heat mapping. These techniques are more narrowly focused to give detailed feedback on what is and isn't working within the UX design.

After you have identified the topics to explore in testing, the next step is to ensure that all assets that will be needed for testing have been created. If you are testing navigation in usability sessions, you need enough wireframes to illustrate key navigational paths. If you are exploring visual design, make sure your visual design is far enough along to demonstrate the vision behind the experience. Finally, if you're measuring the usability of a solution, remember that the usability of an experience can be affected by the choices in copy and nomenclature, browser implementation, and other late-stage design choices, so make sure your designs are complete enough to yield effective insights.

Choosing a testing method

Your testing approach should be defined primarily based upon the type of feedback and input you are looking for and where your project is within the overall UX process. Table 12-1 identifies some key topics you may choose to test, and the commonly used and effective testing methods used to explore them.

Table 12-1	Choosing a Testing Method
Topic to Explore	*Useful Method*
Navigation (early stages)	Card sorting, tree testing or usability
Content categorization/taxonomy	Card sorting or tree testing
Nomenclature	Card sorting, tree testing or usability
Visual design appeal	Concept testing
Design options	A/B testing
Usefulness of content	Concept testing and usability
Ease of use, navigation (late stages)	Usability
Visibility of key features	Heat mapping, usability testing
Quality of implementation	Browser testing, user acceptance testing
Technology performance	Beta testing, user acceptance testing

Be sure to accommodate the work involved in incorporating the feedback you receive from testing into the design process! It is a widespread mistake in planning UX projects to plan for user testing, but to underestimate the time it may take to make revisions. Whenever you put a UX prototype in front of a prospective user, you will receive feedback on the design. If the feedback is significant, it may require fundamental changes to the design choices that have been made. In contrast, some feedback can be addressed by simple changes that can make an enormous and valuable impact on the overall solution. Whichever testing method you choose, make sure to account for the time and resources it will take to accommodate what you learn during the testing process.

Identifying research participants

After you've defined the overall objectives for testing and associated methodologies for doing the testing, you need to identify the people with whom you will test the solution. These users are called the *research participants,* and they should represent your target users as closely as possible. If you have focused your UX solution around a priority persona or two, you should look to find research participants who have similar characteristics.

You can identify your research participants from a variety of sources; existing customer populations, internal marketing databases, and loyalty programs are great sources of potential participants. If your UX project is a redesign of an existing experience, using an online survey to find volunteers for testing is a common tactic. For new products or services, you may need to be more creative in finding participants who are similar to your target user. This shouldn't be hard to do because your UX will be aimed at those users when it is completed, so you should have a good idea of how to reach these types of people.

Many third-party research and testing firms can help with finding participants for your testing, for a fee. Many of these firms create a *participant screener,* a set of guidelines and questions to identify those types of people who meet the research criteria, and conversely, help rule out those people who are not a good fit. The research screener focuses on those characteristics that are most relevant to the experience. For example, for a mobile app focused on wealth management and retirement, the screener ensures participants have enough financial assets and investment experience to be helpful in their feedback on the solution.

Testing your UX solution with the wrong type of participant can be disastrous to the success of your UX! If your solution is intended for a specific type of user — with specific experience, typical behaviors, and understanding of subject matter — make sure your testing sample reflects these key characteristics. Using participants who do not reflect the characteristics of your target personas can skew the results of your testing, and can lead design teams to make decisions that are not appropriate for the overall success of the experience.

During this stage, you also need to define how many participants you need, which is the *sample size.* Some research and testing techniques are based upon smaller samples of data (qualitative), and others are based upon larger sample sizes (quantitative). Qualitative methods provide deep sources of data, but are based upon a small sample size. Quantitative testing methods, on the other hand, focus on more focused data sets but with a much larger sample size. Most UX-related user testing strategies have a qualitative focus because they allow deeper exploration of key components of a user's experience, including her reactions, expectations, feedback, and pain points associated with the experience. Most of testing methods outlined in this chapter are considered qualitative testing methods.

Given the qualitative nature of testing methods, you won't need a large sample of participants. Common user testing approaches include samples that tend to average somewhere between 8 and 16 people, although some testing methods include fewer or more participants. Exactly how many testers you need depends on the uniqueness and complexity of your solution, as well as the range of topics you want to explore with your participants.

It is common to reward research participants with an incentive for their time. The cost of participant incentives is directly related to how difficult it is to find people willing to participate in the testing process. For example, a UX solution tailored for use by heart surgeons typically requires a much higher participant incentive, due the potential difficulty of finding heart surgeons who are available and willing to participate in the testing. Gift cards and gift certificates are typical incentives.

It's a great idea to recruit a couple of extra research participants to account for cancellations and no-shows during the testing process. These extra participants, called alternates, can be scheduled to come to the testing sessions and wait for a short period of time. They are paid for their time regardless of whether they actually participate in the testing sessions. The objective behind reserving a few alternates is to ensure that even if there are a few cancellations during your testing process, you'll have enough alternates to fill in the gaps and the overall user research effort will still yield enough valuable insight to inform the rest of the design process.

Selecting a location for testing

Another important decision in defining an effective research approach focuses on where to conduct the testing itself. In many cases, any appropriate business environment will suffice, such as a conference room or office setting. For more advanced and technologically dependent testing methods, such as heat mapping or A/B testing, a more formal usability lab may be needed. As an alternative approach, it's also common to select an environment that is closely related to the subject of the overall experience, such as conducting testing for an e-commerce experience in an actual store.

Incorporating stakeholders into the process

If third-party stakeholders are involved in your UX project, it can be an effective strategy for the UX process overall to include them in the testing sessions as observers. Stakeholders' presence during the testing sessions can be a great opportunity for them to observe real customers accomplishing sample tasks in context of the solution you are building.

Using Participatory Design Testing Methods

Participatory design testing methods are testing methods that aim to get users directly involved in the UX design process. Participatory design methods break down the separation between the design and testing processes. With participatory design techniques, you design with users' direct input and involvement.

If conducted correctly at the appropriate time in the project life cycle, there are a number of benefits to a participatory design technique:

- **It's agile.** Most participatory design techniques are conducted in a very iterative and agile way, where changes to the design can be made in between each testing session or with minimal impact to the design schedule. The goal of these techniques is not to simply test a design and gain consensus on what's working but to advance the design process through the involvement with actual users. In this respect, you can make changes to the designs during each session with participants and in between the sessions themselves. The state of the design by the end of the series of participatory design sessions is often very different than the state of the design at the start.

- **It generates early-stage input.** Because most participatory design methods are conducted at early stages of a design process, it is frequently easier to incorporate the ideas that are identified during the sessions themselves. Conversely, one of the problems with later-stage testing in UX is that any changes that are identified during the testing can cost significant time and money to address. Early-stage input is much easier to incorporate.

- **It's integrated.** Another common characteristic of participatory design methods is that it gets a variety of team members involved in the testing exercises. Instead of letting third-party research moderators facilitate testing, the goal of participatory design techniques is to get design team members (and other stakeholders) directly involved in the sessions themselves. This way, the design and testing process are truly integrated, breaking down the walls between the two processes and between separate team members.

- **It's user-centric.** Because actual users are involved in design sessions, the eventual experience has the potential to be more user-centered than solutions that are developed without input from users during the design phase. Without using participatory design techniques, even some of the best design teams create experiences that do not reflect the way an actual user would think about it.

Card sorting is one participatory design method, and it's a great way to involve the user in the design process.

Conducting a Card Sorting Exercise

One of the most useful methods of user research in a UX design project is card sorting. Card sorting is a participatory design process that is typically conducted in early stages of the information architecture process. Simply put, the exercise involves asking users to sort the contents of a website or similar UX. Each bit of content is described on a separate index card, and users sort the cards into categories that make logical sense. This ensures that the way that content is organized within an experience makes sense to users. After all, they had a hand in designing it!

Conducting a card sorting session is one of the easiest user testing methods to undertake. Any team member can take the lead in facilitating the session, although it's probably wisest to allow the team member who is focusing on developing the information architecture to take the lead. Follow these key steps to conduct card sorting:

1. **Write each piece of key content or functionality that will be contained within an experience on a 3 x 5 index card.**

   Figure 12-1 shows sample index cards. In this example, all the content for a corporation's website is identified on a collection of 30 to 50 index cards. The cards include written content, and also interactive functionality such as "Apply for job."

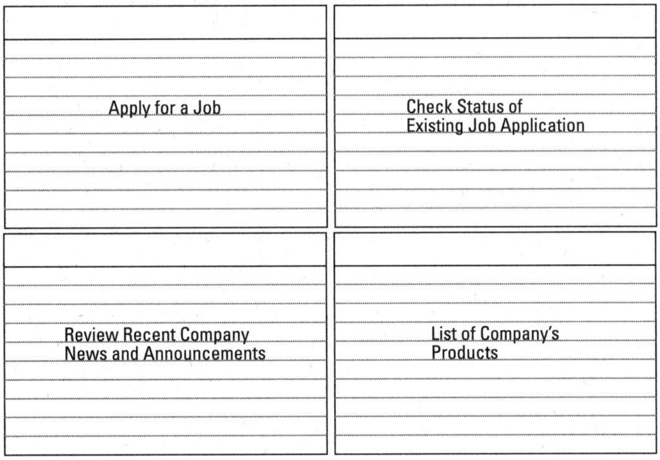

Figure 12-1: Sample content cards.

2. **Put the stack of cards in random order.**

3. **Ask each participant to consider each card and place the cards into categories that she thinks make logical sense.**

   In some instances, you may want to give the participant a few initial uber-categories to work with (such as "Career" information). In other cases, leave the categories entirely up to participants to designate.

   Naturally, you need a large enough desk or table to accommodate the various piles of cards. See Figure 12-2.

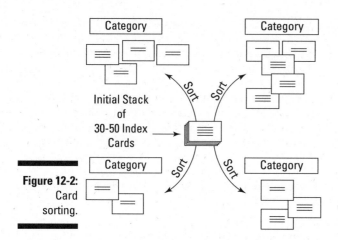

Figure 12-2:
Card
sorting.

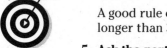

Figure 12-2:
Card
sorting.

4. **As the participant creates her piles of cards, ask her to share her thoughts out loud with the testing moderator.**

   The participant's thought process during the exercise can be just as illuminating as the actual categories she creates. The sorting of the cards can take some time, depending on how many cards you use in the exercise and the nature of the content to be sorted. Content that is easily understood and conveyed takes less time to consider and to sort.

   A good rule of thumb to use is that no sorting exercise should take longer than 30 or 45 minutes, so 50 cards is a good upper limit.

5. **Ask the participant to name the categories she created.**

   The objective is to understand the terminology she would use for each bucket of content. This helps give a guideline for the nomenclature to be used in the navigation. See Figure 12-3.

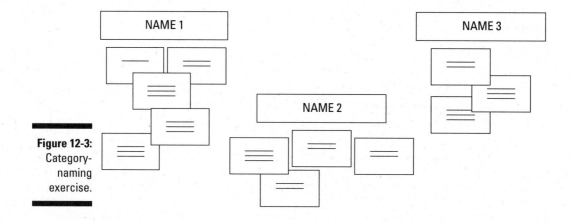

Figure 12-3:
Category-
naming
exercise.

The card sorting method of user testing explores how actual users would construct an experience, and uses that input to guide the creation of the information architecture. It is a simple technique that can be very effective.

The converse to card sorting is a method called tree testing. This approach tests an already designed navigation model or taxonomy. With tree testing, you have the navigation called out and then assign a series of tasks, such as "Find the film *Who's Afraid of Virginia Woolf* on a website that contains music, DVDs, and books." In this type of testing, the user drills down through textual navigation that you provide to find what you ask them to look for. You record what they do and where they go. Tree testing helps you identify any issues with the navigation you have designed. A commercial tool you can use for this type of testing is TreeJack (www.optimalworkshop.com/treejack.htm).

Usability Testing Primer

Usability testing is a cornerstone of the UX process because it aims to ensure that any possible problems with clarity of the eventual solution are identified. Usability can be measured using a variety of assets, from paper-based illustrations to high-resolution, clickable prototypes. The difference comes out in the moderation of the sessions and when the testing is conducted during the project life cycle.

The primary goal of usability testing is to identify what is working and what is not working with an experience. Unlike participatory design techniques, the focus of usability testing is to evaluate and explore a solution without necessarily making design changes on the fly.

Almost any aspect of UX can be tested and evaluated during usability testing. Here are some examples of things you can test:

- ✔ Visibility of content within a page
- ✔ Navigation, including primary, secondary, and tertiary
- ✔ Nomenclature of content categories and features
- ✔ Clarity of content, including instructional content
- ✔ Identification of common pathways through an experience
- ✔ Error identification and error handling

Usability testing may uncover unforeseen problems that the design team may not have anticipated. In addition, it's also probable that users will provide feedback on other aspects of the experience, such as the general usefulness of features, visual appeal, and overall value, although these components are not typically the focus of usability testing because they are not easily addressed in the later stages of the project life cycle.

The following are core steps you need to follow for usability testing. Many of the specific steps outlined here have been covered in some detail throughout this chapter.

1. **Identify scenarios for testing.**

   As you prepare for usability testing, one of the primary decisions you need to make is about which parts of the experience to test. Testing can be focused on the range of top-level content categories across an experience or can be focused mostly within one specific content or functional area. For an e-commerce experience, the product purchase process would be critical to include in usability testing. After you have decided on the scope of your tests, you will need to create sample scenarios that will be used during the testing sessions. For example, to test a gift store's e-commerce experience, a scenario could be defined that includes instructions such as, "Research and find an art book to use as a Mother's Day gift." Scenarios should be based upon the typical tasks that a persona might do within the final experience and are included in the script for the testing sessions.

2. **Create the prototype.**

   Naturally, you need assets to use during usability testing sessions, whether those are simple wireframes or a fully designed prototype. Make sure that you have the depth and breadth of pages within the scenarios you will want to explore during the sessions, but you don't need to have every page or screen built out. Many usability sessions are conducted with just a small set of screens to convey the core components of the design.

3. **Recruit participants.**

   Find the participants you will use during your sessions, making sure they closely mirror the types of people upon whom your target personas were based.

4. **Select a moderator.**

   Identify the person to lead the usability sessions. This can be a team member from the UX design team, but it also can be useful to have someone not associated with the design process who can act as an objective, third-party moderator to the sessions. For large and complex UX projects, external third-party usability testing firms are frequently hired to conduct the usability testing.

5. **Prepare each participant.**

   At the start of each session, begin with a conversation with the participant about her experience as it relates to the type of experience at hand. In addition, it's important for the participant to understand the goals for the testing, and that you are not testing the participant, but using her to test the designs. Furthermore, she should understand that all feedback on the experience is helpful feedback. It's an important message to convey because it helps get participants to give open and honest feedback during sessions. Finally, if you are recording the sessions via audio or video, you must disclose that to the participant.

6. **Conduct the sessions.**

   Conduct the sessions, asking each participant to complete the task that's been given him as part of the scenario. Most usability sessions are run from an interview guide that contains the core questions to ask the participants, the topics to explore, and the scenario itself. The guide helps to ensure consistency across all the sessions. Ask each participant to think out loud during the tasks, so observers can understand the thought process that a user would go through as he browses the experience. Good questions to ask during a user's browsing of an experience include whether he is finding the content he needs to accomplish the tasks, and, and after each click through the prototype, whether he is seeing the content he expected to see.

7. **Analyze the results.**

   As a rule, the team should debrief quickly after each testing session, identifying what was learned during the session and any issues that have been identified. It's not uncommon to make changes to the design in between the testing sessions and to explore whether problems can be fixed with small changes. In addition, it's also helpful to identify if any changes need to be made to how the testing sessions will be moderated moving forward. After all the sessions have been completed, the comprehensive data should be documented, and all top-priority problems should be identified. If testing was conducted by an external usability specialist, a presentation of the findings is typical.

8. **Make changes to the design.**

   Enhancements to the design should be made to reflect all top-priority usability challenges. In addition, non-mission-critical changes can be identified for enhancements to the experience in the longer term post-launch.

9. **Test again, if necessary.**

   If substantial changes were made to critical areas of the experience as a result of usability testing, it may be wise to conduct another round of testing to ensure the problems have been fixed. This follow-up round of testing can be focused on the core changes that were made as a result of the first round of testing, and it can be conducted with a limited sample of participants.

Many software tools on the market aid with usability testing. Some tools allow the usability sessions to be live-streamed to remote locations so that more members of the design team can view the sessions even if they are not in the same physical location as the sessions. Other software tools, such as Morae (www.techsmith.com/morae.html), use the computer's camera and mouse to simultaneously record eye-tracking and mouse-tracking. With these tools, as the sessions are recorded analysts can identify where a user's attention was focused to coincide with the recorded video comments. Finally, a number of online usability and research services can conduct effective usability testing sessions with users who are located in remote locations — even foreign countries. Morae and YouEye (https://www.youeye.com) both allow live-streaming of usability testing to remote locations.

Whatever method — or methods — you choose to test your experience, a final experience is typically only as good as the amount and quality of testing that was integrated into the UX process. Not developing a plan for research and testing is surely setting up your project for failure.

Chapter 13

Measuring Your UX to Keep It Relevant

In This Chapter

▶ Ensuring your UX is always relevant

▶ Learning what to measure

▶ Understanding how metrics work

▶ Discovering which tools and approaches will position you for success

---

If you can't measure something, you can't understand it.

— H. James Harrington

Successful UX is predicated upon meeting users' needs. Frequently, UX is digital, and in today's world technology evolves at an astounding pace, with new inventions entering the market weekly. And as technology evolves so will user behavior, and thus new user needs arise and existing behaviors adapt. Take, for example, wearable glasses that capture video and images and enable users to record exactly what it is that they are seeing. A person no longer needs to take out a camera or phone to snap an image; eyewear with embedded cameras enables her to do it immediately. As more people adopt this type of technology, users' expectations of how they capture video and images will evolve. But measuring UX performance relates to both the audience and the channel.

Trends show that different types of users respond differently to the same situation. For example, Google Insights reports that Generation Z, which represents anyone born in 1996 or after, has a shorter attention span, does not mind scrolling for information on digital displays, and expects high visual stimulation when compared to users who were born in 1995 or earlier. Unlike other generations, such as Baby Boomers, Generation Z-ers possess different expectations around their experience with digital information. Other chapters, such as Chapter 8, explore the implications of different channels and the impact of channel experiences on UX. Different channels and the fact that users tend to use more than one to accomplish a task mean that assessing their behaviors is even more important if you want to optimize an experience across multiple channels. Ultimately, you can get data on what your users do through measurements, but to answer the question of why they do it, see Chapter 12.

Measuring UX Performance as UX Strategy

Measuring UX performance involves more than just looking at what users are doing or whether they are using particular functionality or features within the experience. Measurement of UX means that you understand UX as a strategy and an ongoing process with repeatable steps to ensure it is continuously optimized for unanticipated future user needs, technology constraints, and requirements. Chapter 1 explains the steps included in UX process:

1. Discover

2. Define

3. Design

4. Build

5. Test and launch

6. Maintain

Typically, this process is illustrated sequentially with maintenance as the last step in the process. A performance-driven UX, however, recognizes that maintenance is not just maintaining the experience and making a few updates here or there. Effective maintenance is really about measuring the solution and then making recommendations for optimization. An effective process really is not linear; instead, it is circular, as illustrated in Figure 13-1.

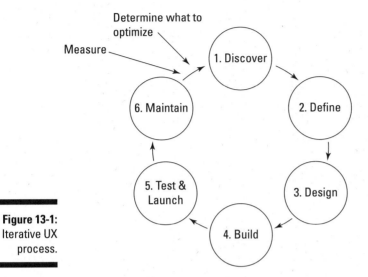

Figure 13-1:
Iterative UX
process.

The implications of the approach illustrated in Figure 13-1 are as follows:

- **Closed loop:** A closed-loop process is circular, repeatable, and sustainable. When the final step is complete, the initial process kicks off again with the information gleaned through measurement and evaluation of the last step in the process. This characteristic allows the process to change and evolve. Thus, after you measure the performance of an experience, you can determine which areas are functioning as expected and satisfying users, which are necessary to archive or remove, and which opportunities exist for future advancement. When you understand these data points, you can then kick off the UX process to discover, define, design, and build the new functionality, features, or content, using either a whole or abbreviated version starting with the discovery phase.

- **Measured and optimized:** An effective UX process can be, and should be, measured. You can measure all functionality, features, and content if you build testing into the process mechanisms to do so. You can determine what users are using and what they do not use, and you can even begin to understand why users engage with the experience. Although in many cases measurements show data and the reason why things occur require testing. Depending on what you learn from the measurement of its performance, the experience can be tested, changed, and optimized.

✔ **Ensured relevance:** By measuring the performance of a UX, you can ensure it is relevant and timely. You should measure the performance and evaluate the results periodically to ensure your experience is up to date and meets user needs and expectations.

✔ **User-centric:** The approach illustrated in Figure 13-1 keeps your UX user-centric because it measures how, where, when, and why a user engages with it.

Understanding Goals, Objectives, and Metrics

In order to measure results, you must first understand how and what you need to measure. Chapter 2 introduces the notion of the business value of UX. UX generally starts with business goals and a set of objectives, looks at the user to determine needs, and then connects the two with an experience. Organizational goals and objectives are obviously important for any organization to function. And organizational objectives can also be measured to determine whether each objective is realized and each goal is accomplished. For example, if a business specifies the primary goal of a website is to help a business sell more products than it previously sold, and the specific objective is to raise revenue by 20 percent, a business can use specific measurements to determine success.

A goal is a general purpose that aspires to achieve something. Here's an example: **Goal:** *This website will be the most-used retail website in the world.* Goals may or may not have measurable outcomes. Goals tend to be loftier and longer term than objectives. In contrast, objectives define clear criteria that must be accomplished. Objectives can always be quantified and measured. Here are some example objectives: **Objective 1:** *Raise sales on the website by 20 percent.* **Objective 2:** *Increase number of website users by a numerical value of 1,000.*

Performance-driven UX, meaning a UX that seeks to achieve results, always has a goal or goals and a series of objectives. Effective UX should combine objectives and goals from a business and user perspective. For example, your goals may state that your new website answers the following questions for the user:

✔ **Why should the user consider our brand or organization over that of another? Why should he use our experience?** The answer speaks to why someone would prefer this brand or organization over another. It could be because the brand has better products or services or meets the customer needs better than others. It could be because the work the organization is doing to impact the world, community, or user is more compelling than that of other organizations. It might also be because the content served up in the UX is premium and the most reliable and relevant.

✔ **Why our product or service?** The answer should point to why the product or service is best, optimal, or ideal for the user.

✔ **Why choose our brand or organization to apply for a job or establish a career?** The answer applies to users who are interested in working for the organization and speaks to why someone would want to work at your organization.

✔ **Why invest in our organization or brand?** The answer should focus on why someone would be interested in investing in the company or providing funds to an organization.

Objectives provide the quantifiable results you seek. For example, for the third goal in the preceding list, you might want to set the following objectives for a new website:

✔ Increase the amount of traffic/number of users to the careers section of the website by 20 percent by January 2015

✔ Increase the amount of qualified job applicants by 20 percent by January 2015

✔ Ensure that 50 percent of your successful job applicants start with the website by 2015

To make a UX successful, you should define the goals and objectives necessary for its execution during the initial stages of work (discovery and define phases). Additional objectives can be teased out from user testing and during the design phase. Many a book exists on how to create effective goals and objectives, but a standard, oft-used methodology is what is dubbed SMART. However, another way of looking at these questions is that an objective or set of effective objectives should answer the following questions: who, what, where, why, how, when, and which? The SMART approach follows:

✔ **Specific:** The more specific your objective, the better. If you incorporate questions such as who, what, where, and so on, then you will most likely achieve the level of specificity necessary.

✔ **Measureable:** Measurable means an objective is quantifiable. A measurable objective includes some type of metric to benchmark it. For example, "We will increase sales of a product with our new experience by 20 percent." The number you will use to measure the performance is 20 percent.

✔ **Attainable/Achievable:** For an objective to be usable, it must be attainable. You should start with a criterion you believe to be realistic. In the beginning of your process, you may have to re-evaluate original notions of what you thought was realistic after a first round of measurement. One of the pitfalls to avoid is setting objectives that are too aggressive. When you are too aggressive, you set up the solution for failure, which disincentivizes your internal organization and stakeholders to improve the solution in the future.

✔ **Relevant:** The objective should always be relevant. Lofty ideals are not relevant or achievable. Relevance means taking into account who needs to achieve the objective and why they need to achieve it. For example, which specific users are targeted and what specifically do you want them to accomplish?

✔ **Time-specific:** For an objective to be measurable, you should always include a time frame for measuring it. For example, "Within a 6-month period the results should be *x*."

By using the SMART approach, you ensure that your objectives can be measured with specific results, and you set up your experience so that it is performance driven. In this case, performance-driven means that future decisions are predicated upon how the UX performs with users against pre-determined objectives. For example, if you plan to increase the number of job applicants but this does not happen, you can begin to look at where the breakdown is for the user and why more people are not using the website to apply for jobs. If certain areas of the experience are successful, you can continue to monitor these areas, but make fewer changes or improvements.

Goals and objectives are relevant, but they must also be translated to specific metrics to measure success. A metric is a measurement and is used in analytics to measure results. A few definitions prove useful:

✔ **Analytics:** This term is used frequently in the world of UX and covers an umbrella for the data collection, analysis and assessment of the performance of an experience. Analytics has grown into a science for UX. You may have heard terms such as *web analytics* or *site analytics.* These practices refer to the measurements and analysis of that data used to understand the performance of a website. Analytics is not just metrics or measurements, it also includes an analysis of those metrics and uses tools such as user testing to answer the question of why users are behaving in a particular manner.

✔ **Metric:** The specific definition of a metric is any type of measurement. Metrics are a key component of analytics and form that basis for how and which data you gather about your experience. Metrics will not tell you why a user does something or behaves in a particular manner but can indicate who, how, where, when, and with what.

✔ **Key performance indicators (KPIs):** KPIs are specific metrics used to determine the performance of a solution. You don't need to understand the intricacies of this term to apply best practices to measuring the success of your solution. You will see this term used frequently if you read more about metrics and measurements, and what you need to know about it is that KPIs are a set of metrics used specifically to measure the progress and success of your objectives. The metrics and approach described in the next section embody a set of KPIs that you can leverage for your success without being an expert in analytics.

✔ **Conversion metric:** In the digital world, a conversion point is any time or place within an interaction that a user accomplishes an objective you set. Conversion points identify a specific criterion for where, when or how the user converts to a desired result. For example, in e-commerce, typical conversion metrics include when and where on a website a user purchases a product or adds a product to an online shopping cart. But conversion metrics are not necessarily just sales-specific. You might set up conversion metrics for when a user applies for a job, downloads a document, or shares a document or piece of media socially. Conversion metrics are specific measurements to determine whether a user successfully completes a task you perceive as relevant for your UX performance.

Putting the Performance Approach to Work

Performance-driven UX includes a series of steps that are repeatable and ongoing. These steps include the following:

1. Consider goals and objectives for each channel.

2. Define what you want to measure and how you will measure it.

3. Capture any specific channel requirements.

4. Put in place a process internally for when you will measure, how you will assess and analyze the results, how you will report the results, and what you will do to act upon the results. Then repeat the process as necessary for the duration of the UX.

The next four sections contain specific direction for accomplishing these steps.

Considering goals and objectives for your experience

The first step in the process of determining what and how to measure is to get specific with your goals and objectives to ensure you have the correct criteria to measure. Review your business goals and objectives and apply each to your UX. In *Search Engine Optimization All-in-One For Dummies,* 2nd Edition (John Wiley & Sons, Inc.), Bruce Clay and Susan Esparza highlight a set of commonly used goals for websites. These goals and objectives are applicable to many different types of UX, not just websites. You can find this list online at www.dummies.com/how-to/content/establish-business-goals-for-your-web-site.html.

Clay and Esparza outline four different types of websites (and in many cases a website might be a combination of all four). They include e-commerce sites, content sites, lead-generation sites, and self-service sites. Each type of site has a goal and set of objectives that correlate to its function. In some cases, more than one goal applies. You should limit the amount of goals, however, because they are high-level aspirations and overarching categories to house an array of UX objectives. In each case, ensure that the goal and objectives tie to your larger business objectives. Using Clay and Esparaza's aforementioned framework, the following demonstrate specific types of sites and goals and objectives each should seek:

E-commerce sites

E-commerce sites are websites that sell products online.

Primary Goal: Increase annual revenue overall with e-commerce website in all digital channels.

Objectives

1. Sell a specific number of products within a specific time frame.

2. Increase the number of repeat customers by X percent over Y time frame.

3. Increase the number of users who have signed up for a profile necessary to complete transactions (which also records previous purchases) by X percent over Y time frame.

4. Decrease the number of returns by providing accurate, relevant, and timely information on a product or service, and by providing online support by X percent within Y time frame.

5. Increase the level of user satisfaction determined by positive online reviews, users' online ratings, and user surveys by X percent within Y time frame.

6. Decrease number of calls to customer support by providing relevant, accurate, and timely information to support the product by X percent within Y time frame.

Secondary Goal: Increase brand/business awareness online over the course of a year within all digital channels.

Objectives

1. Increase the number of users to the site by a specific percentage over the duration of X months.

2. Increase the amount of socially shared content on the site by X percent over the duration of X months. (Socially shared means that users have taken a video or piece of content and shared it with any social network, such as Facebook, Twitter, LinkedIn, and so forth.)

3. Increase the overall number of users to the site by search engine optimization by X percent over Y amount of time, as determined by higher rankings within specific search engines. (For this metric, set an objective for what ranking you want to achieve based on which types of keyword searches you want users to search.)

Content information sites

Content sites are websites with a primary focus on disseminating information, such as newspaper sites, online magazines, or sites that profile organizations with a specific mission, such as nonprofits or government organizations.

Goal: Grow the readership of the site due to quality, compelling, and rich content, which includes retaining the existing user base over the course of a year in all digital channels.

Objectives

1. Increase the overall users to the site by X over Y period of time.

2. Retain X existing users during Y time frame, as determined by those who have a user profile and return to the site.

3. Increase the number of repeat visitors overall with X number of visits per user in Y time frame.

4. Increase amount of time users spend on site — reading or interacting with engaging content — by X percent over Y time frame.

5. Increase the amount of content shared socially by X percent over Y period of time.

6. Increase number of users who visit the site from search engine optimization by X percent over Y amount of time.

Lead generation sites

Lead generation sites generate a lead from a consumer to a business. Typical examples include a car dealership website, a site used for medical services, and furniture sites for small businesses that sell furniture in stores. Also, business-to-business sites, such as those selling a service or product from one business to another, often fall within this category.

Primary Goal: Increase overall revenue by generating more leads annually through all digital channels.

Objectives

1. Increase the overall number of users to the site by X who convert (conversion could be signing up for a profile, contacting a sales associate, signing up for additional information, downloading a whitepaper) over Y period of time.

2. Increase amount of time users spend on site — reading or interacting with engaging content — by X percent over Y time frame.

3. Increase new leads by existing customers as determined by existing customer referrals by X percent over Y period of time.

Secondary Goal: Generate more awareness of the brand online over the course of 12 months and within all digital channels.

Objectives

1. Increase the amount of shared content socially by X percent over X period of time.

2. Increase number of users from search engines to X percent over Y amount of time. (So if you get 100,000 visitors, X percent comes specifically from search engines and this number increases over a specified period of time.)

Self-service sites

Self-service sites offer tools for users to support a purchased product or learn how to accomplish a specific task (for example, a do-it-yourself site where a user learns how to make a doghouse or bake a cake).

Goal: Increase user satisfaction with brand over the course of a year within all digital channels.

Objectives

1. Increase the overall users to the site by X percent over Y period of time.

2. Decrease the total number of calls to customer support center by X percent over Y period of time.

3. Decrease number of product returns due to lack of support or understanding of the product by X percent over Y period of time.

4. Increase the number of positive experiences shared in peer-to-peer consumer ratings sites, such as Yelp, by X percent over Y period of time.

5. Increase positive customer feedback measured by online surveys and surveys of the experience by X percent over Y period of time.

6. Increase number of users from search engine optimization (natural search) from X percent over Y amount of time.

Applying the examples to your site

For each of the preceding examples of objectives identified for the specific site types, you do not necessarily have to use an increase as your primary objective success factor. You can also state the objective in terms of revenue or other types of metrics. For example, instead of increasing sales by X percent, you may want to say achieve X dollars of sales over a specific time frame. You may not always increase your amount of users or sales, but you can assign a realistic number for what you think means a successful user experience.

Not all experiences will conveniently fall into one of the four preceding categories. In many cases, you may have different goals within certain areas of your experience. For example, a website for a hardware business may sell some products online, drive a user to purchase other products to a store, provide support information for products that are purchased, and have a section devoted to do-it-yourself projects, such as reshingling a roof. In this example, you may use the four described website types and apply each set of objectives to different sections of the website according to what each section offers its users.

When you're generating the list of goals and objectives, you will want to vet each with various stakeholders in your organization. You may find it useful to generate a preliminary list and then conduct a workshop with representatives from each major line of business. Different stakeholders might include product line representatives, brand specialists, a member of the SEO and analytics team, a member of the technology team, sales leads, or any person in charge of major decision making for the business or organization. When the list is complete, you are ready to define specific metrics to measure.

Defining specific metrics to measure

In general, there are numerous types of UX metrics. In some cases, metrics measure performance of the UX; in other cases, they measure user behaviors.

Metrics tell you what a user does and measure user behavior. Metrics are not diagnostic. You won't be able to answer the question of "Why did the user behave this way?" from metrics alone. The data culled from metrics can inform you that you need to ask the question of "Why?" and guide you to dig deeper into what is successful in your experience and what is not.

The metrics described in the following sections provide a set of baseline measurements.

User path or clickstream

Here you measure the actual path a user takes to accomplish a task. A *clickstream* embodies the series and sequence of steps a user completes to get to a certain point, when a user actually clicks a link to go from one step to the next. Clickstream is measured in a singular channel experience. For example: What are the clicks or taps within a desktop website or mobile smartphone site or tablet site? *User path* is more encompassing and means the overall steps a user undertakes to complete a task. For example, to purchase a product, what is the user path in the overall experience? Does she engage in more than one channel — jumping from tablet to desktop to smartphone to complete the purchase?

To assess the user path or clickstream metric, leverage the user journeys you identified for the experience and then survey the actual behavior of a user within your UX. (Read Chapter 4 for more information about user journeys.) Does the user engage in a similar path to accomplish the task you called out within the journey? If the user does not follow your presumed journey, you can begin to diagnose issues. By knowing where and what the user does, you can see whether your experience is effective in achieving a desired result. You can also see which content is important to the user and what is not. You can look at which channels are used to accomplish which tasks and make decisions on where and what to optimize and which areas need improvement.

Within the clickstream, remember to try to see where a user comes from when entering your experience.

- ✔ *Direct visitors* are users who come to your site or experience directly. For example, on a website a direct user is someone who types your URL into a browser and lands on your site.

- ✔ *Referred visitors* are visitors who are referred from another site, say by clicking a banner ad and landing on your site.

- ✔ *Search engine referrals* refer to visitors who land within your experience after conducting a search.

All three of these pieces of data are useful and can help you determine the overall user path. Additionally, if you can track where the user goes after exiting the experience, this information is useful, too. For example, if the user jumps to a search engine, you will know he wants to do another search, which can indicate he did not find what he needed on your site. Although you may not know why a person jumped, knowing where he went can help you set up tests in these areas.

If the experience is broken or difficult to use, you can see where within the journey the user stops or jumps to another path or exits the experience entirely. In some cases, you may identify user paths that you did not know existed. This information is critical to helping you determine how your users engage with your experience. For experiences that include personalization, user paths are critical to determine which parts of the experience to personalize and when to do so. By knowing which path the user takes, you can determine how to personalize content along that journey. Later in this chapter, we explain how to conduct these measurements.

Length of visit

Here you assess how long the user engages with a particular experience. This metric may break down to measuring several different sets of information. As a best practice, you should measure how long the user engages with the overall experience (for example, how long he remained on the website); the time he spent on each page within the experience; and, in some cases, the length of time spent interacting with unique modules within the page, such as viewing a video. The length of the visit tells you which content the user interacts with and what modules within the experience are important to him. For experiences that are rich in content, this metric helps you assess whether a user is reading or consuming your content and which specific content he views.

A little amount of time spent within the experience may correlate to various explanations. On a smartphone, a user may want to get the information as quickly as possible, so if the user spends very little time interacting with an experience or page, this may mean the user was able to complete a task effectively and efficiently. However, in content-rich experiences, a short length of visit may mean the user is not interested in the content. A short length of visit may also mean the user cannot navigate or find the information he seeks, and therefore leaves.

Conversion

There are metrics for conversion that capture which areas of conversion are or are not successful. A conversion occurs whenever a user completes a task critical to the UX. A UX may offer several points of conversion. Typical types of conversion metrics include when and where a user does the following:

- Purchases a product (metrics also should track which products are purchased)
- Purchases additional items with a product, such as an accessory
- Completes a registration form or creates a user profile
- Views product information
- Downloads a document, such as a whitepaper, an annual report, or an app

✔ Subscribes to a service, such as activates an app or subscription for a news journal

✔ Applies for a job online

✔ Requests additional information about a service or product

✔ Clicks a map online or taps it on a smartphone to find a store

✔ Clicks (or taps) to call a business from a website on a smartphone

✔ Fulfills a lead from a website by either calling a sales associate or visiting a store

✔ Shares a piece of content socially on Facebook, Tumblr, Instagram, Twitter, LinkedIn, or another social network

As you identify which metrics you want to target, try to call out specific conversion metrics that demonstrate the business value of your experience. Often you can assign a return on investment with conversion metrics, because these generally impact the business or organization overall. For example, a downloaded and/or shared report from a nonprofit organization website means its content is valued and consumed. By tracking the performance of your conversion metrics, you can see where and when a user converts. If users are not converting in the manner in which you desire, you can look into what in the process is not working. You can test these areas of the UX to determine why the users are not converting as expected.

Look at number of conversions within each channel your solution is offered. Understanding the deltas between where and within which channels users convert helps you understand which types of content to serve up per device. Also, for e-commerce sites, ensure that you understand which products or services the user purchases while within each channel.

External search keywords

Keywords in this instance refer to terms a user applies in an online search in a search engine external to the experience, such as Google.com or Bing. com. For example, if a user goes to Google and then searches for *cat toy,* the keywords for the search are *cat toy.*

Any website can use tools to track the keyword searches that result in a user landing on the site. The keywords are particularly important for the following reasons:

✔ You can see which top keyword searches are conducted for your site and know which types of content are important for the user. This data can help justify an investment in specific types of content for the future and also help with decisions about where to surface content. For example, if *cat toy* is the most searched term for your site but cat toys are buried three levels down in the navigation, you might want to surface promotional content on a home page and raise the visibility of cat toys overall within the site architecture.

✔ This metric is an important part of the user path and displays for the first step in the process.

✔ If you notice a trend that users land in specific areas of your site from a search engine and then immediately bounce from your site to someplace else, you can analyze why the user is coming to the site but not having his expectations met.

✔ You can analyze why people are using Google instead of your internal site search.

Onsite search keywords

Here *keywords* refers to the terms your users leverage to conduct a search within your experience. Many different types of UX leverage search functionality. You will find search capabilities in word processing applications, downloaded smartphone apps, on websites, and within a variety of other UX interfaces. When a user conducts a search within an experience, the terms he uses for the search can point to a variety of useful data:

✔ Top searched keywords, which are the key terms used most frequently to find information, reveal that users have interest in specific types of content. Thus, if a majority of users within your UX solution search for *cat toy,* you will know that this content and associated products or information are important for your users. By viewing search logs, which can be done with most analytics types of software, you can understand what users are searching for, and then identify areas or trends in terms of what the users need or want.

✔ In some cases, a user may search for something if he cannot find it or easily navigate to it. So search can point to navigation issues. You should test areas that you feel the user should find within the site navigation but instead uses search, especially for desktop experiences. In mobile devices, users tend to use search more frequently to navigate experiences.

✔ Look for top failed searches, where a user searches for something but no results are returned. These can indicate that a user's expectations are not met with the site's current content. In cases of top failed searches, you may want to offer either alternative content if you do not have what the user is looking for, or state why it is that you do not offer the information.

One example where top failed searches can influence priorities around content is as follows: Many websites that sell products do not contain information about their corporate responsibility. Often, users will search for why a company is ethical, earth-friendly, or socially responsible. How responsible is the company and which initiatives does the business support? After making that determination the user will make a purchasing decision. If those users cannot find this information they are likely to quickly move on to another company.

After you view this type of data and understand which types of lacking information your users want to see, you can make the choice whether to feature more information on that topic.

Watch out for instances where a user searches for a term but identifies the information differently from how you represent it. (Terms a user prefers are called *preferred search terms*.) Preferred search terms means that the user identifies the information or terms in a certain way. These instances can either validate your labels or indicate that you need to test your nomenclature and language on the site or build additional synonyms to represent the content (for example, a user searches for *kitty toy* instead of *cat toy*). If you find multiple instances of users identifying your information differently from how you represent it, particular if they search within your experience within your onsite search, you may consider testing your nomenclature and updating it!

Other metrics

If all the previously mentioned search metrics were not enough, then fasten your seat belt because there are more types of metrics to consider. Although this section may not seem a real page-turner, these metrics are absolutely critical to validate and inform the future success of your experience:

- **Depth of visit:** Here you assess how deep within the experience the user goes. Which pages does she interact with? If you are looking across channels, which channels does she use and how and what does she do within each? Depth of visit is similar to user path, but specifically calls out how deep she goes within each experience.

- **Visits to convert:** How many times does the user visit the experience before completing a conversion task? Within this metric, you will want to see if you can view other channel engagement with your experience prior to conversion. If you cannot access that information, track the number of times a user must revisit a single channel experience in order to convert and also track what the user does at each visit. You can also track the length of time it takes a user to convert. You will also want to look at the number of visits necessary to convert and how many users convert within the first visit of your experience.

- **Value of interaction:** Here you look at the total revenue generated per visit based on the number of visitors divided by the revenue. This metric can help establish baselines for how much your experience is worth.

- **Cost to convert:** Here you determine how much it cost to actually convert. This metric is more for businesses that want to track the overall cost of a campaign, website, or other tool within the conversion process versus the amount of conversions over a specific period of time.

- **Exit metrics:** These metrics look at where and when a user exits from your experience. If a user leaves your experience before completing a specific outcome, you should analyze why the user left the experience. Exit metrics should capture what a user did prior to leaving and whether a task is accomplished. Exit rates can indicate either successful or unsuccessful areas within the UX. For example, a user might exit your experience after he completes a task and has no other reason to remain within the experience.

✔ **Bounce rates:** A *bounce* is a specific metric for websites that indicates a user has entered somewhere within the site, say from clicking on a link after conducting a search on a search engine, and has left immediately after without clicking on other links or spending any time within the page. A bounce rate generally indicates that a user is not satisfied with where he lands or with the content that is within the experience. Bounce rates are important because they often indicate a gap between what the user expects and what is revealed to her once she lands within an experience. If you have certain areas with high bounce rates, you should conduct additional testing in these areas to determine what is not effective or relevant.

✔ **User interaction history:** Here you assess what the user has done in previous visits to the experience and look at the overall behavior within the experience. Interaction history can indicate how a user behaves and what is important to him. For example, for an e-commerce site, previously purchased or viewed items can indicate that the user is interested in specific types of products or content. You can use this information with personalization to serve up more relevant content to the user in the future.

Understanding Channel-Specific Requirements

To determine in which channels your UX surfaces, review your user journeys and include any and all points of channel engagement. You may also want to review which content is served up in each channel to assign specific measurements for its performance. To determine which metrics to measure per channel, follow these steps:

1. **Review your user journeys and content requirements per channel.**

2. **Reference your goals and objectives to identify specific measurements that will demonstrate success.**

3. **Generate a list of metrics per channel.**

4. **Validate the list metrics with your business users to ensure organizational alignment.**

   The preceding section shows typical types of metrics to measure for performance. But remember, different channels may have specific areas to target.

Remember that even if you develop your UX for one channel, users may interact with it in several!

The following sections describe channel-specific considerations.

Desktop experiences

In general, a desktop experience translates to longer engagement time, so looking at what a user does, how much time she spends, and which content she engages with (and to what level she engages with it) helps you prioritize your content and make recommendations for the future. Remember to view what types of activities are critical for conversion. Are longer detailed specifications viewed prior to making a purchasing decision for a product? Are PDF documents downloaded or shared across social channels? These types of questions will help you assess user interaction across a desktop experience.

Smartphone experiences

One of the key metrics for smartphone use is the length of time spent within a site or app for experiences optimized for smartphones. Unlike desktop solutions, the more time spent on a site on a smartphone can indicate that the user is not able to find what he needs. Often length of time correlates to conversion, with shorter amounts of interaction yielding higher conversion rates. Although this rule is not always true, ensure that you evaluate length of time spent within the smartphone experience and pay attention to longer spans of time. Definitely ask whether longer engagement periods translate to higher exit rates prior to conversion.

Ensure you pay close attention to how users search with a smartphone experience. In general, users rely on search heavily to navigate smartphone sites and apps. A decrease in search may indicate that your search solution is not robust or effective. Remember that smartphone search must be simpler than search in desktop solutions.

A change in phone orientation — moving from horizontal to vertical or vice versa — can indicate that a user must change the phone position to view content. So by measuring this metric, you know if your users are able to easily interact with your experience. For smartphones, frequent orientation change may correlate to high exit rates. But note that sometimes functionality requires it, such as viewing a video.

Social media should most definitely be tracked on mobile devices, particularly with smartphones because users of smartphones tend to be much more engaged with social media. Looking at how your users engage with social networks tells you what types of content they like, and what about your experience, product, service, or organization they do or do not like.

Also evaluate the frequency of click-to-call and click-to-map usage. Both metrics are important. Click-to-call metrics indicate the number of users who call your organization or brand. Map usage indicates that users are trying to find you. Users on smartphones tend to use this functionality regularly. Also, a user is more likely to purchase a product or yield a conversion if he talks to you on the phone or visits one of your locations. If these features are not frequently used in your experience, ask yourself why. If they are, try to track how frequently each leads to conversion.

Tablet experiences

A metric to track for apps is how many users choose not to download the app for a tablet and instead view the desktop website within the tablet. This can indicate that you have not properly set expectations on the benefits of the app.

Measure the screen size of the device and which type of device is being used. (This metric actually applies to any type of mobile device.) This information can help you make design decisions around what and how much information to serve up. Remember that, in general, the smaller the screen, the less time users tend to spend engaged in experiences.

For digital content subscriptions, such as for newspapers or magazines or annual reports, how many users view or subscribe to a tablet version or app versus reading it in print.

E-mail/SMS experiences

For any e-mail or SMS efforts, you should track conversion metrics, look at which e-mails and SMS messages lead to additional interaction, and examine how many users opt in to each. Metrics for these are based on the rationale for why you are using e-mail and SMS. If you are using e-mails to reconnect with a user or to acknowledge him, such as with an anniversary or recognition or follow-up after he has engaged with your experience, does the user respond either by e-mail or clicking on any of your links? If you use SMS, does the user follow through with whatever the offer is? Any conversion metrics identified early may apply depending on the content of the e-mail or SMS.

Social media metrics

Social media is also important to consider in metrics. Social listening can yield a lot of information about how users and consumers view your brand or organization. The following present some typical metrics to capture specific to social media:

- ✔ **Post rates:** At what rate is your content being posted within social media? Where is it posted, who is posting it, and what is posted? How often is it reposted, such as retweeted? Content that is posted means that the user appreciates it or wants to share it.

- ✔ **Share of voice:** This metric tracks the number of times you are mentioned within social media versus the number of times your competitors are mentioned. This metric is important in understanding how others view you, and where within the competitive space you rate within social media.

- ✔ **Referral traffic:** Social media referrals indicate that your site or experience is being viewed in social media. Knowing how many users are coming from social media and which social media sites are generating traffic helps you monitor your presence within social media. When you calculate where your users are coming from overall, check to see which specific referrals are from social media sites.

- ✔ **Social sentiment:** This metric informs you of what people are saying about your experience or the content within it. Do they have a favorable view of it? Do they dislike it? Tracking social sentiment is important in understanding the perception of your experience in the social world. You can use a variety of free social metric tracking tools to track this metric, and these are covered in the next section.

- ✔ **Repeat engagement:** Here you look at which users continually engage with your experience by talking about it, sharing it, liking it, and communicating about it within social media. This metric is important as an indicator of user loyalty.

- ✔ **Tracking influencers:** Influencers are people within your industry whose opinions matter and who have a following due to their insights or wisdom. A blogger who is the go-to source for anything to do with running, for example, is an influencer. These people can be very important to you, and if you can get on their radars, they can help generate publicity and awareness of your experience.

Capturing and Reporting on Metrics

Capturing metrics is important, but even more critical for performance-based UX models is having a process and tools to measure, analyze, and report on the metrics. This section explains best practices in capturing and reporting on metrics and offers insight into tools and approaches.

When capturing metrics, make every attempt to review the results on an ongoing basis. As a best practice, you should target quarterly reviews of the analysis, from which you can make recommendations for changes and future state enhancements.

To analyze your metrics, use the following approach:

1. **Use metrics gathering tools that leverage dashboards to roll up the analysis into a report from the raw data.**

   This analysis generally does not provide an answer to "why," but it can show the trends and summarize the overall findings. Most major analytics tools have some type of reporting or dashboard.

2. **Look for trends in user behavior; whenever something does not seem copasetic, make a note that further analysis is necessary.**

   For everything that functions as expected or more than satisfactory, capture the successful metrics. Such metrics are critical in reporting back to stakeholders or others in the organization how the UX is performing.

3. **For problematic areas, first determine whether a usability issue is at fault.**

   In some cases, you may have issues other than usability. Ask the following:

   - Do your competitors offer the same product or service; this may be part of the problem. Are those competitors getting more visits or traffic to their experiences for a reason?

   - Can users find your experience? Analyzing external search engine logs will tell you whether you are getting the traffic you need. If nothing else, you can conduct your own research. Google Analytics offers free keyword reports that will tell you which sites perform best with keywords.

   - Are there negative reviews of the experience, the product, service, brand, or organization? If so, why and what can be done about it? Negative reviews on sites such as Yelp can significantly affect users' perceptions.

   - Is there a usability issue that prevents your users from completing a task? If you cannot determine whether a usability issue exists, you may want to use a test such as System Usability Scale, which rates the usability of your UX. For more information, see `www.measuringusability.com/sus.php`. This scale does not answer why users do what they do, but it can help you isolate usability issues. If you determine that your site has usability issues, you need to test to determine why the issues exist. Refer to Chapter 12 for more information on testing.

4. **Make a list of recommended fixes or solutions.**

   You may want to test these as well to validate the design direction.

5. **Prioritize which enhancements are necessary; then design and release.**

For the quarterly assessment of your UX, use a combination of metrics and user analysis, such as surveys, A/B testing, or multivariate testing. See Chapter 12 for more on these approaches. As a general rule, in addition to metrics, you should use testing when launching new features or functionality or when you're trying to determine problem areas. For example, you can use an A/B test to evaluate which of two designs is most effective for users.

The following are some tools that you can use to capture metrics:

- Google Analytics provides a series of tools to measure and report on metrics. Many of these tools are free, but you can also purchase the service to subscribe to more complex and detailed analysis. Visit `www.google.com/analytics/`.

- Adobe Marketing Cloud (`www.adobe.com/solutions/digital-analytics/marketing-reports-analytics.html`) is a popular tool used by many companies to measure a variety of different metrics. This tool must be purchased.

- HootSuite (`http://hootsuite.com/`) and SocialMention `www.socialmention.com/` are two tools you can find online to monitor social media metrics, and you can use much of their capabilities for free. In addition to tracking your social media presence, you can see where your top site referrals come from and within these tools find out demographic information on age range, country, gender, and so on. This information can be enormously helpful in maintaining your UX in the bot the short and long term. Facebook Insights (`http://www.facebook.com/help/336893449723054`) and Twitter Analytics (`https://analytics.twitter.com/`) offer additional free tools to track social media performance.

- Tree testing validates your navigation and helps locate issues. Test any areas where you determine usability issues exist. A tool that effectively helps you do so is Optimal Sort, which you can find online at `www.optimalworkshop.com/treejack.htm`.

- For user surveys and to test the overall customer satisfaction of your experience, you can use tools such as ForeSee, which is online at `www.foresee.com/`.

Chapter 14

Making It Past the Finish Line

In This Chapter

▶ Identifying when you might need assistance

▶ Knowing when to bring in help

▶ Finding UX help

Access to talented and creative people is to modern business what access to coal and iron ore was to steel-making.

— Richard Florida

*U*X is a particularly multidisciplinary field. As mentioned in Chapter 1, UX design is a healthy mix of both art and science, of creativity mixed with functional requirements, all delivered through technology. The chapters in this book aim to cover many of the considerations that go into the process of UX design, including information architecture, visual design, content strategy, and technology, among others, and to convey a baseline understanding of the diverse world of UX. However, no one person will be an expert at all the disciplines that are part of UX. A Swiss Army knife is good for accomplishing a wide variety of tasks, but you still need other tools for bigger tasks. Furthermore, if a project is complex in nature (with significant interactive or technical functionality), the depth and breadth of expertise needed to successfully execute a project can be significant.

Some small projects are ideal for a single person, but for other projects you'll need additional help. One person may be able to play a Mozart sonata effectively on a piano, but a full orchestra is required to play the entire symphony. With that level of complexity, the role of a conductor for the orchestra becomes paramount.

 One of the best things you can learn about UX is to identify the areas for potential additional subject matter expertise, and, to know when your project might need additional external help. It's a wise person who knows when to call for help, and has already lined up the assistance.

This chapter covers some of the basic areas within UX where deeper subject matter expertise and assistance can be extremely valuable to your project.

Determining When You Should Consider Bringing in Additional Assistance

A single person can be effective at creating simple experiences: simple websites or apps without a significant level of functionality or a challenging visual design. However, in many cases, you'll want to consider working with a broader set of subject matter experts. Here are some situations where bringing in additional help makes sense:

- ✔ The functionality of the experience is significant, such as e-commerce in which product selection, purchase, and shopping cart checkout are required functional processes.

- ✔ The underlying technology is complex — including content management systems, e-commerce architectures, or financial services.

- ✔ The experience is heavily branded, heavily visually designed, or requires an expert's touch with respect to photography, illustrations, or video.

- ✔ The experience contains advanced rich media tools, such as dynamic visualizations, animations, or calculators.

- ✔ The experience will be rolled out onto a variety of platforms, such as desktop website, smartphones, and tablets, or any emerging platform.

- ✔ The user testing needs of the user experience is significant, and you want a third-party facilitator.

- ✔ The subject matter of the experience is deep, such as designing a portal for investment bankers.

- ✔ A project has significant risk, such as a variety of dependencies on other stakeholders, teams, or people.

- ✔ You think that bringing in some experts may give you an opportunity to learn something new.

- ✔ You feel like you are in over your head.

Understanding just what type of additional assistance you need is the first step, and you have a variety of help to choose from. The UX industry supports a large global community of freelancers as well as both small and large design agencies. It is also common to hire additional help for specific expertise that is required for your UX, such as hiring art directors who can create illustrations, or hiring developers who can create browser-side technology tools.

UX is a field where multidisciplinary business generalists thrive, but if you are hiring external UX talent, it's always helpful to understand the specific background of each candidate. UX is a broad field, and many designers who call themselves UX designers are not alike — some are from backgrounds that are more strategy-oriented versus design-oriented, but the field also includes people who come from backgrounds in content, technology, and user research. When you're looking for external assistance for your project, think about the depth of subject matter expertise you need on your project. Then review your possible UX candidates with that in mind. The term "UX" means many things to different people, so it's critical to determine the type of expertise each candidate or team brings to your project.

This chapter outlines the most common areas where bringing in subject-matter expertise or additional UX help can have a significant effect on your project.

Supporting Large-Scale UX Projects with Additional Information Architects

When an experience you use today contains a significant amount of functionality — such as online banking or commerce — you can bet that the core information architecture work was not delivered by one solitary UX professional; large solutions require a team of UX-ers. In this case, the information architecture work is typically broken down into different functional areas, where teams of information architects focus on specific components of the experience. In an e-commerce project, this can mean that shopping cart and checkout processes are handled by one team, while designing the wireframes for a product display page and other components is handled by another. In addition, global information architecture components, such as content categorization and navigation, may be handled by another team.

Most likely, each of these tracks of work is led by a team member who has been designated as the track leader, while junior team members on that team are tasked mostly with conceiving and designing the wireframes and defining what needs to be annotated. The modular nature of most UX solutions lends itself nicely to breaking down complex projects into core functional tracks of work that can be reassembled during the course of the UX design. The team needed to support each functional track can be assembled or augmented with additional UX professionals as the project progresses, so it's a model that is scalable and flexible.

Projects of this scale survive on the amount of communication across each track of work because UX decisions within one track can have a cascading effect on the other tracks. In addition, great UX leadership at the top helps ensure that all tracks come together into one cohesive experience.

Get everyone on the team to understand the bigger picture behind the experience. If you are working on a large-scale, complex project with teams focused on one specific functional area, it is still wise to get every team member to understand the bigger-picture strategy that is behind the experience. Because great design comes from the choices made in the details, it's helpful to have even your most junior UX designer aware of the target user that is embodied in your personas. When UX project teams get large, it's a great idea to have on-going UX strategy sessions where the overall project strategy is shared across all team members, so all the design choices are made in context of the strategy.

Bringing in Visual Design Experts

Visual design is one of the most critical areas for a UX project. Many users of an experience can easily identify a visual design that is appealing, fresh, or compelling, but users aren't always able to articulate why it's so appealing. That is the art of great design. Conversely, visual design that is ugly repels people's subconscious in ways that can be irreparable for an experience. Even the best UX solution that has a poor visual design is still likely to fail.

Visual design is one of the most common areas where people employ a formally trained designer or art director, or even multiple designers for larger-scale projects. Professionally trained designers can offer a variety of benefits to a project:

- ✔ Define the underling system to support the experience, including the grid system that relates to the overall page size
- ✔ Create more abstract artifacts, such as mood boards, which help define the high-level look and feel for the experience
- ✔ Interpret and translate existing brand guidelines, if any, for use within the experience
- ✔ Take the lead in the overall visual design of the solution, creating design concepts, design directions, and page comps
- ✔ Take the lead in creating all visual elements for the experience, including page graphics, button and link styles, and use of visual assets such as photographs
- ✔ Create the style guide

If the project is large and complex, the visual design track may consist of multiple designers under the direction of one lead art director. Multiple designers can be particularly helpful in early stages of visual design where the team is developing multiple visual concepts in parallel with one another, before a leading design direction has been chosen.

Visual design is far more than just coloring in wireframes, so it is important to ensure that visual design team members are closely integrated with the rest of the UX team, including the information architects! Although the visual component of a solution has its own specific needs, the closer the visual design is developed in connection with the rest of the solution, the greater the cohesiveness of the solution overall.

Sources of visual design talent

On UX projects, visual design team members can come from a variety of places. If you are working with an established brand, these team members should have the deepest understanding of the brand's language, identity, and ongoing market positioning. As such, it's common that these team members can come from a background or role with a company's brand or marketing team.

In addition, leveraging a visual designer from an external source to help is common practice. This can be in the form of a freelancer or a team of free-lancers, since there is a widespread global community of designers who prefer to work on a contracting basis. Contracting a third-party agency solely for the visual design of a broader UX solution, however, is rare because the visual design is typically so tightly integrated with the broader effort. Most third-party agencies either take on the larger, more comprehensive UX challenge (including visual design and information architecture), or they don't get involved at all.

Local design schools and design associations such as AIGA (American Institute of Graphic Arts) are great places to look for visual design help for UX solutions.

If you are hiring a visual designer from an external source to add to your project team, make sure the designer has adequate digital or UX experience. Digital and user experience design is a relatively new practice of design, and not all visual designers have deep experience with it. On the other hand, graphic and communication design has formally existed for decades. There is a large community of talented visual designers who have historically focused on print, communication, and brand design, but who don't have significant experience in interactive, UX, or digital design. As you look for design talent to help with your UX project, consider the complexity of your project and how much digital experience you'll need from your visual designers.

As you review visual design candidates for your UX project, here are some questions to consider:

✔ How much digital experience does the candidate have?

✔ How significant is the brand challenge on your project? Has the prospective designer created an experience for an existing brand, interpreting brand guidelines for a new platform?

✔ Does your project deal with an entirely new brand or a new product that needs deep differentiation? Does the designer have experience in the visual design of brands that have not yet existed, where the visual design will need to create an initial brand language?

✔ Is the project content-rich or deeply transactional? If so, does the candidate have experience in the visual design of these types of projects?

✔ How collaborative does the designer like to work?

Developing specific visual assets: Photography, illustration, and video

UX solutions that have a variety of deep visual assets, such as photographs, illustrations, or video assets, also may require you to enlist the help of a trained professional. Great visual components — like custom photographs of products — can help significantly differentiate your experience from your competitors' UX.

These types of visual assets are much simpler to outsource to professionals, and the development of them can exist outside the day-to-day development of the UX solution. This means that you can hire a photographer to create a series of images for your experience, but not require the photographer to work as an integrated member of the broader UX team. The modular nature of the UX design process allows for the easy insertion of key visual components during the build phase, although the look-and-feel guidelines for these images should be developed as the visual design direction is created.

Photographers, illustrators, and videographers possess various subject matter expertise. For example, some photographers specialize solely in food photography or real estate. Likewise, some videographers specialize in short films that profile business leaders. Narrow down the type of expert you are looking for, and then look to local resources as you would for external visual design assistance.

Be careful to choose differentiating visual assets for your experience! Online image libraries are popular sources of visual assets such as images, illustrations, and videos for design projects today. Many of these online sources can be helpful for assets to use as FPO (For Placement Only) images during the design process. Keep in mind, however, that the accessible nature of these stock libraries often makes the content feel too familiar and not differentiated. Think carefully about the importance of visual design assets for your experience and consider bringing in experts to creating custom assets where needed to bring to life your experience's most important components.

You may not need custom-developed visual assets for every page of your experience. It is often cost effective to develop custom assets only for key pages of an experience, such as the home page or section pages.

Assisting with Content and Copy

Another common area for leveraging additional assistance in a UX project is the area of content, which includes content strategy and copywriting, although they are two distinct areas of practice.

Content strategy assistance

Some projects can be relatively simple with respect to their content strategy needs, such as simple websites with content that never gets too deep or detailed. In these cases, by following the guidelines in Chapters 7 and 8 you can prepare you experience to be successful.

However, UX projects with more robust content requirements may need the help of a content strategy professional. Here are some situations where bringing in backup help makes sense:

- ✔ The content solution is complex, meaning that syndicated, high-volume weekly content, curated content, and user-generated moderation of content is required.

- ✔ The experience includes a large set of products to profile and account for, including larger stores (with larger numbers of products and product categories) and business-to-business product sets.

- ✔ The experience relies on a continuous stream of timely, relevant, and meaningful content to support it.

- ✔ Personalization is involved.

- ✔ The experience surfaces in different channels, and optimization of that experience within those channels is required.

- ✔ The product set changes frequently, such as a clothing retailer changing styles every season.

- ✔ The company is global, supporting different products for different markets, in different languages.

- ✔ The internal product taxonomy (such as an internal product catalog that represents how products are internally represented) may not translate easily for external customers (product names).

- ✔ The subject matter of the experience is deep, such as designing the business-to-business experience for an insurance company to support its brokers and sales teams across the company.

✔ Any experience being delivered through a specific content management software application (for larger enterprise solutions), such as Tridion, Adobe CQ, Interwoven or many others.

As Chapters 7 and 8 explain, many different considerations go into an effective solution for your experience's content strategy, including defining a content model, taxonomy, metadata, and general publishing model for the experience overall. The skills that comprise content strategy are specialized, so look within local digital design agencies to find the right fit for the project you are delivering.

Written copy and copywriting assistance

Users of digital experiences absorb and digest copy very differently than they do from a printed experience. In the world of UX, it is said that content should be "written for scan-ability," meaning that users can browse a page and quickly absorb the general nature of the content and then decide to delve deeper if desired. Therefore, writing content for digital experiences is a specific form of expertise: Good digital copywriters know how to break down content into chunks that can be absorbed and comprehended, and yet still give meaning to the experience.

Finding writers for your UX project can be an easier task to accomplish than finding a content strategist. Local contractors, freelancers, and existing internal marketing teams are great places to start looking for these team members. As you look for writers to add to your UX project team, make sure they have adequate digital experience.

Again, if your project deals with a specific subject matter for users to understand, such as financial services, technology, or business-to-business solutions, then make sure you find writers with relevant subject matter expertise. Almost any industry has a large community of technical or expert writers who have experience in bringing to life a specific subject matter in clear, comprehensible, and persuasive written copy.

Supporting User Testing Activities

As explained in Chapter 12, the areas of user testing and usability are common for leveraging third-party assistance. You may want to add some assistance with user testing or usability to your project if you feel your testing needs are complex or if you want to ensure you have an external, unbiased moderator for the research itself.

User testing and usability are commonly supported by external resources. This enables key tasks to be accomplished in parallel to the UX design, including

- ✔ Developing the research protocol, which will identify what to test and which methods to use for testing
- ✔ Addressing all testing logistics, such as testing locations, scheduling, and participant incentives
- ✔ Recruiting and scheduling the research participants, sometimes using an external service to identify potential participants
- ✔ Moderating the sessions
- ✔ Presenting the findings

You can turn to several places to get help with user testing and usability, including independent freelancers, small research firms, and larger, global firms. In addition, if your testing needs are relatively simple, you can leverage a team member with a general UX background to take the lead with the testing process.

Enabling the Technology Architecture through Expert Help

The digital nature of most UX solutions assumes some level of technology as part of the eventual experience. Simple content-oriented websites using off-the-shelf tools may not require the help of a technology professional, but if your solution is more complex in nature then you may need additional technology assistance.

The realm of technology, however, is broad and deep, which means there is a variety of types of technology help you can consider. This section highlights some of the most common areas for which you might seek assistance and provides a high-level understanding of what's involved. Entire books have been written about each of these areas, so if you are interested in delving deep into any of the following technology areas, you should do some more digging.

Complex technology architectures

The field of UX can be used to develop experiences of many different types across a range of different industries, such as banking, shopping, or just keeping in touch with others. Many of the digital services and experiences people use on a daily basis are supported by complex and deep technology systems running underneath them, which are called *technology architectures.* The experience people interact with on the surface is just the tip of the iceberg.

Consequently, you may need to interact with experts and teams who build and maintain the architecture that will support your UX. Most technology professionals in these areas come from the other teams that interact with UX, but identifying the technology architecture that your experience requires should not be the UX leader's responsibility. Some areas of technology architecture that are commonly present in a UX project include those experiences that have the following features:

- ✔ **Commerce and transactional systems:** Online shopping and commerce experiences are typically supported by a variety of technologies, some of which are complex product information management systems (PIMs), e-commerce and payment systems, and applications. Understanding any key enablers or constraints that may affect the UX at the outset is critical.

- ✔ **Content management systems:** Experiences that are deep and robust with content are typically supported by a content management system (CMS), which allows for the efficient creation, publishing, and retiring of content into an experience.

- ✔ **Authentication:** Any experience that requires a user to register or sign in has a system to support customer data and authentication. In addition, if customer payment information or other personal information is stored, proper security systems should be in place.

- ✔ **Industry-specific experiences:** Experiences in industries like banking, investing, and insurance have a variety of technologies — often custom to the enterprise — to support the users' experience.

- ✔ **Performance architecture:** Finally, almost every experience is supported by a variety of technologies to deliver the solution effectively, load pages quickly, and respond to users' interactions. These types of technologies include hosting and general performance, among others.

Platform-specific technology assistance

Digital user experiences are delivered by a variety of client-side technologies that consist of browsers (Safari or Explorer, for example), platforms (smartphone or web), and mobile operating systems (Android or iOS, among others). On your UX team, you'll want to have representation from a technologist who understands the strengths and limitations of each of these client-side technologies, if relevant, and who can help bring the UX designs to life in technology standards such as HTML. These technologists, often called web or interactive developers, are critical to the creative success of your UX solution because they will be the ones translating the design assets into actual technical code.

Keep your interactive developers closely aligned and integrated with the creative team members on your UX project. The earlier these developers are brought into the project process, the easier it will be for them to inform the creative development of the solution. In addition, if your lead developers are involved in your project from the start, they will have a good understanding of the underlying strategy for the overall UX, enabling them to make decisions that will help to ensure the final experience is fully effective.

Rich media asset development

Finally, the last common area for which you may want to enlist external help for your UX is in the development of specific rich media assets, such as interactive tools, calculators, animations, and interactions. These rich media assets are typically the responsibility of more advanced and experienced interactive developers who have worked extensively with technologies such as HTML5, Ajax, Adobe Flex, and others.

Finding help with rich media assets is similar in many respects to finding help with visual design assets like images, illustrations, and video. You'll want to look for a specialist who has the requisite experience and can plug into your UX project with ease.

Where to Find UX Help

User experience design is a relatively new field of practice, estimated to have begun in the early 1990s and borne out of the practice of human-computer interaction (or HCI). As a new and rapidly growing field, the resources available for UX are constantly evolving.

UX For Dummies is intended to be a basic primer for core aspects of UX. As you begin to deepen your understanding of UX design, there are myriad other resources to turn to so you may continue to understand the field. Some of the resources focus on design basics, including interaction design, new technologies, and platforms. Other resources approach UX thinking a little more strategically and focus on managing user experiences, or even using UX-centered thinking to focus on customer experience design.

Following are great resources you can turn to in order to learn more about UX. Each of them will point you to additional sources of insight and inspiration.

Browsing great web resources

The web itself is a real-life illustration of user experience design. Every site and app you use can be an interesting source of education and inspiration for design choices that have been well made, or, in some cases, choices that were not so well made.

UX Magazine

UX Magazine (http://uxmag.com) is a great online resource devoted to all things UX. It has a database of articles that focus on the practice of UX, the business side of UX design, usability, and interaction design, and technology. The Resources section profiles great books, additional online resources, presentations, and software tools. The site also has a robust job posting section, for use by both employers and job seekers.

Smashing Magazine

Smashing Magazine (www.smashingmagazine.com) is an online resource devoted to the web design and UX community. The site is continually updated with new articles, points of view, and best practices in the areas of user experience, e-commerce, mobile design, coding, and visual design. It also has a healthy job board, where employers and candidates can connect.

UX Booth

UX Booth (www.uxbooth.com) is a online publication by and for the UX community. Its content includes core areas of UX, including, interaction design, usability, content strategy, and general user experience topics. It polls articles and topics from the community, so there is a great diversity of perspective within the content.

LinkedIn

LinkedIn (www.linkedin.com) is a great resource for connecting to the UX community, including other practitioners, employers, UX design firms, and industry events. A search of LinkedIn Groups reveals a variety of UX-centered interest groups, including those that focus on mobile UX, interaction design, usability, and other topics.

UX Books

Myriad books focus on UX or the broader practices of experience design and customer experience management. If you are interested in getting to know more about UX, check out these books:

- *The Design of Everyday Things,* Revised and Expanded Edition, by Don Norman (Perseus Book Group): Although this book does not focus on digital UX design specifically, it is a seminal book on user-centered thinking and focuses on usefulness and usability of the everyday products that surround our lives. This is a must read for everyone interested in user centered thinking.

- *The Elements of User Experience: User-Centered Design for the Web and Beyond,* 2nd Edition, by Jesse James Garrett (New Riders): A good primer on the fundamentals of web design.

- *User Experience Management: Essential Skills for Leading Effective UX Teams,* by Arnie Lund (Elsevier): A great book on the management side of UX within a business context and what it takes to effectively lead UX teams, and the diversity of skills included in them.

- *Don't Make Me Think: A Common Sense Approach to Web Usability,* 2nd Edition, by Steve Krug (New Riders): This highlights how users absorb information, and the steps you can take within UX design to create easy, seamless experiences for the user.

- *Experience Design: A Framework for Integrating Brand, Experience, and Value,* by Patrick Newbery and Kevin Farnham (John Wiley & Sons, Inc.): Although this book does not focus on UX specifically, it focuses on the broader, more strategic area of how consumers interact with brands and how the strategic value that is created with those experiences works well for both the consumer and the brand.

- *Outside In: The Power of Putting Customers at the Center of Your Business,* by Harley Manning, Kerry Bodine, Josh Bernoff (New Harvest): This is another book that is not specifically about the field of UX design, but the broader field of customer-centered thinking. It examines the tangible value of customer-centered thinking in business and the strategic value that can be unlocked by widening the proverbial aperture, which forms the cornerstone of the world of UX.

Attending UX conferences

Finally, conferences are another great resource for understanding more about the world of UX. In-person meetings that highlight the practice and ongoing evolution of UX design are great places to connect with others, learn best practices, and deepen your understanding of the field. The following list includes a few of the best conferences:

- ✔ **IXDA (Interaction Design Association):** Conducted annually in January or February. IXDA is a global association of interaction designers that attracts a focused audience of interaction and UX professionals. It is by far one of the best nonprofit conferences focused on the ongoing practice of designing brand interactions and UX.

- ✔ **South by Southwest:** Staged annually in March in Austin, Texas. South by Southwest encompasses a variety of areas including the interactive industry at large, but it has a deep focus on areas such as UX design, innovation, start-ups, and mobile or emerging platforms. The conference attracts more than 10,000 people to the city of Austin each year, and it's a great way to understand the broad landscape of the interactive industry.

- ✔ **Local UX meet-ups:** Almost every city within the developed world has a UX community, some focused solely on specific areas of UX, such as mobile UX. Check local listings, schools, and design associations to see if there is an upcoming event where you can connect with others in the field.

Part IV

The Part of Tens

To read about the top ten UX pitfalls, visit www.dummies.com/extras/ux.

In this part . . .

- ✔ Understand why your user is the most important consideration to the UX process.

- ✔ Ensure your UX is best in class.

- ✔ Define the UX principles that never change, regardless of the type of project.

Chapter 15

Ten Reasons Why the User Is Your Most Important Consideration

In This Chapter

▸ Identifying the benefits of user-centric thinking

▸ Understanding changes in user behavior

▸ Recognizing the importance of the user

*E*ven the best businesses, products, or services can't compensate for experiences that are poorly designed; selling fantastic products through a terrible e-commerce experience will not retain the masses. If your UX is lacking, it is only a matter of time until your competitors offer similar products or services and deliver them through a better experience.

If you aren't thinking about the role that the user plays in your UX then you're probably headed for disaster. This chapter highlights ten golden rules for understanding that the user — your users — is your most important consideration in UX, and potentially in your business overall.

UX Is Based on User-Centered Design

The practice of UX was borne out of the field of human-computer interaction, which aimed to understand how people most effectively interacted with computers and other technologies. In short, the field of UX puts the user entirely at the center of core interactions with your business, brand, products, and/or services. Without the user at the center of your thinking, you lose the benefit of understanding how outsiders view your services. In this respect, the user must always remain your primary consideration.

UX Focuses on How Services Are Used

Unlike communications or advertising, where a user more passively views the communication, UX focuses on designing experiences that people interact with and actually *use.* Effectively designing interactive experiences requires that the experience be supported by an understanding of human behavior. Just like doorknob designers must understand how people open doors in order to create fixtures that work for people, digital UX designers must also understand how people behave as they shop, socialize, or balance their checkbooks. A UX designer creating a new travel app must understand how people plan holidays, business trips, and other types of tasks that the experience needs to support.

Without a focus on the user, it is challenging to ensure that the UX will align with users' behaviors and meet their needs. The more you can align how you sell your products with how customers actually want to buy them, the greater the chance for success. UX helps maximize user understanding in the actual design process.

Users Vary in How and What Content They Consume

Browsing and using digital experiences can be overwhelming. How a user navigates through different experiences — and the information she absorbs and retains while doing it — is difficult to predict when the experience is taken out of real-life context. For example, the best-designed website may fail miserably when users actually use it while on the go in a grocery store instead of using it as they sit in front of their desktop computers. Alternatively, some experiences are designed with detailed information, and later the developers discover that users tend to just scan the top-level information and use other information sources for details.

In the case of websites, internal stakeholders frequently want to overload pages with additional content, options, promotions, or links. Yet users can only focus on one content element at a time, and too much content makes it easy for a user to get to the point of "cognitive overload." What feels like an appropriate amount of content on a page during the design process can be vastly overwhelming to a user in context of real-world use.

Keeping the focus on the user helps ensure that the content can be conveyed clearly, absorbed quickly, and retained easily.

Users Share Their Experiences — Positive or Negative

In this age of social media, every user of an experience has the ability to promote your brand, or tarnish it, based upon his interactions with your brand. A bad design delivers a bad experience, which can make an unhappy customer. Unhappy customers can comment about the experience on peer-to-peer consumer evaluation websites, such as Yelp.com. They can share their experiences across multiple social networks, such as Twitter or Facebook. Because consumers tend to place a high emphasis on what their peers think about brands and organizations — especially when making a purchasing decision — bad feedback can adversely affect your brand and even cost you revenue! Keeping the user focus at the center of your UX efforts helps ensure your experience will be seamless, useful, and usable, and it may just be the reason for users to act as a brand advocate on your behalf.

Users Change Over Time

Your users are constantly evolving. Many experiences originally designed for the web on desktop computers are now being accessed through smartphones and tablets. The technology landscape is constantly changing, which is causing users to evolve. Furthermore, many people who will use the experience you develop also use some of the most popular websites across the globe, including Amazon, Walmart, and Target, which are constantly evolving as user behaviors evolve. Technology also continues to emerge and change. In the past year, wearable technology — such as eyewear that captures video and images and smart watches — has entered the consumer markets. Tomorrow, we may see augmented reality! These types of technology advances will yield changes in user behavior.

Translation: The bar of user expectation is constantly rising. Even after you launch your UX, continually monitor how users are accessing it, and look at which content and features they are using and which they are not. Listen to your users and react to what they are saying. Build a UX strategy that enables you to respond as things change, so your solutions are continually optimized against user needs. Some parts of your experience that are very successful today may be outgrown by users in the next year.

A continual focus on users helps ensure that your experience will remain relevant, useful, and engaging.

User Experience Trumps Brand Messaging

No matter what you say about your brand or how you message it to users, if the experience you offer to interact with it is not good, your message won't matter. In branding, what you say is less important than what you do. Think of your UX as a representation of your brand and message in and of itself that speaks just as loudly as — if not louder than — your brand positioning statements.

Marketing strategies that don't take into account how good the actual user experience is aren't going to be as successful as those that carefully consider the experience itself. For years, the Avis car-rental company's brand message was "We try harder," but that statement would have been meaningless if users didn't actually feel like Avis was trying harder. The user's experience always trumps the message.

Your Competitor Is Only a Click Away

The digital nature of UX design implies that, in most cases, your user is just one click away from your competitor at any given time. Bad UX invites — and, in this day in age, almost implores — users to explore who else might be offering similar products or services in a simpler, more convenient, more timely, more relevant, and even more enjoyable way. Remember, when a consumer is frustrated with your organization, enticing him back is both challenging and costly.

Your Users Are Not You

During the UX process, as much as you try to put yourself in the shoes of your user, you will never be that user. Designing an experience means that you are viewing your business from the inside out. A user, on the other hand, is viewing your business from the outside in. She has a different set of per-spectives, wants, needs, contexts, and pain points than you do. She acts in her interest, which may or may not be in the best interest of your business.

One of the greatest traits in UX design is cultivating empathy for your user. During the design process, the UX team should continually strive to view the experience from the user's perspective. This is called having empathy with the user, and it is a critical ingredient for user-centered design. However, keep in mind that as much as you may try to build a connection with your user through empathy, your perspective is still going to be vastly different than hers. Understanding the strengths — and limitations — of user empathy is an important factor for success.

Experience Is Personal

The digital UX design process focuses on creating websites, mobile apps, and software that will be experienced by users; however, you are not designing the actual experience. For example, the experience that arises out of a user interacting with a website is entirely personal to the person who actually uses it.

For example, two people can use the same mobile app to check the weather forecast for San Francisco. They will use the same app, under the same circumstances, and yet one person might feel she had a great experience and the other might find it to be a terrible experience. In this case, the same mobile app delivered two very different experiences. The reason is the realm of experience is very personal to each person and is dependent on a variety of factors — including expectations, past experiences, mood, and context — that are beyond the control of the UX team.

Understanding that experience is deeply personal helps ensure you continually keep real-world users at the forefront of your process. It also helps to account for differences within the experience using tools such as personas to define why different users may encounter the same experience uniquely. Understanding the personal goals, behaviors, and reactions of the user helps you design a successful solution for the variety of users who may engage with your experience.

Experience-Focused Companies Out-Perform the Market

As outlined in Chapter 1, companies that deliver superior customer experiences are actually delivering higher performance and higher returns to their shareholders.

As noted in Chapters 3 and 12, both quantitative and qualitative research can correlate the effect of good customer and user experiences on the bottom line. Good experiences mean a happy customer, which translates to good business. In addition, Chapter 2 provides some great business rationale for using UX-centered approaches in your business.

Chapter 16

Ten Ways to Ensure That Your UX Is Best in Class

In This Chapter

▶ Identifying success metrics for UX

▶ Understanding the role of users

▶ Getting assessments right

▶ Keeping your experience up to date

Afterwards you have completed your UX project and launched it to the public, you need to continually monitor it to ensure it is achieving the objectives that were originally defined for it. Furthermore, you need to understand just how well your experience performs compared to your competitors' experiences, or compared to best-in-class experiences that are out there.

Just how good is your UX? What are some ways to ensure that your UX is best in its class? This chapter gives you ten simple rules of thumb. They may not all apply to every type of UX, but taken as a whole, they provide some good guidelines for making sure you create and maintain a great and effective UX.

Ask Your Users

The number-one method for determining how well your UX is performing is based upon your top priority: the users themselves. Asking users about the experience — on an ongoing basis — helps to determine the state of health of your UX and when it may be time to enhance it.

Online surveys, intermittent research studies, or guerrilla testing can be great methods of gathering feedback on any existing UX. The results themselves can help determine how well your experience is performing, and whether it remains the best in its class. Consider completing surveys or testing at least twice a year to ensure your users' needs and expectations are met. This approach will also help you to optimize your experience on an ongoing basis contingent upon what you learn from your users.

Conduct a Heuristic Assessment

Another way to determine how well your UX is performing is to conduct a heuristic assessment. *Heuristic assessments* are audits of products, services, or experiences based upon a predefined set of standards, but without the input of users. In layman's terms, they can be called "expert assessments," in which the criteria to evaluate the services are defined by experts. That's not to say you need a UX expert to conduct the actual audit; you can define the characteristics that you think best-in-class experiences should demonstrate, and then use them as criteria to evaluate the competitive landscape. Any available insights on users or secondary research can help you do so. And after you've defined the heuristics, you become the expert in evaluating how the UX stacks up against others. Naturally, you need to maintain a truly objective perspective during this process, and it may help to work with someone who truly has objectivity in evaluation.

Monitor Your Analytics

Websites, mobile and tablet apps, and software all have the capability to provide an ongoing stream of data with respect to which content and features are being used, which are not, and where users may be having problems. Continually monitoring the analytics that come out of your UX helps you ensure your UX is performing at the level that your business requires and desires. Your analytics should measure which content your users engage, when and if they complete a task such as purchasing a product, and what their actual journeys are to accomplish specific tasks.

Several types of analytics can measure the performance of your UX. Conversion metrics, for example, can show where and when a user purchases a product, what journey he follows to make the purchase, which content he interacts with and which he does not, when he signs up for a user profile, and even whether he applies for a job with your company. Figure out which analytics are important to measure before you launch an experience and how often you need to respond to what you learn from the analysis.

Consider monitoring and reporting on these analytics quarterly. You can meet quarterly with your technology, content, marketing, and digital teams to review the reports and make recommendations for enhancing the experience. This level of engagement is particularly necessary if you have personalization built into your experience. Understanding the user journey and how a user engages with your experience helps you figure out what types of experiences and content to deliver to her. Also, remember the importance of social listening in this analysis. *Social listening* is where you look at and "listen" to what users are saying and doing with your organization or brand within their social networks. It also includes seeing which elements of your experience users comment on and share with others.

Focus on the Enjoyment Factor

One of the primary goals of UX is frequently defined as making complex interactions seem simple, seamless, and even enjoyable.

If your UX is actually providing a delightful experience — regardless of the type of experience it is — it is a great indicator that users consider it best in class. For example, a new smartphone app may actually make grocery shopping simple, quick, and enjoyable, or an interaction that puts the user in control of her financial health can result in an experience that consumers no longer dread, but actually enjoy.

Keep the Experience Fresh

The best experiences are those that evolve, that are continuously updated. Stale content is an indicator that the experience is not well-maintained and sends a message to your users that the experience is not critical to your business.

On the other hand, fresh content helps give users reasons to continually come back to the experience and to use the service. Best-in-class experiences have a system in place to maintain the content and keep it fresh.

By listening to your users and monitoring which content they use, you can invest in delivering them content that is useful to them. Longer form articles and videos that may not directly sell your service or product but offer the user useful and interesting information can go a long way in making your experience enjoyable. Offering this type of content on an ongoing basis can differentiate your experience from your competitors' and provide additional lead-ins to your product or service. For example, offering weekly low-glycemic recipes for people with diabetes or those on low-carb diets can generate an entirely new following for your experience if you own a grocery store chain.

Structure the UX to Reflect User Needs

Best-in-class experiences are structured in ways that reflect how users think and behave, not necessarily how the business thinks of itself. Navigation, content categorization, and taxonomy should all be based on an outsider's view of the business. What you call one of your products or how you organize it internally within an organization may not be how the user thinks of it.

Frequently, a user's approach to content differs from how the business is actually organized, causing some hurdles in the UX process. But superior and effective experiences reflect users' wants, needs, behaviors, and pain points. An outstanding experience also reflects how users identify with and think of products and services it promotes. If you organize your products in a hierarchy that your users don't understand, they may not be able to find what they want when they need it.

Reuse Components

Best-in-class UX are based upon a system of components that allows the actual content to be separated from the presentation of it. Furthermore, the presentation of the content is enabled by a system of pages, templates, and content modules.

If your UX is reusing components extensively, it is a great indicator that the UX is not only an efficient solution for the business, but also that it is providing a high level of consistency to the user.

Structuring content where it is separate from presentation, and using templates and modules to serve up the experience, enables you to be adaptive to multiple channels — desktop, smartphone, tablets, kiosks, and so on. The benefits are numerous. You can tag and measure the performance of specific modules; you can make modules shareable so that users can share the module socially; and you can ensure that the content is accessible in multiple channels rather than being channel dependent. This approach gives your users control over how, where, and when they access your content.

Support Multiple Platforms

We live in a multi-platform world, where most UX solutions need to exist on a variety of devices, including desktop computers, mobile phones, and tablets.

Best-in-class UX solutions have the flexibility for components of content and design to scale to support multiple platforms. Supporting all platforms seamlessly can require a lot of effort, but the more the solution enables multi-platform access, the stronger the solution will be. Also, the more you consider how users engage with each channel and optimize your experience accordingly, the more you will ensure they use your experience throughout their entire journey.

Don't Lose Your User

A user should always have a clear understanding of where she is as she navigates through the experience. Clear visual cues should be given at every stage of the experience so the user knows where she is, how she got there, how to get back to where she was, and where else she can go from there.

Bread-crumbing is a term used to describe navigation that shows a visual trail of the pages the user visited within a section. It helps convey way-finding within the experience and provides shortcuts to navigate back to previously visited pages. Remember, however, that many mobile experiences don't enable bread-crumbing: The navigation is simplified because of the size of the screen.

In many UX solutions, Back button activity by a user can signify that the UX solution isn't providing visible, useful, or in-context navigation. In other words, a user may click Back to escape the navigational system provided within the experience itself. Consider how often your desktop users feel the need to click Back to ensure your navigation is working as hard as it should for them. In contrast, for mobile experiences, provide a mechanism for users to return to the previous screen: Navigation controls are limited on many mobile devices.

Create the Experience That Competitors Copy

Imitation is the sincerest form of flattery. In the world of digital UX, it's very common that the best UX ideas and solutions are imitated and replicated by competitors, in the form of similar UX patterns, functions, or features. Although the experiences may not be identical, if your competitors are copying or creating concepts or patterns that are similar to yours, it's a great sign that your UX is setting the standard within your industry. Naturally, though, if you do see imitation of your UX by your competitors, it only raises the bar for you to continue to innovate within your own UX, so that you maintain your competitive advantage!

Chapter 17

Ten UX Principles That Never Change

In This Chapter

▶ Understanding some core truths about UX

▶ Defining useful rules of thumb guidelines to inform any type of project

▶ Emphasizing UX as the "user approach"

*U*X is a relatively new field — less than 20 years old. Since its inception, UX has changed greatly as new digital devices, platforms, interaction models, and services have become available. But some core truths to UX have remained constant. Here are ten UX principles that will never change even though our world continues to evolve.

The User Is Rarely Wrong

You may have heard the old adage, "The customer is always right." Well, the world of UX has a similar mantra, although this refrain does not manifest entirely the same as it does with the traditional customer experience. One can say that the user is always right, but in truth, the user can be wrong. Still, when a user does err, it is typically is not the user's fault. If several users are making the same mistake frequently, the fault lies within the UX.

The goal of UX is to make complex interactions simple for users, to guide them along a journey and support them as needed, where needed. Common user errors might signify that something is wrong with the UX — that the experience is not behaving in a way that the user expects.

Usability Is an Absolute Requirement

One of your most important goals in UX design is creating experiences that are free of usability problems, in short, ones that work. Usability issues dilute the success of your project. Good usability is, simply put, a requirement — not an option.

Remember, though, that good usability alone does not guarantee success. Your UX needs to do far more: It also must provide useful content and features; illustrate an engaging visual system; and differentiate your brand, organization, products, and service offerings.

Content Is King

The best design in the world will not guarantee success. You need great content, features, and functionality. And, you need to keep that content fresh.

As stated in Chapter 1, great UX are useful, usable, and engaging. Usefulness is directly related to the content and features that the experience provides: Are they what the user needs and wants? Are they provided when the user needs them? Without good content, your experience will not be useful or relevant to your users.

Your experience is only as good as the content that supports it: Users consume content to make decisions and perform tasks. Your UX needs effective, rich, relevant, and timely content. Without it, your UX is not compelling and may not be usable or useful.

Don't Underestimate Visual Design

Great visual design can make the difference between a UX that is merely adequate to one that is actually delightful, fresh, compelling, and engaging.

In the world of UX, it can be easy to get caught up in the functional aspects of your experience: the content, information architecture, or technology, for example. Yet, great experiences also come to life through great visual design. Users will not always remember an experience that offered nothing more than seamless operation, but they may remember one that works seamlessly and actually provides a visual style that stands out from the rest. Never underestimate the power of great visual design in your UX process.

Prototypes Are Powerful Tools

Regardless of the type of experience you are designing, bringing it to life early and often in any form of prototype will help illustrate its strengths, weaknesses, and progress. Prototypes take many forms, including hand sketches, wireframes, and clickable high-fidelity experiences.

Prototypes can be leveraged by the broader UX design team, business stakeholders, and actual users. The ability to bring to life a UX concept that is currently under development should never be underrated.

UX Is an Art and a Science

UX design is arguably one of the most multidisciplinary fields of practice. It is inherently creative, so it is an artistic practice at its core, and yet it takes into account a variety of perspectives — research, content, technology, business strategy — that the creativity can mask. You need to understand that healthy doses of both art and science go into good UX. Make sure your approach to the work supports both aspects.

Good UX = A User's Approach

User-centered thinking provides the backbone to UX design. It requires that all business processes, goals, and problems be understood from the user's perspective. As a retailer, you may be focused on selling products, but the user's perspective requires that you also focus on buying products. How you sell products should be brought to life in ways that reflect how and why shoppers buy them: It forms the basis of "outside in" thinking. An effective UX connects the needs of the user with the goals of the business. Each business objective should be clearly tied to a user's need and his desired outcome.

Less Is More

Users can be continually overwhelmed with information. This state is called *cognitive overload*.

"Less is more" applies to the world of UX design and information architecture. When you include white space on your pages, the page contents can breathe. Users also appreciate simple and consistent ways to navigate through site. Too many choices within a navigational system may render the whole system useless because users can process only so much information at any given time.

Sometimes experiences demand that a surplus of information be made available and transparent. For example, financial services and insurance companies may require lengthy and cumbersome disclaimers and legal policies. A good UX finds ways to present this information only when and where it is necessary, giving the user an option to view it if he wants to see it, or making a forced viewing of it less unwieldy. Even if you have long-form content, such as lengthy articles or detailed specifications, you can summarize the most important points and provide that information initially at the top levels of the experience. The user can then choose whether he wants to view the summary or the detailed information.

Consistency Is Key

Designing a system that a person will interact with requires that you consider how the system will behave as a user engages with it. Is the content where the user expects it to be? Does it behave as the user expects?

A great rule of thumb in UX design is to always provide consistency to the user — for example, place navigation in the same area in every page and use consistent content modules. Using templates helps maintain consistency, which means users won't have to spend their time trying to figure out how the site functions, but instead can focus on the reason they visited your site.

The Experience Is the Brand

The actual user's experience of any brand will trump what the brand says about itself. "The Experience is the Brand" is a quotation widely attributed to Clement Mok, designer and author, who points out that any brand is defined by the experience it provides to consumers. It is not only what the brand says; it is what the brand does and how the brand behaves.

In this respect, UX design thinking is one of the most powerful tools in building and differentiating a brand today; it forms the backbone of how brands behave in an interactive world.

Glossary

A/B testing: A technique used where two different variables are tested to see how each affects a user's behavior. For example, two different types of navigation buttons may be used to see which button results in the most clicks. See also *usability testing*.

abandonment rate: The rate at which an action is abandoned prior to completion (conversion). For example, if a typical conversion is purchase of a product, the rates at which users abandon or leave a journey prior to completing the purchase.

accessibility testing: Testing for how easy to use a solution is for all types of users; generally, testing is designed to ensure a solution is accessible for all users, such as those who are visually impaired or deaf.

agile methodology: A project management and software development process that is highly iterative, in which tasks occur concurrently and often without the completion of previous tasks. Generally, agile development is more nimble and faster (but not necessarily a better approach in all cases) than a waterfall approach, which assumes certain tasks are complete prior to engaging in subsequent tasks. See also *waterfall methodology*.

analytics: The process of evaluating metrics, user research, and the overall performance of an experience to make recommendations for optimization. See also *metrics*.

authentication: The process of confirming a user's identity. For example, a user authenticates herself when she provides her credentials (username and password) to log into a user profile on a website. Authenticated users generally have a user profile stored in the experience.

beta testing: Tests that occur after a prototype or beta version of the experience is complete. A beta is released for a group of users who are asked to complete a series of tasks (such as log into a screen), and then data and bugs are recorded.

below the fold: A concept used in UX to indicate any information that falls under the visible area of a user's browser — basically, any information the user must scroll to see. Information above the fold generally has the highest priority because it is what a user sees first, requiring no interaction.

brand guidelines: A set of documented standards for rules on how to represent a business' corporate identity with visuals, text, and overall design within the UX. Guidelines often address logos, colors, typography, rules for voice and tone, and editorial conventions. For example, brand guidelines might specify which logos to use and where to place each within a page.

browser testing: Testing how a digital UX renders on a particular browser or platform, such as how a website renders in Internet Explorer and Safari. Browser testing ensures that an experience renders appropriately across several different browsers and platforms.

card sorting: An exercise conducted to see how users group and identify categories of information. This exercise is used to test how content should be organized for the purposes of designing taxonomy and navigation.

channel: The various physical means through which an experience can be rendered, such as desktop, smartphone, tablet, in-store kiosk, and e-mail.

cognitive overload: A point at which too much information is provided to a user to easily accomplish tasks or too many tasks are provided so the user cannot single out the most important for himself. Cognitive overload generally results in user frustration and abandonment.

competitive benchmark: An evaluation of the competitive landscape to determine what competitors' experiences offer. Competitive benchmarks uncover areas of opportunity, such as identifying functionality that can prove competitively differentiating as well as provide a baseline for what should be included within a future state experience.

concept testing: Technique used to explore and test designs early within the design phase of an experience to help identify which ideas are more effective with users than others.

content brief: Outlines the vision, goals, and objectives for the content experience.

content experience: Includes all content within an experience, including rules for when and to whom content is served, such as personalization rules. A content experience frames which content a user consumes, where and when she consumes it, and through what means she consumes it.

content inventory/audit: Looks at the content within a current experience and uncovers how much content exists and the quality of it. The tool can also be used to perform a competitive audit. The inventory and audit help define which content should remain in the future state experience and identify opportunities for new content.

content management system (CMS): A publishing application used for acquiring, creating, managing, reviewing, publishing, measuring (its impact post-publish), optimizing, and archiving content. A CMS is often necessary for any high-volume or high-frequency content solution and can be used to ensure standards in content production.

content matrix: A tool developed by a content strategist that documents which content will go into an experience and provides nomenclature rules. Often a content matrix is captured in a spreadsheet, such as Microsoft Excel.

content model: A tool developed by a content strategist that provides a blueprint for making decisions about how, why, and when content surfaces within an experience. This tool is a key component in content management system design, specifying the rules for content use in wireframes and validation of visual comps. Typically, it is created in a spreadsheet, such as Microsoft Excel.

content strategy: The approach for figuring out which content is required for an experience. A content strategy defines the future-state content experience. It also includes the content life cycle and the governance model required to support a content experience.

contextual interview: A form of user analysis in which a user's behavior with a UX is examined in the context where the user would use it, such as within his home. The user is interviewed as he interacts with an experience. Because the user is examined within his natural environment, contextual interviews can provide detailed insight into user behaviors, wants and needs.

conversion: A business measurement of task completion in a user experience. Some conversion type examples are purchasing a product (converting leads to actual sales), signing up for a user profile, downloading a document, or sharing a piece of content socially on Twitter or Facebook.

conversion metric: Measures the rate at which a user completes a task identified as a conversion. See also *key performance indicator (KPI)*.

critical success factors: The criteria by which you determine the success of your experience or within the actual product to design and build the experience. Critical success factors can translate into objectives for the experience and help your UX project team align around a vision of what will translate to success.

customer journey: See *journey*.

customer segmentation: A group of categories used to designate different types of users based on demographic and user information, such as age (generations such as Generation X, Baby Boomers), purchasing behaviors, or specific socio-economic categories. Segmentation models help frame what types of users engage with an experience and can inform the design process.

design direction: A designed example of the look and feel of the eventual experience; similar to an architectural model for house construction.

ethnography: An observational research technique, where users are observed accomplishing key tasks (not solely interviewed). Ethnographical research looks at anthropological and sociological influences in user behavior and assesses how users act in an attempt to assume what they are thinking during the process.

experience models: A graphical representation that captures how a user envisions a system. Experience models are used to represent how a user thinks about a UX and her engagement with it.

feature phones: Mobile phones without touchscreens with which the user interacts. See also *smartphones*.

focus group: A group interview conducted with a specific and small group of people, during which participants are encouraged to discuss a series of topics relating to their perceptions, thoughts, reactions and behaviors. Commonly used in advertising; less frequently used in UX design.

footer: The bottom of a page or template. Footers generally include information and navigation elements that are less important than main navigation items, but still important, such as privacy policies of a company.

future-proofing: The process of designing a system that can support significant change and evolution in the future. Creating a system or experience that is sustainable, and easy to adapt to future changes.

grid: A type of page layout design where a grid is superimposed on a template and then elements are ordered within it. Grids can help identify layout, sequence, and priority of content.

guerrilla testing: A form of rapid testing in which participants are selected informally and asked to answer a few questions or complete a few tasks, in context of an environment (for example, interviews of shoppers at a grocery store). Guerilla testing allows for quicker, less-formalized testing, but it can still yield much data depending on the tasks tested. See also *contextual interviews*.

header: See *masthead.*

heat maps: A form of testing that results in a display of the areas within an experience with which users find most visible, or interact with most frequently. Heat maps show which areas of the screen and experience users engage most.

heuristic assessment: An evaluation that provides a scorecard for how an experience performs against what are known best practices, in lieu of actual user testing. Heuristic evaluations illuminate strengths and weaknesses of an experience according to commonly defined standards.

HTML (HyperText Markup Language): A universal standard for creating web pages. HTML is used in web and app development.

information architecture (IA): The science behind organizing and designing information, navigation, and interaction. The underlying structure and design of the experience.

interaction design: The design practice focused on how users interact with an experience, such as through touch, swipe, and mouse click. Interaction design also involves defining how the system will react to a user's interaction.

journey: The end-to-end series of steps a user takes to complete a specific task — for example, the steps a user takes to download a job application from a website.

key performance indicator (KPI): A metric used to measure or quantify the success of a business objective. Conversion metrics fall under KPIs because conversion is generally tied to a business objective.

landing page: A primary page within an experience where a user lands at or near the beginning of a journey. A landing page can stand alone as the entry point of a journey and generally has several pages under it. A careers home page may be a landing page in a corporate website for the careers section and all material that falls within it, such as a job application and testimonials about working for the organization.

market research: A type of research that looks at industry trends and how a product, service, brand, or organization is performing against a competitive landscape within an industry. Market research generally explores what competitors are doing and how well they are performing.

masthead: The top of a page within a design. Generally, the terms *masthead* and *header* can be used interchangeably, although masthead can indicate an area where the title and specific information of a page is captured. A masthead of a newspaper, for example, includes the name of the paper, the date of publication, and publisher.

metrics: A specific measurement of something. In UX there are specific measurements used to evaluate the effectiveness of the experience such as the number of pages viewed or number of visitors to the experience.

modular design system: System of design that relies on the creation of templates or standardized page types that are populated with reusable, standardized content modules. Modules allow for reuse across the experience and also standardize the look and feel of content.

mood board: A tool used in visual design to help capture the themes related to a design direction. Mood boards generally are a collage of information, such as pictures from magazines, pasted on a board to visually represent a series of visual themes and feelings the design is meant to evoke.

multichannel: An experience that is rendered in more than one channel, such as a website that can be accessed on mobile phones, tablets, and desktops.

navigation: The process and steps a user undertakes within an interactive experience to get from point A to point B. Navigation can also refer to the navigation menu that a user can use to maneuver through an experience.

omnichannel: An approach that looks at every channel a user employs to engage with a brand or organization. Omnichannel places the user at the center and looks at which channels he interacts with, how and where he interacts with them, and which content he consumes within each.

page comp: A design tool that captures a visual illustration of a page or template, showing the look and feel of the page. It shows what visual elements fall on a page (images, photos, colors and typography), where the elements are placed, and what size and shape each element is.

participatory design: An approach to design where those who will use the experience are invited to participate during the early stages of the design process to weigh in on how the design should function. See also *card sorting*.

pathway: Indicates the user journey that represents the user's information needs. Pathways meld the business or organizational needs by creating a journey that will give the user what she needs to accomplish a task.

personalization: Crafting an experience that is customized to a specific user based on who the user is, where she is, what she is doing, how she does it, why she is doing it, and when she is doing it.

persona: Tool that brings to life a fictitious target user who is modeled from an understanding of a group of users defined by common behaviors, wants, and needs. A persona generally denotes a specific user type personified by a fictional character, but given a name and photo.

prototype: An illustration of how the future UX might look, feel, and behave. Several types of prototypes exist — from a paper sketch to a clickable prototype. Prototypes are employed in user testing and stakeholder reviews and help determine the eventual direction of the UX.

responsive design: A UX design that is programmed to assess a device (for example, smartphone versus laptop computer) and automatically render the experience appropriately. Responsive design is used for multichannel experiences and provides a mechanism for sharing one design across several devices, such as smartphones, desktop computers, and tablets.

rich media: Any type of multimedia formats used in an experience. Rich media can include animated images, videos, interactive modules and tools, infographics, audio files, and media.

scenario: Captures a story about a user related to the completion of a task (for example, "Sheila's Car Purchase Scenario"). Scenarios are used to help inform the design process and determine what types of features, functionality, and content are necessary to support the UX.

screen resolution: The number of pixels that a screen can display within a given area. Screen resolution is used to determine how large of a screen designers have to work with, and, just how detailed the designs can be (defined by the number of pixels).

sitemap: A tool, generally created by an information architect, used in the design process. It provides a high-level representation of the organization of the content on a site and implies how a user might navigate through an experience. A sitemap displays a map of the experience, showing the home page, landing pages underneath it, and subsequent pages or templates.

smartphone: Mobile phones with touch screens and often more advanced functionality and options than feature phones. See also *feature phone*.

stakeholder interviews: Discussions with the primary individuals with a vested interest in the experience for the purpose of uncovering requirements, ascertaining issues or gaps within the existing experience, and defining criteria for where the future needs to be.

style guide: A tool that captures either the content or visual rules for an experience, or both. Content style guides include the voice and tone guidelines for an experience. Visual style guides convey the rules of visual design, including typography, placement of templates, colors, branding elements, size of the underlying grid, icons, and other details.

taxonomy: A hierarchy of information and the terms used to label it. Generally, a taxonomy classifies information into categories and provides the labels for what those categories are called. An example is a product hierarchy, such as Clothes⇨Women's⇨Suits⇨Pants.

tree testing: A type of test that looks at the information hierarchy within an experience, and how a user would find information within it. Tree testing can help identify issues within navigation and taxonomy.

templates: A standardized set of page designs for a type of page or content. Template examples include a product page, a home page, and category landing pages. Templates help standardize the look and feel of an experience and also facilitate the use of reusable content modules.

typography: The font and style of the textual letters. This includes the size and spacing of fonts.

user: A person who interacts with an experience.

usability testing: A process of testing how usable an experience is, which can identify usability issues as well as strengths within the solution. Usability testing is generally an umbrella category for many different types of more specific testing, such as tree testing and participatory design.

user acceptance testing (UAT): A type of testing conducted after an experience is built, but before it is launched. In UAT, a set of tasks or scenarios is tested to uncover bugs or usability issues. UAT can help catch issues not uncovered earlier because it tests in the fully designed system.

user journey: See *journey*.

user modes: The different modes for user interaction. A few examples include an authenticated (logged-in) user, unauthenticated (not logged in) user, a new user, or a previous user.

user profile: The set of information a user provides about herself when setting up a profile of who she is. User profiles generally are completed when a user registers with a business or organization and includes specific information about who she is and her preferences and/or previous purchasing history.

user scenario: See *scenario.*

visual design: The process to create and design the final look and feel of an experience. This includes color, typography, images, and overall placement, size, and rendering of elements within each page of an experience. See also *page comp.*

waterfall methodology: An approach to project development that requires a set of specific activities within a project and one activity does not begin until a previous activity ends. Within the UX high-level process, the define phase starts after the discovery phase, the design phase starts after the define phase, and so forth. See also *agile methodology.*

wireframe: The layout, placement, and hierarchy of information of a page type or template, used to highlight information, functionality, and prioritization of information similar to how blueprint sketches are used in construction. A wireframe does not address visual design.

Index

• A •

A/B testing, 223, 225, 289
abandonment rate, 289
accessibility
  content audit, 123
  multichannel design, 182
  testing for, 223, 289
achievable goals, SMART approach, 240
acquisition of content, content
      life cycle, 144
ad space in style guide, 214
adaptive approach, 180
adaptive design, 85, 86, 282–283
Adobe Flash apps, 190
Adobe InDesign software, 167
Adobe Marketing Cloud (website), 256
aggregated content, 144
agile methodology
  channel UX design, 176, 177
  defined, 289
  participatory design testing methods, 228
alternate research participants, 227
analysis of data. See data analysis
analytics. See also metrics
  assessment of UX, 96–98, 280–281
  data gathering, 39–40
  defined, 240, 289
  personalization, 68
annotating wireframes, 169–171
announcement in content life cycle, 147
annual report as content type, 133
anonymous user, journey, 67, 68
Apple iPhones, 190
Apple Siri, 178
archive content, content life cycle, 145
article page
  as content type, 133
  template, 164, 166

assessment of UX
  analytics, monitoring and reporting,
      280–281
  asking users about their experience,
      279–280, 281
  of competition, 102–105
  component reuse, 282
  content-first approach, 282–283
  of current/future state, 92–102, 105
  enjoyment factor, 281
  fresh experience, 281
  goals of, 94
  heuristic assessment, 94–96, 105, 280
  imitation and innovation, 283
  multiple platform support, 282–283
  navigation, 283
  performing, 93–96
  scenario-driven, 99–100
  user-centric structure, 282
  visual systems audit, 98–99
  website analytics, 96–98
assistance for project completion.
      See expert assistance
assumptions of book, 2
attainable goals, SMART approach, 240
audience
  content audit, 124
  content brief, 114–115
audit
  of brand, in define phase, 23
  of content. See content audit
authentication
  complex technology architecture
      assistance, 266
  defined, 289
  technology architecture, 16
authenticity, social media experience, 200
author in content inventory, 122
Axure software, 167

• B •

back button, 190, 283
bandwidth for mobile phones, 186, 187,
     192–193
BBC Global Experience Language style
     guide resource, 213
behavior
  behavioral segmentation, 44, 45
  data analysis, 42
  determine target users, 38–39
below the fold content
  channels, 176
  defined, 289
  wireframe, 168
benchmark
  competitive benchmark, 79, 290
  current experience, define phase, 22
  visual design, 203–204
Bernoff, Josh (author), *Outside In: The
     Power of Putting Customers at the Center
     of Your Business,* 158, 269
best practices, mobile phone UX design,
     186–191
best-in-class UX. *See* assessment of UX
beta testing, 223, 225, 289
biographies as content type, 133
blog posts as content type, 133
Bodine, Kerry (author), *Outside In: The
     Power of Putting Customers at the Center
     of Your Business,* 158, 269
books as resource, 270
bounce, defined, 251
bounce rate metric, 98, 251
brand experience
  affinities for, persona, 51
  audit in define phase, 23
  competitor survey, 103
  content audit, 122
  experience as, 288
  look and feel, 17
  navigation, 172
  visual systems audit, 99
brand expression, UX importance, 13
brand guidelines, 204, 290
brand messaging compared to user-centric
     experience, 276

brand representative on strategic
     team, 83
branding elements in wireframe, 167
breadcrumbs, 191, 283
browse by category, navigation, 172
browse path, sitemap, 160–161
browser testing, 223, 225, 290
build phase, UX process workflow
  described, 22, 23–24, 80
  metrics, 236–237
business
  benefits to, as reason to use UX, 28–35
  content strategy relationship model,
     113–115
  evolution of, data gathering, 40
  future-proofing requirements, 84
  plan goals, 29
  questions for data analysis, 43
business goals and objectives
  content brief, 114–115
  in define phase, 22, 79–81
  journeys, 64–65
  UX, 15
business strategist/analyst on strategic
     team, 83
button style
  mobile phone UX design, 190, 191
  smartphone, 187
  style guide, 214, 215
  visual design, 208

• C •

calculator watch, 176
calendar
  editorial, 132, 152–153
  governance, 151–152
  UX strategy, 83
captions, voice guidelines, 216
capturing metrics, 254–255
car purchase example, 54–56, 70–73
card sorting
  defined, 290
  taxonomy, 141
  test and launch phase, 222, 225,
     228–231

Cascading Style Sheets (CSS), 85, 86, 182
categorization in taxonomy, 141
centralized governance model, 149, 150
channels. *See also specific channels*
  agile design, 176, 177
  benefits as reason to use UX, 26–28
  conversion metric, 248
  defined, 290
  design considerations, 175–200
  metrics, 241, 251–254
  multichannel focus, 177–199
  performance-driven UX, 241
  social networks, 199–200
  technology assistance for project
    completion, 266–267
  trends in, 176–177
  types of, 175
  visual design, 203–204
character count in content model, 139
choices in testing strategy, 222–227
clarity, consistency, and ease of use
  heuristic assessment, 95
  usability, 14
  visual systems audit, 99
Clay, Bruce (author), *Search Engine
    Optimization All-in-One For
    Dummies,* 242
clickstream metrics, 246–247
click-to-call, 186, 191, 193
click-to-map, 186, 191, 193
closed loop
  content life cycle, 127
  described, 237
  metrics, 237
  UX strategy, 79, 80, 237
CMS. *See* content management system
code
  flexible, 87
  interoperable, 87
  responsive design, 85, 86
  standarized, multichannel design, 182
cognitive overload
  defined, 290
  usability, 14, 274, 287–288
color
  style guide, 214
  visual design, 203, 207

color depth, 203
columns, mobile phone design, 187
comfort level, determining, 20–21
company information
  as business goal, 30
  as content type, 133
competition
  assessing for UX design, 102–105
  competitive landscape, 15–16
  future-proofing, 84
competitive benchmark, 79, 290
complete the project. *See* project
    completion
complex technology architecture expert
    assistance, 265–266
complexity of needs
  behavioral segmentation, 44, 45
  profile, 43
component reuse, 282
comps, visual design comps, 23
computer, desktop. *See* desktop
    experience
computer, laptop. *See* laptop experience
concept testing, 222, 225, 290
conceptualizing visual design,
    209–211
conferences for UX, 269–270
consistency
  ensuring, getting started with UX, 20
  as key to UX, 288
  visual design, 209
constant evolution, user-centric
    experience, 275
contact information as content type, 133
content. *See also specific topics*
  competitor survey, 103
  define and prioritize, 105–106
  defined, 111
  development of, 24
  guidelines for persona creation, 50–52
  guidelines for voice and tone,
    215–216
  inputs for UX design, 18–19
  as king to UX, 286
  large-screen experience, 183–184
  mobile phone UX design, 187–191
  multichannel design, 180–181

content *(continued)*
  multichannel experience, 179–180
  organization and information
    architecture, 10
  prioritization, 157–158
  refresh in maintain phase, 24
  requirements for, 105–106, 125–128
  social media experience, 200
  template, 162, 163
  usability, 13
  visual design, 211–212
content assessment, sitemaps, 157–158
content audit
  completing, 122–125
  content strategy, 115, 116, 122–125
  in define phase, 23
  defined, 290
  report, content strategy, 128–129
content brief, 114–115, 290
content categorization. *See* taxonomy
content experience, 112, 290
content experience strategy, 132, 137
content features
  define and prioritize, 105, 107–109
  evaluating, 108–109
  road map, 82
  voice guidelines, 216
content information sites, metrics
  goals for, 243
content inventory
  completing, 116–122
  content strategy, 115–122
  defined, 290
  taxonomy, 141
  templates, 165–166
content life cycle
  content strategy, 112, 126–128, 132, 136,
    143–148
  governance model, 149
content management system (CMS)
  complex technology architecture
    assistance, 266
  content inventory, 117, 122
  content life cycle, 145
  defined, 291
  governance model, 149
  sitemap, 162
  technology architecture, 16

content matrix, 18, 149, 291
content model
  content strategy design, 132, 138–140
  defined, 291
  governance model, 149
  UX design, 18
content modules, wireframe, 167
content strategist on strategic team, 83
content strategy
  assistance for project completion,
    263–264
  audit report, 128–129
  content audit, 115, 116, 122–125
  content brief, 114–115
  content experience strategy, 132, 137
  content inventory, 115–122
  content life cycle, 112, 126–128, 132, 136,
    143–148
  content model, 132, 138–140
  content requirements, 125–128
  content types, 132–136
  defined, 10, 112, 291
  defining, 111–113
  designing, 131–153
  developing, 111–129
  editorial calendar, 132, 152–153
  future-state point of view,
    128–129
  governance model, 148–152
  missing assets, 93
  non-working current assets, 93
  production workflows and tools, 132,
    152–153
  relationship model of user, content,
    business, 113–115
  stakeholder interviews, 116,
    125–128
  steps in process, 131–132
  taxonomy, 132, 140–142
  UX as iterative approach, 92–93
  working current assets, 92
content survey, 135
content type
  content inventory, 120–121
  content life cycle, 145–146
  content model, 139
  content strategy design, 132–136
  defined, 120

content-first approach, assessment of UX, 282–283
content-rich experience, length of visit metric, 247
contextual content, 157
contextual features, tablet UX design, 194
contextual inquiry, data gathering, 42
contextual interviews, 100–102, 291
contextual navigation, 172
conversion
  as business goal, 32
  defined, 291
  metric for, 241, 247–248, 250, 291
conversion rate metrics, 98
Cooper, Charles (author), *Managing Enterprise Content: A Unified Content Strategy,* 180
copy
  expert assistance for written, 264
  visual design, 211–212
  voice guidelines, 216
copywriting, expert assistance, 264
cost
  cost to convert metric, 250
  information architecture, 156
  to serve users, 43
  testing, 220
coupons, 191
creating content in content life cycle, 144
Creative Commons (website), 208
critical success factors, 80, 291
cross-selling, content model, 138
CSS (Cascading Style Sheets), 85, 86, 182
curated content, 144
current experience, benchmark in define phase, 22
current state, assessing for UX design, 92–102, 105
customer journeys. *See* journeys
customer loyalty, 12
customer retention, 29, 32
customer satisfaction, 12, 30
customer segmentation, 51, 137, 292
customer support costs, reducing, 31

• D •

Darwin, Charles (scientist), 77
data
  age and relevance, 40
  analysis. *See* data analysis
  gathering. *See* data gathering
  review questions, 40–41
  visualization, tablet UX design, 195–196
data analysis
  behavior, 42
  business questions, 43
  desire, 42–43
  determine target users, 38, 42–48
  example, Broadway theater ticketing, 44–49
  metrics, 254–256
  pain points, 43
  profile creation, 42–45
  similarities and differences, 42–45
  usability testing, 233
data gathering
  appropriateness of fit, 40
  data review questions, 40–41
  determine target users, 38, 39–42
  ethnography and contextual inquiry, 42
  focus groups, 42
  online surveys, 41
  sources of existing, 39
  user interviews, 41–42
  website analytics, 39–40
dead-ends in usability, 14
decentralized governance model, 149–150
define phase, UX process workflow
  described, 22–23, 79–81
  metrics, 236–237
defining
  content strategy, 111–113
  persona creation, 52
definitions as content type, 133
delete content in content audit, 124
delivery. *See* channels
demographics, persona, 51
depth of visit metric, 250
description in content inventory, 118–119

design best practices, mobile phones, 186–191
design considerations
  changes, usability testing, 233
  channels, 175–200
  inputs for UX, 16–17
  multichannel experience, 177–199
  UX design. *See* UX design
design direction, 210–211, 292
The Design of Everyday Things (Norman), 269
design phase, UX process workflow
  described, 22, 23, 80
  metrics, 236–237
designers, qualities of good, 21
desirable solutions from UX design, 9
desire
  data analysis, 42–43
  user-centric experience, 274
desktop experience
  as channel, 27
  larger screen size design, 183–185
  metrics of channel, 252
  as option in mobile phone UX design, 189–190
  tablets compared to, 193–194
  visual design, 203
differences, data analysis, 42–45
differentiating, persona creation, 52
direct visitors, clickstream metrics, 246
discovery phase, UX process workflow
  described, 22–23, 80
  metrics, 236–237
display, content model, 139
document format in content inventory, 121
Don't Make Me Think: A Common Sense Approach to Web Usability, (Krug), 269
drop-off rate metric, 98
Drucker, Peter (management expert), 37

• **E** •

e-commerce
  complex technology architecture assistance, 266
  fundamental requirements, 106–107
  metrics goals for, 242–243
  technology architecture, 16

edited global content, multichannel design, 181
editorial calendar
  content strategy design, 132, 152–153
  governance model, 149
efficiency in information architecture, 156
Einstein, Albert, 7
electricity and mobile phones, 192–193
The Elements of User Experience: User-Centered Design for the Web and Beyond (Garrett), 269
e-mail experience
  metrics of channel, 253
  multichannel, 197–198
embedded video, style guide, 215
emulators for multichannel testing, 182
engagement
  repeat, social media metrics, 254
  scenarios, 61
enjoyment factor, assessment of UX, 281
error prevention and handling, heuristic assessment, 95
Esparza, Susan (author), *Search Engine Optimization All-in-One For Dummies,* 242
ethnography, 42, 292
evolution of UX, 77–87
examples
  Broadway theater ticketing, 44–49, 52–54
  car purchase, 54–56, 70–73
  data analysis, 44–49
  persona creation, 52–54
Excel. *See* spreadsheet
exit metric, 250
expectations, scenarios, 60–61
experience as the brand, 288
experience design, 7
Experience Design: A Framework for Integrating Brand, Experience, and Value (Newbery and Farnham), 269
experience models, 57–75
  defined, 292
  goals for experience, 57–58
  journeys, 62–75
  scenarios, 58–62
  UX design, 18

expert assistance
  complex technology architecture, 265–266
  content strategy, 263–264
  copywriting, 264
  industry-specific experience, 266
  information architecture, 259–260
  platform-specific technology, 266–267
  sources of, 267–270
  technology architecture, 265–267
  visual design, 202, 260–262
  written copy, 264
external search keywords metrics, 248–249

● **F** ●

Facebook (website), 184, 186, 199–200
Facebook Insights, 256
FAQ pages as content type, 133
Farnham, Kevin (author), *Experience Design,* 269
feature phone, defined, 292
feature phone experience
  global use of, 185–186, 192–193
  interface, 185
  UX design for, 185–193
federated governance model, 149, 150
financial performance, experience leaders, 12
Flash apps, 190
flexible design, 85–87
Florida, Richard (thought leader), 257
focus groups, 42, 292
font. *See* typeface and font
footer
  defined, 292
  navigation, 172
  wireframe, 168
ForeSee (website), 256
form fields, mobile phone design, 190
form pages as content type, 133
format free multichannel design, 180
fresh experience, assessment of UX, 281
functionality
  competitor survey, 103
  content inventory, 121

mobile phones, 186, 191–192
  template, 162
future state, assessing for UX design, 92–102
future-proofing, 82, 84–85, 178, 292
future-state content types, 135–136
future-state for content strategy, 128–129

● **G** ●

Garrett, Jesse James (author), *The Elements of User Experience,* 269
Gates, Bill (philanthropist), 111
gathering data. *See* data gathering
general description of persona, 52
Generation Z, 235–236
getting started with UX
  considerations prior to start, 19–21
  deciding on new project or redesign, 19
  defining, 8–13
  determining your level of comfort, 20–21
  ensuring consistency, 20
  identifying technology, 20
  inputs and building blocks, 14–19
  maintaining the experience, 20
  typical process workflow, 21–24
  understanding target users, 19
  and usability, 13–14
getting started with UX, 7–24
Gigya app, 200
global content, multichannel design, 181
glossary as content type, 133
goals and objectives
  business. *See* business goals and objectives
  for experience, 57–58
  journeys, 64–65
  metrics, 238–245
  for metrics, 238–241, 242
  performance-driven UX, 238–239, 241, 242–245
  scenarios, 59–60
  SMART approach, 239–240
  UX as a strategy, 79–80
Google (website), 178, 194
Google+, 200

Google Analytics (website), 256
Google Glass, 84
Google Insights, 177, 235
Govella, Austin (information architect), 166
governance calendar, 151–152
governance charter, 150–151
governance in content strategy, 112, 148–152
governance model, 148–152
graphic design, 202. *See also* visual design
graphics. *See* images
grid
  defined, 292
  master, visual design, 205–206
  style guide, 214
guerrilla testing, defined, 292
The Gutenberg Galaxy: The Making of Typographic Man (McLuhan), 178

• *H* •

handbooks as content type, 133
Harrington, H. James (business process expert), 235
Harvey, Greg (author), *Microsoft Excel 2013 All-in-One For Dummies,* 117
HCI Human Computer Interaction (HCI), 7
header. *See* masthead
headlines, voice guidelines, 216
heat maps, 223, 225, 293
help
  as content type, 133
  heuristic assessment, 95
heuristic assessment
  assessment of UX, 94–96, 105, 280
  defined, 293
heuristics, 94
high-level sitemaps, 158–160, 169
home page template, 164, 165
HootSuite (website), 256
horizontal display, mobile phone, 187–188, 190
how service is used, user-centric experience, 274

HTML (Hypertext Markup Language)
  defined, 293
  metadata in content inventory, 119–120
  multichannel design, 182

• *I* •

IA. *See* information architecture
icons
  in book, 2–3
  mobile phone UX design, 191
  style guide, 214
  visual design, 208
illustrations. *See* images
image libraries as resource, 262
images
  large-screen experience, 183
  mobile phone UX design, 187
  style guide, 214
  visual design, 208
  voice guidelines, 216
imitation, assessment of UX, 283
InDesign software, 167
industry-specific experience, expert assistance with, 266
influencers
  journey, 67
  social media metrics, 254
infographics, 134, 183
information architecture (IA)
  assistance for project completion, 259–260
  benefits of good, 156
  content strategy, 132, 135, 136, 138–140
  defined, 10, 155–156, 293
  design and building, 155–174
  sitemap, 156–166
  visual design compared to, 202–203
  wireframes, 166–174
information discovery, seamless, as UX benefit, 33–34
innovation
  assessment of UX, 283
  competitor survey, 103, 105

inputs
  early, participatory design testing
    methods, 228
  getting started with UX, 14–19
  UX as a strategy, 78–79
  UX design, 16–17
insights
  ease of extraction, data gathering, 41
  Facebook Insights, 256
  future-proofing, 84
  Google Insights, 177, 235
inspiring, data gathering, 41
instructional copy, voice guidelines, 216
instructions as content type, 134
integration, participatory design testing
    methods, 228
intelligent content, 138
intent, content experience strategy, 137
interaction design, 10–11, 293
Interaction Design Association (IXDA)
    conference, 270
interaction value metric, 250
interoperability, multichannel
    UX design, 197
interoperable code, 87
interviews with stakeholders. *See*
    stakeholder input
interviews with users
  asking about their experience,
    279–280, 281
  contextual, 100–102
  for data gathering, 41–42
inventory. *See* content inventory
IXDA (Interaction Design Association)
    conference, 270

• J •

journeys
  clickstream metrics, 246–247
  content types, 132–136
  defined, 62, 293
  experience modeling, 62–75
  goals for, 64–65
  multichannel design, 178, 180
  omnichannel experiences, 72–75

persona and, 64–65
  personalization, 66–68
  purchase decision task, 69–71
  scenarios and, 63
  stakeholder input, 64
  task identification, 65–66
  user path metrics, 246–247
  UX design, 16, 17

• K •

kevinpnichols.com (website),
    125, 126
key needs/goals, persona, 51
key pages or screens, design phase, 23
key performance indicators (KPIs),
    15, 241, 293
key terms in taxonomy, 140–141
keyword metrics
  described, 97
  external search, 248–249
  onsite search, 249–250
keywords
  defined, 249
  metadata in content inventory, 120
  for onsite search, 249–250
kiosks as channel, 8, 27, 197
knowledge of users, usability, 11
known user, journey, 67
KPIs (key performance indicators),
    15, 241, 293
Krug, Steve (author), *Don't Make Me
    Think,* 269

• L •

LaFontaine, David (author), *Mobile Web
    Design For Dummies,* 176
landing page, 165, 293
landing page analytics, 97
laptop experience
  larger screen size design, 183–185
  tablets compared to, 193
larger screen size design, 183–185
larger teams for project completion,
    258–260

launch phase. *See* test and launch phase
Laurel, Brenda (video game expert), 219
layout, visual design, 202–203
lead generation sites, metrics
    goals for, 244
legal disclaimers/notices as content
    type, 134
legal representative on strategic team, 83
length of visit metric, 247
level 2 title in content inventory, 118
lighting, mobile phone UX design, 190
link styles
  mobile phone UX design, 190, 191
  style guide, 214
LinkedIn (website), 200, 268
local meet-ups, 270
location
  tablet UX design, 194
  for testing, selecting, 224, 227
log out as content type, 134
login in wireframe, 167
logo
  style guide, 214
  wireframe, 167
long forms, large-screen experience, 184
lorem ipsum text, 171
Louis XIV (King of France), 57
lower-level pages or screens,
    build phase, 23
loyalty of customer, 12
loyalty programs/cards, 191
Lund, Arnie (author), *User Experience
    Management,* 269

• *M* •

MacDougall, Alice, 25
magazines as resource, 269
maintain phase, UX process workflow
  described, 22, 24, 80
  metrics, 236–237
maintaining
  the experience, getting started
    with UX, 20
  sitemaps, 171
  wireframes, 171

managing content in content life cycle,
    145, 147
*Managing Enterprise Content:
    A Unified Content Strategy* (Rockley
    and Cooper), 180
Mann, Thomas (author), 43
Manning, Harley (author), *Outside In: The
    Power of Putting Customers at the Center
    of Your Business,* 158, 269
manuals as content type, 134
market research, defined, 293
marketing representative on strategic
    team, 83
master template and grid, visual design,
    205–206
masthead
  defined, 294
  template, 162, 163
  wireframe, 167
McLuhan, Marshall (author), 175, 178
measureable goals, SMART approach, 239
metadata
  content audit, 123
  in content inventory, 119–120
  defined, 120
  multichannel design, 179
metrics. *See also* analytics
  analysis and reporting, 254–256
  business objectives, 15
  capturing, 254–255
  channel requirements, 241, 251–254
  content life cycle, 145
  defined, 240, 245, 294
  goals and objectives for, 238–245
  key performance indicators (KPIs), 15,
    241, 293
  multichannel design, 181
  performance-driven UX, 238–239, 241–251
  personalization, 68
  SMART approach, 239–240
  types of common, 246–251
  UX as a strategy, 236–238
*Microsoft Excel 2013 All-in-One For
    Dummies* (Harvey), 117
migrate in content audit, 124
mobile apps, UX in, 8

mobile phone experience. *See also* smartphone experience
as channel, 27
competitor survey, 103
design best practices, 186–191
functionality and UX, 186, 191–192
multichannel design, 185–193
tablets compared to, 193
Mobile Web Design For Dummies (Warner and LaFontaine), 176
mobility of mobile phones, 186
moderator in usability testing, 232
modular content in multichannel design, 179, 180
modular design system
defined, 294
templates, 164–166
monitoring, assessment of UX, 280–281
mood boards
defined, 294
design phase, 23
visual design, 209–210
Morae (website), 234
Morgan, Robin (poet), 131
mouse for navigation, 184, 203
MS Excel. *See* spreadsheet
multichannel, defined, 294
multichannel experience
channel benefits, 26
content, 179–180
design considerations, 177–199
e-mail and SMS, 197–198
future-proofing UX, 178
kiosk, 197
larger screen size design, 183–185
mobile phone design, 185–193
print materials, 198–199
smaller screen size design, 185–196
steps to ensure, 180–182
support for, assessment of UX, 282–283
tablet design, 193–196
trends, 176–177
multiple channels
adaptive design, 85, 86, 282–283
flexible design, 85–87
responsive design, 85, 86

N

name in persona, 51
NASA website, 187–190
National Cancer Institute website, 194–195
navigation
assessment of UX, 283
defined, 294
generally, in UX, 172
information architecture, 10
large-screen experience, 184
mobile phone UX design, 189
mouse, 184, 203
template, 162, 163
testing, 225
touch navigation, 194–195, 203
usability, 13
visual design, 203
voice, 178, 216
wireframes, 167, 171–173
new customers as business goal, 29
new employees as business goal, 30
new project or redesign, deciding on, 19
new visitors metrics, 97
Newbery, Patrick (author), *Experience Design,* 269
news as content type, 134
newsletter as content type, 134
newspaper as channel, 27
nodes in taxonomy, 141
Norman, Don (author), *The Design of Everyday Things,* 269

O

omnichannel, defined, 294
omnichannel experience
channel benefits, 26–28
journeys, 72–75
omnichannel user tasks, 28
OmniGraffle software, 167
Omnimedia, 26
online surveys for data gathering, 41
onsite search keyword metrics, 249–250

optimization
  content life cycle, 145
  metrics, 237
  multichannel, 180, 184
*Outside In: The Power of Putting Customers
    at the Center of Your Business*
    (Manning, Bodine, and Bernoff),
    158, 269
Owl's Head amusement part, 30

• P •

page comp, 210–211, 294
page template. *See* template
page title in content inventory, 118
page type, sitemap, 160
pages
  competitor survey, 103–104
  structure of, style guide, 214
  templates compared to, 161–164
pain points in data analysis, 43
participant screener, 226
participants. *See* research participant
participatory design
  defined, 294
  testing methods, 222, 227–228
pathway, defined, 294
payment systems, expert assistance
    with, 266
peer-to-peer reviews, 29
performance architecture, expert
    assistance for, 266
performance-driven UX
  channel requirements, 241
  define specific metrics, 241, 245–251
  defined, 238
  goals and objectives, 238–239, 241,
    242–245
  metrics, 241–251
  regular process for, 241
  steps in, 241
  types of common, 246–251
persona
  compared to profile, 50
  content experience strategy, 137
  defined, 49, 99, 295
  develop in define phase, 22

goal of using, 50
  journeys, 64–65
  scenario-driven assessment, 99–100
  use of, 50
  UX design, 16–17
persona creation
  content guidelines, 50–52
  for defining and differentiating, 52
  determine target users, 38, 49–54
  example, Broadway theater ticketing,
    52–54
  keep it simple, 52
personalization
  content model, 138, 139
  defined, 66, 295
  e-mail or SMS messages, 198
  journeys, 66–68
  print media, 199
phones
  feature phone experience, 185–193
  mobile. *See* mobile phone experience
  smartphone. *See* smartphone experience
photographs
  persona, 51
  style guide, 214
  visual design, 208
placeholder text
  replacing, visual design, 211–212
  in wireframe, 171
platforms. *See* channels
podcast as content type, 134
pop-ups, mobile phone UX design, 190
post rates, social media metrics, 253
predictability in heuristic assessment, 95
preferred search terms, 250
press releases as content type, 134
price comparison on mobile phones, 192
primary content, 157
primary navigation, 172
primary research, 41
principles for UX, 285–288
print materials, 198–199
priorities and prioritization
  content audit, 123
  content experience strategy, 137
  content types, 132–136
  road map, 81–82

user segments to determine target users, 38, 48–49
visual priority of page elements, 10
priority of content, 10
process workflow. *See* UX process workflow
product category pages as content type, 134
product comparison, 184, 192
product detail pages as content type, 135
product guides/instructions, 184
product interfaces, UX in, 8
product packaging as channel, 27
product section of wireframe, 168
product user guides as content type, 135
production workflows and tools, content strategy design, 132, 152–153
profile
  complexity of needs, 43
  creation, data analysis, 42–45
  determine target users, 38
  persona compared to, 50
  UX design, 16–17
profit as profile consideration, 43
project completion
  complex technology architecture assistance, 265–266
  content strategy assistance, 263–264
  copywriting assistance, 264
  information architecture assistance, 259–260
  larger teams, 258–260
  multidisciplinary business generalists in, 258–259
  platform-specific technology assistance, 266–267
  rich media asset development, 267
  single-person teams, 257, 258
  size of projects, 257–260
  sources of UX assistance, 267–270
  technology architecture expert assistance, 265–267
  testing and schedule, 221
  user testing activities, 264–265
  UX strategic team, 82–83
  visual design expert assistance, 260–262
  written copy assistance, 264

project workflow. *See* UX process workflow
promise of good, UX design, 9
promotional space, style guide, 214
prospective customers, determine target users, 38
prototypes
  defined, 221, 295
  test and launch phase, 220, 221, 232
  usability testing, 232
  as useful tool, 287
publishing in content life cycle, 145
purchase decision task, journeys, 69–71
purchase funnel, 32, 69
purchase tools on mobile phones, 192

• Q •

qualitative testing methods, 226
qualities of good designer, 21
quality of content, content audit, 122–123, 124
quantitative testing methods, 226
quote, persona, 51

• R •

radio as channel, 27
recognized user, journey, 67
redesign, deciding on, 19
referral traffic, social media metrics, 254
referred visitors, clickstream metrics, 246
registration, technology architecture, 16
related information, template, 162, 163
relationship model for content strategy, 113–115
relevance
  of goals, SMART approach, 240
  of metrics, 238
repeat engagement, social media metrics, 254
repeat visitors metrics, 97
repeater, journey, 67
reporting
  assessment of UX, 280–281
  metrics, 254–256

research
  determining target users, 37–56
  primary research, 41
  secondary research, 39
research participants
  defined, 225
  for testing strategy, 224, 225–227
  usability testing, 220, 232–233
resources
  books, 270
  conferences for UX, 269–270
  image libraries, 262
  magazines, 269
  for UX assistance, 267–270
  websites, 269
responsive design, 85, 86, 181, 295
retention of customers, 29, 32
reusable content, multichannel
    design, 177, 179
revenue
  as metric, 98
  UX importance, 12
review
  of products, mobile phones, 192
review content, content life cycle, 144, 146
reviews
  as content type, 135
  peer-to-peer, 29
revise, content audit, 124
rich media
  asset development, 267
  defined, 295
  standardized, 166
road map, 81–82
Rockley, Ann (author), *Managing
    Enterprise Content: A Unified
    Content Strategy,* 180
rollover buttons, mobile phone
    UX design, 191

● *S* ●

Saffer, Dan (interaction designer), 169
sales of product/service
  as business goal, 30
  as UX benefit, 30, 32

sample browse path, sitemaps, 160–161
sample content, sitemap, 160
sample size, 226
satisfaction
  customer, 12, 30
  information architecture, 156
scannability, content strategy, 10
scenarios
  assessment driven by, 99–100
  defined, 58, 295
  defining the user expectations, 60–61
  defining the user in, 59
  defining the user's goals in, 59–60
  experience modeling, 58–62
  journeys and, 63
  reasons for user engagement, 61
  usability testing, 232
  use cases compared to, 58
  in UX design, 16, 17
screen resolution, 203, 206, 295
screen size
  interaction time and, 177
  mobile phones, 186
  multichannel UX design, 183–196
scrolling, below the fold concept,
    176–177
search box, wireframe, 167
search engine
  Google, 178
  referrals, clickstream metrics, 246
*Search Engine Optimization All-in-One For
    Dummies* (Clay and Esparza), 242
search listing, template, 166
secondary content, 157
secondary navigation, 172
secondary research, 38, 39–42
section page, template, 165
segmentation
  customer, 51, 137, 292
  user segments, 38, 44, 45, 48–49
self-selection, e-mail or SMS
    messages, 198
self-service sites, metrics goals for,
    244–245
semantic technology, 178
SEO quality, content audit, 123

sessions for usability testing, 233
share of voice, social media metrics, 254
ShareThis app, 200
shopping lists, 191
similarities, data analysis, 42–45
simplicity
  heuristic assessment, 95
  persona creation, 52
  visual systems audit, 99
single-person teams for project
    completion, 257, 258
Siri, 178
site analytics, defined, 240. *See also*
    metrics
sitemaps
  content assessment, 157–158
  content types, 136
  creating high-level, 158–160, 169
  creating sample browse path, 160–161
  define phase, 23
  defined, 295
  design phase, 23
  information architecture, 156–166
  maintaining, 171
  templates, 161–166
size of projects, project completion,
    257–260
smaller screen size, multichannel
    experience, 185–196
SMART approach to metrics, 239–240
smartphone, defined, 295
smartphone experience. *See also* mobile
    phone experience
  interface, 185
  metrics of channel, 252–253
  UX design for, 185–193
  visual design, 203
  wireframe for app, 167–169
Smashing Magazine, 268
SMS message experience, 197–198, 253
social listening, 199
social media experience
  feedback, user-centric experience, 275
  metrics of channel, 253–254, 256
  multichannel UX design, 197
  sharing, 200

social networks
  channels, 199–200
  tablet UX design, 194
social presence, 200
social sentiment, social media metrics, 254
software, UX in, 8
source analytics, 97
sources. *See also* resources
  of existing data, 39
  of UX assistance, 267–270
South by Southwest conference, 270
specific goals, SMART approach, 239
spreadsheets
  content inventory, 117
  content life cycle, 145–146
  journey, 68
  taxonomy, 141, 142
stakeholder, defined, 296
stakeholder input
  content brief, 114–115
  content life cycle, 146, 148
  content requirement questions, 126
  content strategy, 116, 125–128
  fundamental requirements, 107
  journeys, 64
  metrics goals, 245
  mood boards, 210
  on strategic team, 83
  taxonomy, 140
  testing strategy, 227
  visual design, 210, 212–213
Stewart, Martha (entrepreneur), 26
stickiness, 37
structured content, multichannel
    design, 179
style guide
  creation and use, 213–216
  defined, 296
  governance model, 149
  visual design, 213–216
subsection page, template, 165
SurveyMonkey online survey (website), 41
surveys
  content survey, 135
  data gathering, 41, 102–105
sustainable, defined, 82

sustainable model for UX, 82–85
swim lane, content life cycle, 146
swiping, smartphone, 187
syndicated content, 144
synomyms in taxonomy, 141
System Usability Scale (website), 255
Szuc, Daniel (usability expert), 91

• T •

tablet experience
  design, 193–196
  metrics of channel, 253
  UX in, 8
  visual design, 203
target users
  behavior, 38–39
  data analysis, 38, 42–48
  data gathering on, 38, 39–42
  determining, 37–56
  example, Broadway theater ticketing,
    44–49, 52–54
  example, car purchase, 54–56
  persona creation, 38, 49–54
  prioritizing users, 38, 48–49
  profiles, 38, 42–48
  prospective customer considerations, 38
  steps to understand, 38
  stickiness, 37
  understanding, 19
  user experience compared to customer
    experience, 38–39
tasks
  accomplish desired, as UX benefit, 34
  identification for journeys, 65–66
taxonomy
  content audit, 123
  content strategy design, 132, 140–142
  defined, 296
  testing, 225
  UX design, 18–19
technical requirements for visual design,
  203–204
technology
  assessment in define phase, 23
  evolution of, data gathering, 40

expert assistance, 265–267
future-proofing, 84, 87
persona, 51
testing, 225
UX architecture, 16, 265–267
technology lead on strategic team, 83
television as channel, 27
templates
  content audit, 123–124, 125
  content governance model, 149
  content inventory, 117–118, 122
  content model, 139
  defined, 296
  inventory, 165–166
  in modular design system, 164–166
  pages compared to, 161–164
  sitemap, 160, 161–166
  style guide, 214, 215
tertiary content, 157
tertiary navigation, 172
test and launch phase
  card sorting, 222, 225, 228–231
  described, 22, 24, 80
  importance of testing, 219
  metrics, 236–237
  participatory design testing methods,
    222, 227–228
  prototypes, 220, 221, 232
  testing myths, 220–221
  testing strategy choices, 222–227
  usability testing, 220, 223, 231–234
  UX process workflow, 219–234
testing. *See also* usability testing
  choices, 222–227
  choose a test method, 224–225
  importance of, 85
  mobile phone UX design, 189
  multichannel design, 181, 182
  project completion, 264–265
  research participants, 224, 225–227
  select location for testing, 224, 227
  stakeholder incorporation, 227
  steps in, 224
  user testing, 181, 189, 264–265
  what to test, 224
time-specific goals, SMART approach, 240

timing, content life cycle, 146
tone, guidelines, 215–216
top failed search metrics, 249
top level in content inventory, 118
touch navigation, 194–195, 203
tracking
  influencers, social media metrics, 254
  user data, 197
traffic
  referral traffic, social media metrics, 254
  traffic per transaction metric, 98
  UX importance, 13
transactional systems, expert assistance
    with, 266
tree testing
  defined, 296
  taxonomy, 141
  visual design, 222, 225, 256
TreeJack (website), 231
trends, multichannel experience, 176–177
Tufte, Edward (professor), 201
tutorial as content type, 135
Twitter, multichannel UX design, 199–200
Twitter Analytics (website), 256
typeface and font
  character count in content model, 139
  lorem ipsum text, 171
  mobile phone UX design, 187
  style guide, 214
  visual design, 207
typography, defined, 296

• U •

UAT (user acceptance testing),
    223, 225, 296
unique content in multichannel design, 181
United Nations website, 184–185, 195–196
updates in content inventory, 122
up-selling, content model, 138
URLs in content inventory, 119
usability
  as absolute requirement, 286
  clarity, consistency, and ease of use, 14
  cognitive overload, 14, 274, 287–288
  competitor survey, 103

content, 13
dead-ends, 14
defined, 11
getting started with UX, 13–14
information architecture, 156
knowledge of users, 11
navigation, 13
and UX, 13–14
usability testing
  defined, 223, 296
  test and launch phase, 220, 223, 231–234
  visual design, 225
usable solutions from UX design, 9
use cases, compared to scenarios, 58
useful solution from UX design, 9
user. *See also specific topics*
  content strategy relationship model,
      113–115
  defined, 296
  defining in scenarios, 59
  impacts of UX, 33–35
  interviews for data gathering, 41–42
  as rarely wrong, 285
user acceptance testing (UAT),
    223, 225, 296
user experience, defined, 8. *See also* UX
user experience design (UXD), 7
*User Experience Management: Essential
    Skills for Leading Effective UX Teams*
    (Lund), 269
user insights. *See* insights
user interaction history metric, 251
user journey. *See* journey
user mode, 160, 296
user path metrics, 97, 246–247
user persona. *See* persona
user profile. *See* profile
user scenario. *See* scenarios
user segments
  behavioral segmentation, 44, 45
  prioritizing, 38, 48–49
user testing. *See also* testing
  mobile phone UX design, 189
  multichannel design, 181
  project completion, 264–265
user-centered as key to UX, 287

user-centered design, 7
user-centric experience
  assessment of UX structure, 282
  compared to brand messaging, 276
  constant evolution, 275
  design based on, 34–35, 273
  how service is used, 274
  importance to UX, 273–277
  metrics, 238
  participatory design testing methods, 228
  social media feedback, 275
  variation in user desires, 274
user-generated content, 147, 200
users
  asking about their experience,
    279–280, 281
  target. *See* target users
UX
  art and science of, 287
  assessment of, 279–283
  as a broad field, 258–259
  business benefits, 28–35
  as business goal, 29–30
  business objectives, 15
  channel benefits, 26–28
  competitive landscape, 15–16
  completing the project, 257–270
  considerations prior to start, 19–21
  customer experience compared to, 38–39
  defining, 8–13
  design. *See* UX design
  evolution of, 77–87
  getting started, 7–24
  inputs and building blocks, 14–19
  as iterative approach, 92–93
  metrics for, 235–256
  modeling the experience, 57–75
  multidisciplinary business
    generalists in, 258–259
  principles for, 285–288
  project completion, 257–270
  rapid pace of change, 77
  reasons to use, 25–35
  as a strategy, 78–87, 236–238
  target users, determining, 37–56
  technology architecture, 16

  testing, 219–234
  typical product workflow, 21–24
  and usability, 13–14
  user impacts, 33–35
  user-centric experience, 273–277
UX as a strategy
  flexible design, 85–87
  goals for, 79–80
  inputs, 78–79
  metrics, 236–238
  process workflow, 79, 80
  road map, 81–82
  sustainable model, 82–85
UX Booth (publication), 268
UX design
  adaptive design, 85, 86, 282–283
  areas impacted by, 8
  brand look and feel, 17
  channels, designing specific, 175–200
  competition assessment, 102–105
  components of, 9–12
  content features, define and prioritize,
    105, 107–109
  content inputs, 18–19
  content model and matrix, 18
  content requirements, define and
    prioritize, 105–106
  content strategy, designing, 131–153
  content strategy, developing, 111–129
  current/future state assessment,
    92–102, 105
  experience models, 18
  flexible design, 85–87
  information architecture, building,
    155–174
  inputs, 16–17
  promise of good, 9
  qualities of good designer, 21
  reducing interface cost, as UX benefit,
    31–32
  responsive design, 85, 86
  taxonomy, 18–19
  understanding, 91–109
  user focus, 33
  user-centric experience, 34–35, 273
  visual design, 201–216

UX lead on strategic team, 82–83
UX Magazine, 268
UX process workflow. *See also additional details at specific phase*
  build phase, 22, 23–24, 80
  define phase, 22–23, 79–81
  design phase, 22, 23, 80
  discovery phase, 22–23, 80
  maintain phase, 22, 24, 80
  metrics, 236–238
  test and launch phase, 22, 24, 80, 219–234
  typical, 21–24, 79, 80
UXD (user experience design), 7

● *V* ●

validating
  mobile phone UX design, 187–188
  multichannel design, 182
  taxonomy, 141
  tools for, 182
  visual design, 211–213
value of interaction metric, 250
van Der Rohe, Mies (architect), 155
variation in user desires, user-centric experience, 274
vertical display, mobile phone, 187–188, 190
Visio software, 167
visit length metric, 247
visit metrics, 250
visit to convert metric, 250
visitor duration metrics, 98
visitor metrics, 97, 98, 246
visitors, new, as metric, 97
visitors, referred, clickstream metrics, 246
visitors, repeat, metrics, 97
visual design, 201–216
  basics of, 204–209
  benchmarking, 203–204
  brand guidelines, 204
  channel considerations, 203–204
  color, 207
  components, 207–209
  conceptualizing, 209–211
  consistency, 209

  defined, 11, 297
  design phase comps, 23
  expert assistance, 202, 260–262
  fonts and typeface, 207
  importance of, 286
  information architecture compared to, 202–203
  layout, 202–203
  master template and grid, 205–206
  style guide creation and use, 213–216
  tablet UX design, 195–196
  technical requirements, 203–204
  templates, 161–162
  testing, 225
  validating, 211–213
visual priority of page elements, information architecture, 10
visual systems audit, 98–99
voice
  guidelines, 215–216
  as interface, 178
  share of voice social media metrics, 254

● *W* ●

W3C (World Wide Web Consortium), 123, 182, 204
Warner, Janine (author), *Mobile Web Design for Dummies,* 176
waterfall methodology, 297
wayfinding, indoor/outdoor maps, 191
ways to shop navigation, 172
web analytics. *See also* metrics
  assessment of UX, 96–98
  data gathering, 39–40
  defined, 240
websites. *See also specific websites*
  cheat sheet online, 3
  Dummies UX online, 3
  for expert UX assistance, 268
  resources, 268–269
  UX in, 8
white space in visual design, 211
wireframes
  annotating, 169–171
  components of, 167–169

wireframes *(continued)*
  content model, 138
  creating, 167
  defined, 166, 297
  design phase, 23
  focus of, 166–167
  information architecture, 10, 166–174
  limitations, 173–174
  maintaining, 171
  navigation, 171–173
  visual design, 210
Wirify (website), 162
Wodtke, Christina (information
    architect), 166
World Wide Web Consortium (W3C),
    123, 182, 204
written copy assistance for project
    completion, 264

• X •

XML, multichannel design, 182

• Y •

YouEye (website), 234

• Z •

Zeldman, Jeffrey (web designer), 155
Zoomerang online survey (website), 41

About the Authors

Donald Chesnut has spent almost 20 years as a user experience designer. In Donald's work, he takes customer-centered thinking and applies it to a variety of business problems, from communications to commerce, including the design and development of content, community, and digital services. Donald is SapientNitro's chief experience officer, the global lead for SapientNitro's experience design practice. Donald has worked with some of the world's leading brands, including Disney, Target, HSBC, *The Wall Street Journal,* American Express, United Airlines, Citibank, *Rolling Stone,* Unilever, Hilton, QVC, JetBlue, IBM, Staples, and many others. He and his teams have won numerous awards for creativity and business effectiveness. He speaks frequently on topics related to UX and customer experience.

Many of Donald's projects have had a global scope, and he spent two years working in Europe helping to build SapientNitro's presence across Europe. He got his start in the industry with a graduate degree from NYU's interactive telecommunications program, back when the new media industry was actually "new." He spends his free time in and around New York and has a variety of interests and hobbies, most of which have little to do with digital design or UX.

Kevin Nichols has worked in Internet and web technologies for more than 18 years. In 1995, while completing his graduate studies at Harvard, he interned at the Sabre Foundation. He went on to work in Bosnia and Herzegovina, where he conducted media relations and acted as webmaster for the Physicians for Human Rights website. Returning to America, Kevin worked as a contract consultant before taking a position at Sapient. Kevin then went on to play a key role in launching MITOpenCourseWare, where he designed a substantial part of the publication process and managed the production team. Later, as a senior consultant at Molecular, Kevin was responsible for accounts of Fortune 100 global brands, such as HP. In 2007, Kevin started his own consulting firm. He is currently a director and the Practice Lead for Content Strategy at SapientNitro. When he is not gracing United Airline 757 cabins or Hilton's queen-size beds with his presence, Kevin likes to spend his time on Cape Cod, writing the next "Great American Novel." Kevin is committed to international human rights, especially those of refugees and victims of war. Kevin is also author of *Enterprise Content Strategy: A Project Guide* (XML Press, 2014).

Author's Acknowledgments

First, we'd like to thank both the folks at SapientNitro and John Wiley & Sons, Inc., for giving us the inspiration and opportunity to write this book.

Thanks goes to the following people who provided some fantastic design assets used in this book: Justin Berg, Kristin Berggren, Todd Cherkasky, Gerardo Garcia, James King, Clement Mok, Matt Neenan, Dan Peters, Brett Rooks, Jennifer Tattenbaum, Tom VandeKerckhove, Kevin Warner, Gaston Legorburu, and Christina White. The assets, insight, and ongoing inspiration from you made writing this book a much more enjoyable experience.

Special thanks to Craig Harrington for his patience while I wrote this book, and to my parents for giving me a great start.

— Donald Chesnut

I am grateful for a variety of folks who have lent their expertise and eyes on this project: Eddie Gomez, Alexa O'Brien, Anne Casson, Ben Royce, Ann Rockley, Lisa Copeland, Mark Chelius, AJ Dalal, Rahel Anne Bailie, David Cohen, Cynthia O'Brien, and Market Street Bookshop in Mashpee, MA. Also I want to specifically recognize Rebecca A. Schneider (Azzard Consulting) for her various inputs and insights, which greatly informed this work.

Heartfelt thanks to Dr. Mark J. Hirsch and my family for their continual support.

— Kevin Nichols

Publisher's Acknowledgments

Executive Commissioning Editor: Craig Smith

Senior Project Editor: Sara Shlaer

Project Editor: Charlotte Kughen

Copy Editor: Debbye Butler

Technical Editor: Lisa Copeland

Editorial Assistant: Anne Sullivan

Project Coordinator: Melissa Cossell

Cover Photo: ©iStockphoto.com/SpiffyJ